The Bedside
Guardian 2022

The Bedside Guardian 2022

Edited by
Julian Coman

guardianbooks

Published by Guardian Books 2022

2 4 6 8 10 9 7 5 3 1

First published in Great Britain in 2022 by
Guardian Books
Kings Place, 90 York Way
London N1 9GU

www.guardianbooks.co.uk

A CIP catalogue record for this book is available from the British Library

ISBN 978-1-9162047-3-7

Cover design by Guardian News & Media Ltd
Typeset by seagulls.net

Printed and bound in Great Britain by
CPI Group (UK) Ltd, Croydon CR0 4YY

Contents

WINTER

SPRING

SUMMER

trustful communication, and 'spectacle' displaces strategy and argument. Where there is no trust in some shared stake in how things go, argument readily deteriorates into noise-generating – ultimately into violence. Hadley Freeman's mordant piece on the Oscars observes that 'to have opinions you have to have principles'; you have to have some criteria for making sense of behaviour – yours and other people's – larger than how you feel, how you want to feel, who is leaning hardest on you, who will like you. Ignore this and you are easy prey for the varieties of denial that are marketed so aggressively all around.

Denial is one of the themes recurring in these pieces – not just the deafeningly obvious denials around the climate crisis, denials persisting even when (as Bill McGuire starkly underlines) we are already experiencing just a flavour of what will in a couple of decades no longer be 'extremes' of weather but a steady pattern of lethal fluctuations of heat, storm, flood and drought. Denial seems to be everywhere: in the stubborn refusals of Russians to see what is done in their name in Ukraine (look at Andrew Roth's snapshot of what the 'street' is saying in Moscow), in the bizarre fictions peddled by Donald Trump's acolytes, in our indifference to the marketing of English football to the oligarchs of Russia and Saudi Arabia (Chelsea, Newcastle), in the painful difficulty we find in acknowledging toxic racism in cherished institutions (like Yorkshire cricket). It permeates our relations with China, allowing us to look away from domestic repression and global ambition. It is (ironically) present in the indignant complaint that people who advocate a critical look at how we have publicly commemorated the heroes of our colonial past are 'cancelling' authentic history (the surprise acquittal of those who pulled down Colston's statue in Bristol suggests that there are plenty among the general public who can spot the flaws in this sort of rhetoric). It skews our remembrance of the Covid pandemic, persuading us that we coped so much better than we did. And denial has been abundantly in evidence in the Tory leadership campaign – the opportunistic rewriting of recent events, the ludicrous focus on a narrow range of culture wars issues, the alarming tone-deafness to the actual threats facing the most vulnerable of our citizens.

What the leadership contest has highlighted is how easy it is to deny *pain*. Several items here do what both good journalism and good art do, which is (among other things) to make us look at pain without reassuring bromides. It may be the pain of individual loss, compounded by the heartlessness of public lies (Rory Kinnear's moving narrative of his sister's death on the day of one of the infamous parties in Downing Street). It may be the pain and bewilderment of a refugee facing deportation to Rwanda after a traumatic journey from bloodshed and privation; the pain of those heroic women working to continue education for girls in Afghanistan, as reported by Emma Graham-Harrison; the pain of all those in the UK facing a future of unmanageable food prices and spiralling insecurity, in an environment where affordable housing is a vanishing hope. Where has all this been in the last few months of public preening and snapping? Once again, the word that comes to mind is not just 'dishonest' but 'dishonourable', disgraceful: it is a refusal to acknowledge the world others inhabit and the fears and privations they are voicing. Has the political opposition in the UK any compelling narrative to push back at all this? Surely it should at least insist that the overriding priority for society should be to recognise and address these kinds of pain, not to pretend that such acknowledgment is a kind of defeatism or, worse, treachery.

It has become a cliché to talk about the negative effect of online discourse here. The first glacially slow steps are being taken in challenging the huge moral laziness of the tech giants casually diffusing poisonous untruth. But the culture overall is still deep in addiction (Adrian Chiles offers a rueful sidelight on the online marketing juggernaut). It is another version of not being 'answerable'. At the simplest level, the online warrior never has to undertake the frustrating job of finding what needs to be done (and can only be done) *together with* those others whom they so casually demonise. Performative grandstanding is easier than patient problem-solving. Francine Prose's thoughtful piece on the *Roe* v *Wade* debacle notes that the original judgment acknowledged the depth of feeling and the complexity of argument on both sides – in sharp contrast to the brutal simplicities and thinly veiled misogyny which have framed more recent processes and decisions. She takes a clear position, but above all laments the loss of a *method* of debate and decision – a lament that might be shared even by those with different views.

Speaking (or writing) as if no one could legitimately, morally or intelligently question you or answer you is a way of reducing or destroying anything outside your own head. In the last 12 months we have seen more clearly than ever how the routine abuse and exploitation of the natural environment spills over into overt violence against human beings. The appalling story of the murder of Dom Phillips is only one episode in the record of a pretty systematic war, waged by major industrial interests, regularly backed by kleptocratic governments, against local (often indigenous) communities, whose livelihood, habitat and dignity are under threat. It was an issue insufficiently flagged at the Glasgow Cop26 summit – an event where denial almost, but not quite, succeeded in derailing progress towards honouring the promises made in previous meetings. But it was a minimalist outcome. The timetable remains slack; we still fail to register that postponing action is *not* simply leaving the problem till tomorrow but *changing the nature of the problem* that we shall have to address. Thank God the *Guardian* keeps it in focus daily; but how many governments still calculate nothing beyond the pressures of the next electoral cycle?

Journalism and art should be reminding us of pain; but they should also be reminding us of how we manage and make sense even of pain. Rhiannon Lucy Cosslett's wonderfully candid and courageous piece on motherhood does not make pain easy, but she does not deny joy. For that, of course, is another form of denial. We can let ourselves be taught to think less of our humanity than it deserves. There is plenty here to bring us back to why it matters to treat ourselves and each other in terms of 'honour' – candour, consistency, modesty, patience. This is the dimension in our understanding of humanity that sits at the heart of how we can imagine ourselves and our future – and for people like myself it has everything to do with what we mean by religious commitment. But religious humanism is (notoriously) not the only form of humanism (and it is all too often obscured by religious anti-humanism). Andrew Manze's spirited celebration of that devout agnostic, Vaughan Williams, shows that what some have taken to be innocently 'pastoral' music was forged in both personal and collective trauma. It is a hard-won beauty – an honest and an honourable beauty, we might say, not looking away from pain, but not paralysed by it. It relocates us in a world that is not an accidental playground for our whims and passions, but a landscape whose pulses we share, whose life is bound with ours. Choosing honesty is ultimately choosing this generosity of vision. Those who value the *Guardian* value it because at its best it makes those choices; it tells us that we can make them too, as we so urgently must in 'low, dishonest' times.

Introduction

JULIAN COMAN

How to anthologise a year that seemed, at times, to lurch terrify-
ingly out of control? The past 12 months have been a wild, chaotic
and frequently alarming ride. Stagflation, 1970s-style, returned
to Britain and a cost of living crisis upended the economic
assumptions that govern our everyday lives. A law-breaking
prime minister was defenestrated and a radical risk-taking free-
marketeer entered No 10. In the same week, the Queen died, after
a 70-year reign which for many epitomised a vanishing sense of
decency and honour in public life. And overshadowing all these
defining events, war broke out on European soil. For the people
of Ukraine, this was the year that the extent of Vladimir Putin's
murderous, revanchist ambitions became clear.

Luke Harding's February dispatch from Kyiv, delivered in the
early hours of Day One of Russia's invasion, vividly conveys the
sense of shock at the scale and breadth of the assault. In the capital's streets, the first notes of citizen defiance are sounded – a
foretaste of what would become Ukraine's heroic and ongoing
resistance. Shaun Walker's bravura reportage captures the confusion and pathos of Kyiv's central train station as hundreds of
refugees struggle to board a train. 'Look at these faces around
us,' says an art historian hoping to leave with her 15-year-old
daughter. 'They are exactly the same as in the photographs from
the Second World War ... Can you imagine what will happen in

a month?' In a searing subsequent piece from the eastern town of Trostianets, Walker provides a kind of answer, describing 'a grim panorama of several mangled tanks, the whitened carcass of a self-propelled howitzer and a shot-up yellow bus with blood smeared on the seats'.

The war in Ukraine, and the resulting energy crunch in the West, formed the grim backdrop to domestic political turbulence that gradually morphed into a full-blown economic crisis by this autumn. Under the withering gaze of Marina Hyde, and relentlessly pursued by the prose of John Crace, Boris Johnson had no hiding place as he sought to duck, dive and evade the consequences of 'Partygate'. Rory Kinnear's furious account of following Covid guidelines on the day of his sister's funeral, which coincided with the 'bring your own booze' garden party in 2020, sums up why the prime minister had to go.

Characteristically, he took a disgracefully long time to accept the fact. It was not until July, as Dan Sabbagh narrates, that Johnson realised the game was finally up for a leader whose behaviour and moral standards were unfit for the office he held.

As the Conservative party chose a new prime minister for the third time in six years, soaring inflation, unaffordable energy prices and high-profile rail strikes gave a retro 1970s feel to a long, hot summer. Polly Toynbee, way back in November 2021, had been the first to spot that a much-maligned decade was making a kind of cultural comeback. Her spirited defence of the era that gave us the first National Women's Liberation Conference and the Open University, as well as ABBA and floral midi dresses, provides an invaluable eyewitness corrective to rightwing caricature. Zoe Williams's fascinating August interview with the RMT leader, Mick Lynch, captured the sense of a shifting zeitgeist in which the virtues of collective solidarity and the value of strong trade union representation have begun to be appreciated once again.

As the cost of living crisis inflicts hardship on millions of families, John Harris and Aditya Chakrabortty chronicled the stories, dilemmas and fears of those obliged to live at its sharp end.

When such powerful headwinds blow, occasions of hope, humour and inspiration are treasured all the more. With such a talented cast of writers to draw upon, this year's anthology did not have to work too hard to find such moments. Emine Saner's interview reminds us of why Rose Ayling-Ellis was perhaps the most popular *Strictly* winner of all. Suzanne Wrack's celebration of the Three Lionesses' triumph at the Women's Euros 2022 is also a moment of personal reflection and vindication for this veteran writer on the women's game. Simon Hattenstone's tortured but triumphant encounter with Shane MacGowan is a comic masterpiece made up of awkward silences, monosyllabic responses and – in the end – a kind of wry truce between interviewer and interviewee. Sirin Kale's account of going on *Mastermind* is a cautionary tale for anyone who has performed well enough at pub quizzes to wonder 'how hard could it be?'.

Careful readers will note that this book has two endings. The advent of Liz Truss as Britain's new prime minister was originally intended to provide a satisfying sense of narrative closure. The subsequent sad death of the Queen then opened up and widened the debate about the state of the nation, the meaning of its history, and what its future should hold. The succession, as Martin Kettle notes, takes place in a country transformed during Elizabeth II's long reign, and in which she had become one of the few unifying forces. In the context of the global climate emergency, geopolitical realignment triggered by war and a related economic crisis, the country thus embarks on a hazardous, unpredictable journey into 2023 and beyond. As this volume demonstrates, *Guardian* journalists will be there to read the signs of the times with passionate curiosity, courage and insight. There could be no better exemplar of these qualities than the *Guardian* contributor Dom Phillips, who was murdered while investigating illegal resource extraction in the Amazon rainforest. Our global environment editor, Jonathan Watts, remembers him here. May Dom rest in peace.

Editing *The Bedside Guardian* is an honour that presents many invidious choices. There are fine pieces of journalism which undoubtedly deserved a place in this anthology, but have not been allocated one. Apologies to those unjustly omitted. I would also like to thank the *Guardian*'s editor-in-chief, Katharine Viner, for giving me the opportunity to immerse myself in the work of so many gifted writers, and Lindsay Davies for her expert judgment and guidance as we put the book together. I hope it does justice to a remarkable year, and to the colleagues who chronicled it with such distinction.

Autumn

'Moral bankruptcy': whistle-blower offers scathing assessment of Facebook

DAVID SMITH

It might, as one senator put it, be remembered as 'the big-tobacco jaw-dropping moment of truth'.

The truth-teller was former Facebook data scientist Frances Haugen, appearing on Capitol Hill on Tuesday to testify that the online platform knowingly harms children, just as cigarette makers did before they were brought to heel.

The whistle-blower's inside knowledge and clear, crisp answers to senators' questions – with elaborate hand gestures for emphasis – were all the more damning because of her measured tone and lack of hyperbole.

'Facebook knows that they are leading young users to anorexia content,' she said in a voice of authority that may prove a tipping point in government efforts to curb the power of big tech.

She was clearly preaching to the converted as senator after senator joined her in scathing criticism of Mark Zuckerberg, the founder and chief executive of Facebook, for putting profits before people.

Zuckerberg was memorably played by Jesse Eisenberg (later the supervillain Lex Luthor in *Batman v Superman*) in the Aaron Sorkin-scripted film *The Social Network*. Should a sequel be made, the role of Haugen might go to a similarly top-notch actor like Reese Witherspoon.

Having burst into the public consciousness on the flag-ship *60 Minutes* current affairs programme on Sunday, Haugen passed a chorus of clicking cameras to enter the compact Senate committee room at 10.02am.

The 37-year-old sat down at a long table with a blue folder marked 'whistle-blower aid' in gold letters. She unscrewed a green bottle of Mountain Valley water and took a sip. Above her hung a giant chandelier and ornately moulded ceiling and cornicing. Light shimmered off marble panels around the room. Haugen's face was beamed back to her from three giant TV screens. Her microphone came with a red digital countdown clock for each senator's questions.

A former product manager on Facebook's civic misinforma-tion team, she has come forward with tens of thousands of pages of internal research documents she secretly copied before leaving her job in the company's civic integrity unit.

The impunity of Facebook, which has 2.8 billion users world-wide and nearly $1 trillion in market value, is a rare issue that unites Democrats and Republicans, so she was never likely to face a tough cross-examination.

Democrat Richard Blumenthal, chair of the Senate commerce subcommittee, gavelled the session in and argued that Facebook knows that its products are addictive, like cigarettes. 'Tech now faces that big-tobacco jaw-dropping moment of truth,' he said.

He added: 'Our children are the ones who are victims. Teens today looking in the mirror feel doubt and insecurity. Mark Zuck-erberg ought to be looking at himself in the mirror' – but instead, he noted, Zuckerberg was going sailing.

Haugen was a compelling witness. 'I joined Facebook because I think Facebook has the potential to bring out the best in us,' she said. 'But I am here today because I believe Facebook's products harm children, stoke division and weaken our democracy.'

She described Facebook's lack of transparency and said it shows the need for congressional oversight. 'Almost no one outside of Facebook knows what happens inside of Facebook. The company intentionally hides vital information from the public, from the US government and from governments around the world.'

The hearing was taking place just a day after an extraordinary technical glitch put Facebook offline and, somewhat humiliatingly, forced it to communicate via Twitter.

Haugen observed: 'Yesterday we saw Facebook taken off the internet. I don't know why it went down, but I know that for more than five hours, Facebook wasn't used to deepen divides, destabilise democracies and make young girls and women feel bad about their bodies.'

She agreed with the big tobacco analogy, noting that Facebook's own research into Instagram found children saying that it made them feel bad but they could not give it up and always craved the next click. She also warned that Facebook's engagement-based ranking system is 'fanning ethnic violence' in Ethiopia and other countries.

The mood could hardly have been more different from when Zuckerberg himself has testified before Congress, offering robotic answers that exposed members' lack of digital savvy. Haugen observed: 'There is no one currently holding Mark to account. The buck stops with Mark.'

She argued that the company should declare 'moral bankruptcy' if it wants to seek healing and reconciliation.

Haugen's website says she was born in Iowa City, Iowa, the daughter of two professors, and grew up attending the Iowa caucuses with her parents, 'instilling a strong sense of pride in democracy and responsibility for civic participation'.

She has a degree in computer engineering and a master's degree in business from Harvard. Before being recruited by

Facebook in 2019, she worked for 15 years at tech companies including Google, Pinterest and Yelp.

She said: 'Congress can change the rules Facebook plays by and stop the harm it is causing. I came forward, at great personal risk, because I believe we still have time to act. But we must act now.'

About 30 aides, journalists and members of the public watched from two rows of seats behind Haugen and, as so often at such hearings, senators drifted in and out over the three hours. Senator Roger Wicker sought to reassure Haugen: 'You see some vacant seats. This is a pretty good attendance for a subcommittee.'

Blumenthal gavelled the session out at 1.22pm, thanking Haugen for 'doing a real public service'. She smiled, calm to the end, and departed clutching two bottles of water. Her work was done and Facebook's already very bad week had just got worse.

Many observers were asking: if this is not enough now for Congress to act, what is?

5 OCTOBER

Access to the Tory party is being bought by a new class of tycoon funders

PETER OBORNE

One big theme has dominated the conference in Manchester this week: levelling up. Boris Johnson, we are told, is on a mission to rescue working people who have been forgotten and left behind in today's Britain.

According to this powerful narrative, Keir Starmer's Labour party is a manifestation of a 'woke' metropolitan elite utterly alien to the 'red wall' voters who flocked to the Tories at the last election.

The Pandora papers revelations undermine that Tory story. Yes, there are struggling people who have been forgotten by the system. Yes, it's a worthy cause to give them a much bigger say in public life. But no, the Tories don't generally represent such people.

Johnson's Conservative party essentially belongs to the super-rich. The billionaires. Those with privileged access to the prime minister and the chancellor of the exchequer. To the large and, in many cases, insalubrious cast of men and women with walk-on appearances in the Pandora papers scandal.

This class of Conservatives does not seem to see the British state – as Tories have historically claimed to do – as something to which you dedicate a life of service. They seem to see it rather differently: as something to be plundered and used for self-enrichment.

Take the honours system. Traditionally, honours have been used to reward people who have contributed to the good of the nation. In recent history, however, honours have become a commodity that may be bought and sold.

Take public contracts. Traditionally, they are won in open public competition. Not any more.

Certainly Johnson supports levelling up. He wants to level up the billionaires. They've grown richer than ever before under his premiership. This may help explain why Tory donors are so much more likely to win Covid contracts than others. Access, it seems, helps win contracts, and access can come in return for a fat donation.

Let's take an example of another country suffering from fuel queues: Lebanon. It's no surprise at all to find the newly appointed prime minister, Najib Mikati, and the central bank governor, Riad Salameh, among several Lebanese political and financial officials named in the Pandora papers as having wealth hidden in offshore tax havens. While they are not accused of any wrongdoing, this comes at a time when ordinary Lebanese are having their savings wiped out. Lebanon has long been run as a private fiefdom for the super-rich.

The Pandora papers show that Britain is heading the same way. Access to British politics – and in particular the Johnson Tories – has been bought wholesale by a new class of tycoon funders. They may be British citizens, but in many cases they pay very little tax in this country, and they are in large numbers essentially based offshore.

Their existence has been an open secret for years but not publicly understood, perhaps in part because some of Britain's wealthy newspaper owners themselves have a notorious reluctance to pay taxes.

It's important to understand that this new system has sprung up only recently. Go back only a few decades and the Tory party could count on a mass membership for the bulk of its funds, in the shape of small donations. In recent years membership has gone into freefall, and the donors have largely taken over.

Tony Blair (little surprise to see his appearance in Pandora) helped create this model during his famous period in opposition before 1997. Eager to sideline the unions, the ambitious young Labour leader and his aide Jonathan Powell encouraged fundraising from wealthy donors.

The Tories followed suit. They may have felt they had little choice. Money was hard to come by, and the membership was dying. Suddenly party donors became important figures, men and women of note.

But it is Johnson who has been the most shameless by far. On becoming Tory leader he appointed Ben Elliot, whose former business clients include Mohamed Amersi, who looms large in the Pandora papers, as Tory co-chair. This changed the structure of the party. And it is no surprise to learn, courtesy of the Pandora papers, that Elliot jointly owned a secret offshore film-financing business.

At first sight, Eton-educated Elliot looks like a copper-bottomed establishment Conservative. A nephew of the Duchess of Cornwall, Prince Charles's wife, he is the son of Simon Elliot, a Dorset landowner.

If you look more closely, the appointment seems odder and odder. Tory chairs are normally powerful politicians in their own right – think Theresa May, David Davis or, further back, Norman Tebbit, William Whitelaw or Peter Carrington. Significant figures by any standards. The role of Conservative party chairs, from Carrington to May, was to represent the views of the Tory grassroots and explain the actions of their leadership.

I have found no serious evidence that Elliot does much of this important but gruelling political work, if any. Take the Hartlepool and Batley and Spen byelections. A traditional chair would have been prominent in organising the campaign and explaining the results on television. Elliot kept a very low profile.

Elliot is not even an MP and I can discover no significant record in British politics until he became treasurer for Zac Goldsmith's campaign for the London mayoralty in 2016. Yet he's at the heart of Johnson's Tory establishment. He's not there to talk to the grassroots. He's there to manage the donors – the people who matter. Traditionally, that has been the role of the party treasurer, a relatively lowly party official. In the modern Tory party the job has become so important that the treasurer has been promoted to party chair, and effectively become the boss.

Elliot's model for the party is based on his business, Quintessentially. It is a concierge service for rich people who want introductions and invitations at the top level of society. Amersi has deliciously called the system 'access capitalism', a term that deserves to find its way into a dictionary of quotations. You buy your way in. Elliot will be remembered for turning politics into a financial commodity. Now he needs to come out in public and answer urgent questions: who investigates Tory donors? Does it matter if they don't pay tax? Do you care if they have a murky past? Where do you stand on tax havens?

It's not just Elliot who needs to break the habit of a lifetime and answer questions, now that Pandora's box has been well and truly opened. Johnson, the big winner from this rotten financial system, needs to explain to British voters why the Tory party appears to be funded by a new class of super-rich tax avoiders.

And to tell us what they get in return.

15 OCTOBER

'Easy on Me' review – reliably, relatably Adele-esque

ALEXIS PETRIDIS

Adele's statement this week announcing the coming release of her fourth album, *30*, appeared on social media. In it, the singer doesn't talk much about music, more about her emotional state during the album's making, provoked, one assumes, by the breakdown of her marriage: 'absolute mess and inner turmoil … consumed by grief'. She compared the album she made to friends coming over with 'a bottle of wine and a takeaway' and offering earthy, astrological advice: 'It's your Saturn return, babes, fuck it.'

It all sounds thoroughly grim, but it also has a hint of reassurance about it for her fans, who come to Adele in record-breaking numbers for relatable heartbreak – the musical equivalent of an old friend in the pub, tearfully relating the latest chapter in their reliably disastrous love life as they down the pinot grigio.

For one thing, it underlines that she has fresh heartbreak to write about – on her last album, *25*, she was forced to rake over the same relationship that had inspired its predecessor. For another, her fans might have cause to be alarmed by what the cover of *Vogue* refers to as 'a new look, a new love, a new sound'. How reliably relatable can Adele now be, with her home in LA, her squad of Hollywood A-list pals and, the *Vogue* profile suggests, an employee on hand with a different pair of shoes should the singer want to change out of her heels?

Her statement, consciously or otherwise, sends out a message: 'Business as usual, babes, fuck it.'

That's certainly the same message sent out by 'Easy on Me', a single so Adele-esque it's quite hard to make a qualitative judgment about: you hear it and think: 'Yes, that's definitely Adele, doing the stuff that Adele does,' and adjust your response according to whether or not The Stuff That Adele Does is your idea of musical nirvana.

It offers mournful piano that gradually becomes more strident as the song progresses – suggesting a hint of cathartic empowerment – gently supported by subtle touches of bass: the figure it plays during the verses has a vague hint of the opening to the old theme from *Hill Street Blues*. Her voice, as powerful as ever, sounds initially wounded, then soars. You'd have your work cut out arguing that her vocal during the final bridge is anything other than fantastic.

The lyrics – as on 'Someone Like You', or 'Hello', or 'Send My Love (To Your New Lover)' – address the other party in a failing relationship, asking for forgiveness and understanding while underlining that it isn't really her fault – 'you can't deny how hard I've tried' – which has a realistic tang: it's very much an emotional note people strike when they're offloading.

This is reliably relatable business as usual, which is exactly what the millions of people who buy Adele's albums want, especially at this particular juncture in history.

17 OCTOBER

Inside Insulate Britain: on the road with the disruptive climate protesters

DAMIEN GAYLE

The riskiest time in Insulate Britain's roadblock protests is before the police arrive, its activists say. When they targeted a busy junction of the A1090 in Thurrock, Essex, on Wednesday the police didn't appear for nearly an hour. No serious injuries were reported, but it was close.

The first lorry, hurtling towards the T-junction, did not look like it was going to stop: it came to a halt inches from three activists. Cars and vans mounted kerbs and central reservations to evade them. Motorists emerged from their vehicles, pink with rage, snatched protesters' banners and dragged them from the road like ragdolls.

'Am I stopping you from insulating Britain?' one lorry driver berated them. 'No I'm fucking not. Go to the millionaire oligarchs who own the fucking shit and tell them to put the price down.'

In five weeks of disruptive road protests in and around London, Insulate Britain has polarised the country. Ministers have waxed apoplectic at 'eco-warriors' who are 'destroying people's lives', and Boris Johnson has called for powers to 'insulate them snugly in prison'.

But their key demand, that the government 'gets on with the job of insulating Britain's homes' by 2030, is on everyone's lips. Keir Starmer vowed at the Labour party's conference to make home insulation a 'national mission'. It is a huge impact for a group that claims at most 120 active members.

Now with the climate activist group announcing a 10-day pause in the campaign to give the government time to consider its demands, the question is what it will do next. With the crucial Cop26 climate summit opening in Glasgow at the end of the month, the chances are that it will be dramatic.

The night before Thurrock, 18 Insulate Britain members assembled in a rented house in south-east London. They were all in late middle age, inconspicuously dressed and well spoken – far from the 'crusties' evoked in the prime minister's denunciations. For one reason or another they were all in a position to dedicate themselves to the cause full-time.

'It's a bit of a privilege thing,' said Louise Lancaster, 56, who quit her job as a teacher to join the group. 'There are obviously people in our society who have no way of doing this because they have to put food on the table and they can't take time out of work.'

Those whom the *Guardian* spoke to had all been involved in Extinction Rebellion, but some felt it had lost its way. 'I've been on all these XR things; I'd go out every day and get arrested,' said Chris Parish, 69, from Tower Hamlets. 'But ... it's like a carnival. I don't want to criticise it, but I feel like something more needs to be done.'

What sets Insulate Britain activists apart is not necessarily their willingness to go to prison but their determination to do so. They hoped to have 50 climate prisoners jailed by the start of Cop26. 'It would look so embarrassing for Boris Johnson to have elderly vicars in jail,' Lancaster said.

The group says 124 people have been arrested 629 times in 13 actions, according to its own estimates. But so far none have been held on remand for longer than a week. Police have said it is 'very difficult' to bring charges against them, and the government has responded with injunctions banning them from protesting on the M25, around the port of Dover and on critical London roads.

In the kitchen some helped prepare a meal. Others gathered around the dining table, where they studied hand-drawn maps and computer printouts.

'One of the key elements in nonviolent direct action is the need to disrupt,' said one activist, who preferred not to be named. 'What we are really trying to do is bring economic pressure to the government through disruption, so an element in the choice of the site is trying to maximise economic disruption.'

They planned to hit a junction close to an area of warehouses, including Amazon and Co-op distribution centres and the *Daily Mail* printworks. From there lorries would be leaving to join the M25 to deliver goods all over the south-east.

Efforts were made to avoid sites such as hospitals and schools, said another activist who also asked to remain anonymous. 'Then we go to check them out,' she said. 'Today there was another site I thought we could use, but there were a lot of children coming out of school and I didn't want them to be caught up.'

Activists said that as far as they knew – and they had made inquiries, they said – no ambulances or genuine medical emergencies had been 'seriously delayed' by their protests. 'If we notice or hear the sirens for an ambulance, there are people who are generally moving about, coordinating and watching,' one said. Sketching arrows in pink highlighter on a hand-drawn map, she showed the route an ambulance could take through the blockade they had planned.

The next morning, looking for all intents and purposes like a church rambling group, activists travelled to Purfleet station in Essex on public transport. The last leg they made on the number 44 bus, arriving at about 8.30am at a desolate-looking junction by an industrial estate. The eyes of Jackie Doyle-Price, the area's Conservative MP, watched from a large poster. The horizon was dominated by the Dartford Crossing. Assembling in a circle, they took a few final instructions.

'Remember: trust in each other, trust in yourself,' said one. They waited for a gap in the traffic, and walked out into the road.

19 OCTOBER

Dedicated and tireless, David Amess was a paragon of a good constituency MP

SIMON JENKINS

British politics rightly commemorates its own. David Amess, killed in his constituency last week, was eulogised yesterday in the Commons and St Margaret's church in Westminster as what the prime minister called 'one of the kindest, most gentle people in politics'. He was not a star of the parliamentary firmament, but rather that paragon, a 'good constituency MP'. The solemn minute's silence held in the House of Commons and the tributes to Amess from MPs testified to a profession under collective threat. It is one that lies at the heart of representational democracy: that of intermediary between the rulers and the ruled.

Amess's death comes at what many see as a critical juncture in democracy's theatre of public debate. MPs are exposed to criticism and attack as never before, thanks in large part to the glaringly inadequate regulation of social media. Male and female MPs, particularly female ones, are being subjected to appalling anonymous trolling. An Amnesty survey in the run-up to the 2017 general election found the MP Diane Abbott was in receipt of an average of 51 abusive tweets a day. Her colleague Jess Phillips has to keep in constant touch with the police. The atmosphere in which an MP must work is thus increasingly poisonous, with no effective action taken by either Facebook or Twitter.

One of the chief legacies of Amess's death must surely be action by the government and MPs alike to regulate the titans of the social media industry, whose creations are now haunting politics on both sides of the Atlantic. The evil they do both to individuals and to democracy as a whole far outweighs the benefits of non-regulation. The way democracy orchestrates public debate needs constant refreshment.

In Britain that is not happening. Parliament's combative debating chamber and absurd 'upper house' of lords desperately need reform to accommodate the digital age and wholly new patterns of political activity. Yet rather than instigate such reforms, the two houses are planning to spend huge amounts of taxpayers' money on moving their chambers and voting lobbies into Victorian facsimiles while they repair, rather than update, their old ones. The Commons is never remotely full except on Tuesday, Wednesday and Thursday. The rest of the time MPs are in their constituencies, where most are nowadays fully occupied.

The praise heaped on Amess was precisely for this commitment to his constituency, Southend West. He sought no ministerial office. He made no attempts at headline grabbing within his party or in government. The tributes paid to him have all shown his work in a remarkably domestic light. One constituent could not get a school bus, another's council tax was wrong, another could not find her mother a care visitor, one needed help with a homeless charity. Amess would drop everything to help people like this – and to support the local church choir, the fire brigade, a cancer charity. His final campaign was to have his beloved Southend declared a city – an ambition realised yesterday, when Boris Johnson confirmed the move in honour of Amess.

Other modern democracies would find it odd that tasks such as these should fall to a member of the nation's central assembly. In the 1950s, the MP Duncan Sandys was criticised for never appearing in his Streatham constituency. He blandly replied that he was elected to represent 'Streatham at Westminster, not Westminster at Streatham'. It was a repeat of Edmund Burke's similar retort to his Bristol electors. Parliament was where the nation's affairs were discussed, not Streatham high street.

Amess presented an image of an MP who was more similar to a local parish priest or GP. Yet his tasks were essential. The reason why they had to be performed, and why they would seem strange to other democracies, is that the services found lacking in his constituency are in Britain centrally ordained, while elsewhere they are a local democratic responsibility.

A British MP is thus thrust into the role of sole identifiable buffer between a citizen and the state, the last resort, the human port of call in time of distress. In France, Germany or Scandinavia, that buffer takes many forms: a mayor, a councillor, a local service ombudsman. I recall a survey from some years ago that found almost all Germans could name their mayor, while virtually no Britons could name their council leader. Local elections across most of Europe often enjoy huge turnouts, while Britain's are rarely much above 40 per cent.

An MP is thus the nearest to a proper mayor. David Cameron's elected mayors were nothing of the sort, instead mere regional lobbyists for groups of towns with no responsibility for services. MPs, on the other hand, are seen as having seniority and authority. Amess's peculiar genius was to know which door to knock on and, if necessary, break down. To an official, appeasing a popular MP was a wise act of one-off discretion, preferable to possibly having to upheave a defective policy. To an MP it is a path to local popularity and re-election.

In grand bureaucracies such as the health service or social care, the citizen confronts what can seem an overwhelming power. Each edifice is barricaded behind zombie phone lines of recorded voices and websites awash in codes and passwords. All are designed to deter any but the most determined assault. The modern state is an electronic fortress. The only humans who seem trusted by the public to lay siege to it are MPs.

This should not be so. On coming to office, every government pledges to decentralise, localise and diversify accountability. None delivers on that pledge. This gives MPs a prominence that, to many of their constituents, wrongly leaves them as recognisable embodiments of the state. To many people in Southend, Amess must have seemed the local face of the British government, albeit in a friendly guise. He was a point of live contact. As such, he could have seemed a natural focus of antagonism and hatred.

MPs must fill a vacuum in local accountability that detracts from their job of debating and scrutinising the executive in parliament. Such scrutiny has never been more needed than at present. It stands to the credit of Amess and the many MPs like him that they have such a rapport with their constituencies.

They are democracy's finest champions. But their most important and primary job remains at Westminster. Until a government is elected ready to divest power and accountability to other tiers of democracy, MPs will find themselves having to serve two masters. Amess too faced that dilemma.

Conservative MP Sir David Amess was stabbed to death on 15 October 2021 during a surgery at his constituency in Essex.

27 OCTOBER

Ready to quit your job? Come and join me in the anti-work movement

ELLE HUNT

In hindsight, this is embarrassing to admit. But, pre-pandemic, I might honestly have told you that work was the most rewarding part of my life. Even as a child I couldn't wait to get started with my 'career', rushing through school and university to get on with the main event. Through my twenties I broke up with boyfriends as soon as they started to encroach on my primary relationship: my job.

That relationship was one of the many to fall apart in lock-down, however. By freeing up every hour of my day to devote to work, the pandemic swiftly revealed it to be unsustainable, unhealthy and ultimately unrewarding. In two years, I have gone from an out-and-proud careerist to actively cultivating a mindset that might be called 'anti-work', and online I have found my community. On Reddit, the anti-work forum has seen enormous growth: the number of subscribers has increased almost 400 per cent in a year to reach 900,000.

The forum aims 'to start a conversation to problematise work as we know it', to resist an approach that values 'the needs and desires of managers and corporations above and beyond workers', and to imagine a world 'with unemployment for all, not just the rich!'. It shares recommended reading – the anthropologist David Graeber's indictment of 'bullshit jobs', Bertrand Russell's 1932 essay 'In Praise of Idleness' and 'fiction with anti-work themes' – plus anti-work quotes and a playlist (from Dolly Parton to Rage Against the Machine).

But r/antiwork's real value might be in the support it extends to those exploited in their jobs. Moderators are pooling resources to back hospitality and retail workers in a planned boycott of Black Friday next month. Last week, a bartender in the US shared messages from their boss demanding that they come into work at short notice on a Saturday for a ninth consecutive day. When their boss threatened to take away their company benefits, the bartender resigned.

'This [forum] gave me the motivation to finally quit my abusive job,' they posted. 'I may not have health insurance, but I feel so free!' Now, they said, they are in touch with a labour rights lawyer. Although, as ever with the internet, there are doubts as to the veracity of the exchange, the discussion speaks to the erosion of workers' rights – and people's mounting intolerance of it.

The recent explosion in activity on r/antiwork aligns with the growth in union membership in the US and UK through the pandemic, and the 'Great Resignation' as people quit their jobs or retrain. It seems to run deeper than just a desire for change, to acute dissatisfaction with the nature of work itself.

Nearly every industry is experiencing a talent shortage as people resist returning to the grind for as long as they can afford to do so. The US government puts the global shortfall at 40 million skilled workers, with forecast losses of trillions. Hiring managers are complaining of people not showing up to scheduled interviews or even their first day on the job. As the 'Ask a Manager' columnist Alison Green commented, the many people who have been ghosted after an interview might be permitted some schadenfreude.

So much of the societal transformation that we hoped would be precipitated by the pandemic hasn't come about, but there are reasons to be cautiously optimistic about the potential for change in our approach to work. As the culture reporter Charlie Warzel has written, while the topsy-turvy job market does not make up for weakened workers' rights, it does suggest 'the beginnings of a changing power dynamic ... Employees have a tiny bit of leverage right now and many are trying to use it to send a message about how the status quo of modern work feels exhausting and unsustainable.'

The key is for all workers to align as a class of people, and keep up the pressure on employers to make work work for us. Will the revolution begin on Reddit?

30 OCTOBER

Cop26: the time for prevarication is over

KATHARINE VINER

Summits do not always live up to the name. They can easily get bogged down in detail and disagreement, never really reaching altitude.

That is often the case with the annual UN climate conferences known simply as Cop, which have earned a reputation since the first was held 26 years ago for being bewildering marathons that overrun and underdeliver.

This year, perhaps more than any other year, the world needs the summit that starts tomorrow in Scotland to hit the heights. We've had make-or-break moments before, of course, when the climate movement has teetered on the brink of collapse at a Cop only to be rescued by a deal (or fudge) in injury time.

But Glasgow 2021 feels even more do-or-die, because the climate emergency is more finely balanced than ever before between hope and despair, and the effects are already all around us.

One path, the path of short-sighted national self-interest, leads us deeper into the crisis that *Guardian* reporters are covering now with ever greater frequency around the world: the heatwaves of Russia, eastern Europe and the west of North America this year; the floods in China, Germany, India, England, Greece, Thailand. The drought in eastern and southern Africa, threatening hunger, even famine, in places such as Madagascar. The wildfires in Australia, the United States, Canada, Europe, recurring with greater intensity, greater destruction.

Increasingly, at certain times and in certain places, the Earth is literally becoming unlivable. And this is a world warmer by just 1.2°C over pre-industrial levels. A world two or even three degrees warmer in which our descendants will swelter in a few decades' time if we carry on regardless is a terrifying prospect.

But the word 'crisis' has a second, less well-known meaning, from the original Greek – a turning point, an opportunity. What is perhaps different about this Cop, this moment, is that the opportunity is greater than ever.

There has never been as much innovation, investment and interest in green technology. The revolution in renewables, which have soared from a niche interest 30 years ago to a cheap, global alternative energy source that now provides more than one quarter of the world's electricity, is one of humanity's most remarkable achievements.

Heat pumps and hydrogen are becoming household words, if not quite yet everyday household appliances. Batteries, zero-carbon ships and aeroplanes, meat-free food and electric vehicles and other emissions-cutting technologies are all still in their infancy, full of potential. Science, so vital in our dogfight with Covid, is once again playing its part.

Now we need the politicians to play their part too. The fate of billions rests in their hands. Business and consumers are showing willing – but people take their cue from the government, from policy, from binding commitments.

So the Cop26 climate summit, which starts in Glasgow tomorrow, must be the moment when the hope generated by the Paris deal in 2015 becomes real.

The conference needs to find agreement on deep cuts to emissions. It needs to provide serious funding for developing nations to help them cope with the impacts of extreme weather which are already being felt. It needs to commit to ending the razing of forests.

And, most importantly, it needs to set targets for short-term progress and agree on a roadmap for action for the next decade. Every minute decisions are delayed, greenhouse gas emissions continue to rise – and the task ahead becomes more difficult, and urgent.

Taken together, ambitious measures in these areas could keep alive the goal of limiting global heating to 1.5°C. It will be hard. The UN climate convention operates by the consensus of all nations, and geopolitical shifts have fractured international cooperation in many areas in recent years.

But we all live under the same sky. We must hold on to the fact that if the necessary systemic changes take place – from energy to transport to food – we could build a cleaner, healthier world.

As Nicholas Stern, the British economist and author of the seminal 2006 government study into the costs of climate change, says, a just transition to a low-carbon economy is the only viable future for humanity.

The time for prevarication is over.

History will never forgive this generation for the inevitable legacy that would come from inaction.

1 NOVEMBER

Yorkshire CCC are institutionally racist. For me there is no other conclusion

JONATHAN LIEW

Yorkshire County Cricket Club are institutionally racist. There: that wasn't so hard, was it? For years Yorkshire enabled, tolerated and normalised a dressing-room culture of racist discourse. They failed to create a welcoming environment for Muslims and other ethnic minorities. They employed and continue to employ staff who have made racist comments.

When a former player raised serious allegations of long-standing racist behaviour three years ago, the club initially did nothing and then reportedly offered him a six-figure payout to keep quiet. Under investigation, they have chosen at every turn to prioritise their own reputation and their own people. It is true that an investigative panel found that Azeem Rafiq's exclusion from the team was based on his cricket, and not his race. It is also true the panel may not have found sufficient evidence to conclude that Yorkshire are institutionally racist. But frankly, to me, to draw any other conclusion is not simply a refutation of the available evidence but a form of moral cowardice.

So far, so cathartic. For all the comic ineptitude and farcical missteps Yorkshire have displayed in the handling of their racism investigation, anger remains the prevailing emotion here: anger at how long all this has taken, anger at the stories that have emerged, anger at the culture of shameless corporate self-interest that infects so much of this country's executive class.

Above all, you feel angry on behalf of Rafiq, a man who just wanted to bowl some off-spin and win some cricket games for Yorkshire, and who instead has found himself co-opted into a cruel fight for justice that has robbed him of his time and his joy, his human complexity, his dignity and occasionally his sanity.

One of the hallmarks of this episode is that every time you feel Yorkshire have plumbed their own capacity for moral decrep-itude, they somehow manage to drill even lower. Yesterday morning was another such moment: according to ESPNCricinfo, a current senior Yorkshire player admitted regularly addressing Rafiq using the P-word, but was cleared by the investigation of wrongdoing on the basis that it was 'not reasonable for Azeem to have been offended'. Such words, the panel argued, fell under the banner of 'good-natured banter between friends'.

If these latest revelations teach us anything, it is that the report commissioned by Yorkshire almost 14 months ago, dragged through a mangle of delays, and released (in summary) during the chaotic cancellation of the fifth Test between England and India, is barely worth the USB drive it was uploaded to. Key figures were not interviewed. Since Rafiq first went public with his testimony in a wisden.com interview in August 2020 – an account backed up by numerous former teammates and staff – the Yorkshire chairman, Roger Hutton, has not given a single public interview.

The sadness is that there are plenty of decent, principled, appalled people still working at Yorkshire today, but very few of them are in positions of real power. According to the *Yorkshire Post* some senior figures at the club are disgruntled it has not taken a more hostile line against Rafiq. This is a good example of how the struggle against racism is part of a broader fight against entitlement and entrenched privilege, be it through status or wealth or gender or connections. The point being: all this goes far deeper than simple acts of racist abuse. This is about how institutions protect themselves and resist change, about where power lies in our game and how it replicates.

In 2003, when Darren Lehmann was banned for calling a Sri Lankan opponent a 'black cunt' during a one-day international for Australia, his county, Yorkshire, refused to take any action. 'You can't say it was malicious, far from it,' said Colin Graves, the chairman at the time. 'I'm disappointed the ICC has taken it down this route. He is not a racist.' Case closed: ancient history. Except Graves ended up running English cricket. Lehmann ended up coaching Deccan Chargers and Australia and this year was welcomed back to Headingley as coach of the Northern Superchargers. Imagine all the cricketers of colour who will have played under them, the staff who owed their livelihoods to them, the youngsters who went through the pathways they controlled. Imagine how little power they had and how much Graves and Lehmann enjoyed by comparison. That is institutional racism in action.

Yorkshire acted shamefully, but didn't act alone. Senior white England players avoid discussing racism out of squeamishness.

The England and Wales Cricket Board, now making its own inquiries, spent years turning a blind eye to racism in the English game before deciding in 2020 there might be good PR in all this George Floyd stuff. Even now, with its T-shirt gimmicks and a communications department bigger than many countries' coaching staff, it gives the impression of a body less concerned with improving the game than with being able to say it has improved the game.

As another month ticks by, Rafiq continues to wait for justice. He really was a very decent bowler in his prime, a clever spinner with an underrated batting technique, an England Under-19s captain who with a little love and luck could easily have developed into an international cricketer. He's still only 30. And yet right now, his defining legacy in the game is as a victim of someone else's racism. In a crowded field, that may well be the biggest injustice of all.

15 NOVEMBER

Ratchets, phase-downs and a fragile agreement: how Cop26 played out

FIONA HARVEY

As weary delegates trudged into the Scottish Event Campus on the banks of the Clyde on Saturday, few realised what a mountain they still had to climb. The Cop26 climate talks were long past their official deadline of 6pm on Friday, but there were strong hopes that the big issues had been settled. A deal was tantalisingly close.

The 'package' on offer was imperfect – before countries even turned up in Glasgow they were meant to have submitted plans that would cut global carbon output by nearly half by 2030 to limit global heating to 1.5°C above pre-industrial levels. Although most countries had submitted plans, they were not strong enough and analysis found they would lead to a disastrous 2.4°C of heating.

The gap between countries' targets and the emissions cuts scientists say are needed had been known before the talks. What was crucial in Glasgow was to find a roadmap to closing it, which involved forcing some highly reluctant countries to agree a time-table of swift revisions. Finally, after two weeks of wrangling, a 'ratchet' had been settled, with countries agreeing to return next year, and the year after, with amendments.

As the Cop26 president, Alok Sharma, approached the podium, the gavel was poised by his folder, ready to push through an agree-ment between all of the nearly 200 countries gathered in the room. But there was a last-minute hitch.

What followed reduced Sharma almost to tears. China and India wanted to reopen a vital clause in the agreement that enjoined countries to 'phase out' coal-fired power generation. No dates were given for the phase-out, and no more commitment than 'accelerating efforts towards the phase-out of unabated coal power and inefficient fossil fuel subsidies'.

Abandoning coal, the dirtiest fossil fuel, is essential to staying within 1.5°C, a level scientists regard as a 'planetary boundary' beyond which some impacts of climate breakdown will become catastrophic and irreversible. The International Energy Agency has said 40 per cent of the world's existing 8,500 coal-fired power plants must be closed by 2030 and no new ones built to stay within the 1.5°C limit.

Sharma had made 'consigning coal to history' a personal mission through his presidency of the UK talks, and made numerous speeches on it. He had determined long before the start of the summit that he wanted a commitment on coal in the text.

It may not seem controversial for an agreement on the climate to refer to the need to cut out fossil fuels. Yet since the Kyoto protocol was signed in 1997, there has been no such reference in a Cop decision, at the behest of the major fossil fuel producers and users, who hold a great deal of sway in a process that relies on consensus. The inclusion of such a commitment in the Glasgow outcome was a major step.

At the last minute, China and India – both major coal users and producers – made known that they objected to this wording. Sharma, who had been surviving the day on a diet of Lucozade tablets as he had no breaks for food, convened a meeting in the space behind the auditorium. As the Indian delegates discussed the wording among themselves, Sharma answered them in Hindi to press the case for its retention, but to no avail. The two countries were adamant: a phase-out was unacceptable: a phase-down, implying a longer-term future for some coal at least, was the most they would sign up to. The carefully crafted agreement was now in peril.

'My fear was we would lose the whole deal,' Sharma told the *Guardian* later. 'This was a fragile agreement. If you pull one thread, the whole thing could unravel. We would have lost two years of really hard work – we would have ended up with nothing to show for it, for developing countries.'

The man jokingly nicknamed 'No Drama Sharma' by his team was on the verge of tears. To be forced to accept the change was bitter, and he was 'deeply frustrated' according to an aide.

From the start, Sharma has seen himself as the champion of the most vulnerable developing countries at these talks, the only forum in which the poorest nations can confront the biggest emitters and producers of fossil fuels with the consequences of their actions. Choking back emotion, he addressed them directly:

'I apologise for the way this process has unfolded. And I am deeply sorry. I also understand the deep disappointment. But as you have also noted, I think it's vital that we protect this package.'

Developing countries felt the disappointment just as keenly, but they understood the difficulties Sharma faced. 'Although this is far from a perfect text, we have taken important steps forward in our efforts to keep 1.5°C alive, and deliver the much-needed outcomes on adaptation,' said Milagros De Camps of the Dominican Republic and the Alliance of Small Island States. 'We acknowledge it was not an easy task.'

Sharma insists that the deal as it stands shows 'we are on the way to consigning coal to history'. Nicholas Stern, a climate economist, concurs: 'The last-minute watering down of this statement is unfortunate but is unlikely to slow down a strong momentum past coal, a dirty fuel of an earlier era.'

John Kerry, the UN climate envoy, was also visibly annoyed, telling journalists afterwards: 'Did I appreciate we had to adjust one thing tonight in a very unusual way? No. But if we hadn't done that we wouldn't have a deal. I'll take "phase it down" and take the fight into next year.'

For the UK, it was a bitter pill but did not scupper the hard-fought diplomatic struggle to 'keep 1.5°C alive'. The Paris agreement of 2015 marked the first time that developed and developing countries agreed to take the necessary action to limit temperature rises, to 'well below' 2°C above pre-industrial levels, and to 'pursue efforts' to limit heating to 1.5°C. Since Paris, however, scientific warnings on climate have intensified. In October 2018, the Intergovernmental Panel on Climate Change – the leading authority on climate science – showed that going beyond 1.5°C would produce changes that would rapidly become irreversible. The melting of the ice caps would accelerate, sea levels would rise to inundate islands and coastal areas, coral reefs would die and extreme weather would wreak havoc.

Johan Rockström, the director of the Potsdam Institute for Climate Impact Research and one of the world's foremost climate scientists, warned that the 1.5°C target was not like other political negotiations, which can be haggled over or compromised on. 'A rise of 1.5°C is not an arbitrary number, it is not a political number. It is a planetary boundary,' he told the *Guardian*. 'Every fraction of a degree more is dangerous.'

At Cop26, 30,000 participants from nearly 200 countries roamed the halls, some in colourful national dress, others in sombre suits, all in masks. In these meetings, the people suffering on the frontline have an opportunity to confront those responsible for the emissions causing climate change. It is a powerful moral lever, notes Tina Stege, a climate envoy for the Marshall Islands, an archipelago with 60,000 inhabitants that leads the High Ambition Coalition at the talks. 'We are a small nation, but we have moral authority – our position on the frontline gives us that,' says Stege. 'We need to raise our voice, as these changes will affect the whole world in time.'

16 NOVEMBER

Here's the irony of racial progress in Britain – it's now harder to call out racism

NESRINE MALIK

Britain's racism crises now seem to come around as predictably as the seasons. As certain as Wimbledon heralds the summer, the next scandal is sure to appear on the horizon, and with it a storm that darkens Britain's sunny view of its racial progress.

But, like all storms, it will pass, leaving little but a sort of atmospheric discomfort, and even that eventually dissipates. Because it seems to have been decided, at some meeting to which an awful lot of people weren't invited, that Britain has been cured of its racism ills. The occasional flare-up is something to be extinguished, rather than an indication that there is a larger undiagnosed issue underneath.

Periodically, a public figure of black or other minority ethnic background will reveal something horrifying about how they were treated by colleagues or superiors in their profession. Consistently, their demands for redress take too long to be met, which becomes an injury in itself. Whether it's the footballer Eni Aluko being told by the England manager to make sure that her Nigerian relatives weren't carrying the Ebola virus or, most recently, the cricketer Azeem Rafiq allegedly being called the P-word by his teammates, investigations are drawn out, then quickly closed, leaving little room for reflection on the climate that enabled the abuse.

For all the sound and fury of each incident, little changes because the country gives itself a pass. It either minimises the affair's seriousness or chooses to believe that, while there is a problem, it is the fault of a 'small minority'. It's something that should not be 'amplified', rather than something endemic that calls for uncomfortable questions and meaningful reform.

It's banter or bad apples. Take your pick. For these are pretty much the only explanations offered for scandals that have engulfed a variety of institutions over the past five years: the Home Office, the police, the Football Association, with Yorkshire County Cricket Club just the latest. List them and they seem less like anomalies and more like features of contemporary Britain

– miscarriages of justice towards members of the Windrush generation, excessive use of police force, racial abuse towards footballers and cricketers. That's a lot of banter, a lot of bad apples.

The incidents occur separately, to different people at different times and in different places, but still there is a subtle pattern in how the allegations are received. There is an incredulity, a push-back – hesitant at first then increasingly confident – followed by an assertive and well-rehearsed damage limitation exercise that seeks to reassure the public that, however bad matters seem, things are in fact very much in hand.

Part of this is best explained as the paradox of racial progress: the more diverse and liberal a society becomes, the more that white people, more secure in their values and proximity to people of colour as friends, colleagues or family, are likely to reject claims of racist treatment. And the result of that is a destigmatisation of slurs and behaviours that should have been heading to extinction.

When a formal inquiry, in 2021, concludes that someone calling you the P-word is all 'in the spirit of friendly banter', what we are witnessing is a regression. One in which people have decided, without asking those being insulted, that we are post-racial and that people should just be able to take a joke.

Another step forward that has propelled us two steps back is a neighbourhood-watch-style understanding of racism: one that assigns white individuals the task of policing their own behaviour. This emphasis, although welcome, also regrettably serves as a diversion from all the higher and broader ways in which institutional racism operates.

Whenever one of these racism scandals hits, it seems to me that the biggest fight is to challenge the complacencies and complicities of progress. To talk not in terms of the spirit or the good intentions behind the words of Rafiq's teammates, but what recent histories they echo, how they land, what hostility or inhospitality they create for players like Rafiq.

More representation and diversity is always touted as the answer, but they are not ends in themselves. They are merely part of a process of learning in which we figure out once again how we coexist in a country that is becoming more diverse – and beneficially so – but has decided that the hard graft is done and its journey towards equality is over. It isn't.

18 NOVEMBER

Dining across the divide: 'I think some of the ideas are horrible – but it's nice to sit and talk'

SAM WOLLASTON

STIJN, 47, NORWICH
Occupation Humanitarian aid worker
Voting record Stijn, who is from Belgium, can't vote in general elections in the UK, and couldn't vote in the EU referendum. In Belgium he voted Green
Amuse bouche After a typhoon in the Philippines, Stijn organised karaoke: 'People cried from feeling human again'

DAVID, 72, CAMBRIDGESHIRE
Occupation Owns a property portfolio
Voting record Ukip when there has been a candidate, otherwise Conservative – he stood for Ukip in local elections

Amuse bouche David reads the *Guardian* online every morning and agrees with very little of it

FOR STARTERS

STIJN I told him I am Belgian and my wife is German. My job is not in the UK. I'm here because I like it. I love Norwich.

DAVID I found him a little hard to understand. Normally Dutch speakers have a very good command of English.

STIJN My mother tongue is Dutch, second language French. I made him ask questions – an achievement as he tends to talk rather than do that.

DAVID When I travel in Europe, people like to practise their English on me. Some even invite me to correct them.

THE BIG BEEF

STIJN I didn't see a very pro-EU stance in the referendum campaign. I saw the leave campaign, which was basically: 'Press this button and the whole thing blows up', while the other side said: 'Let's not press this button because it's scary.' It's easy to point out that the EU is a mess, badly organised and inefficient – you won't find anyone in Belgium or Germany who disagrees. We take that as the price to pay for sitting down and working something out.

DAVID It's very strange when people who are leftwing like Stijn are pro the EU when the common agricultural policy, which even now is nearly 40 per cent of the EU budget, is a huge transfer of money from the poor to the rich. In the year of the referendum, the biggest subsidy receivers in the country were the Queen, the Duke of Westminster and James Dyson.

STIJN He said the bigger the institution, the more corrupt it is. I've worked around the world – there's a lot of small-town nepotism and corruption, and here there is a government that likes to give contracts to their fellow Etonians and other friends. Corruption has many faces.

DAVID I think a common market is great. A free trade area is excellent. What we don't need is political union.

STIJN I have a lot of criticisms of the EU, but I also want national governments to be accountable, and for citizens to be not only at the mercy of their own governments. Working around the world, I see how that can be for minorities, for poorer communities, for refugees. I want institutions above that.

SHARING PLATE

DAVID When I went to Ukip meetings, I made a very deliberate effort to go to Conservative, Labour and Lib Dem meetings, too – and Stijn said he was pro that kind of approach.

STIJN Polarisation is not necessarily a big problem. I don't think the ideal is that everyone gets along – there should be strong disagreement in society.

FOR AFTERS

DAVID We talked about the anglophone world – dominated by the US in GDP and by India in population. There is an inescapable cultural link between these countries that we don't necessarily have with our European neighbours.

STIJN An imperial state of mind is still very present in England. He talked fondly about the anglophone world – I was like: 'Yeah, but it's the result of colonisation and mass migration.'

DAVID My instincts have always been for small government. He said that's great for people who do well, but bad for people who fall through the cracks. He's got a point, but you have to decide which is a better big picture to run with. I'm in favour of equality of opportunity, but not equality of outcome.

STIJN He looks at the world from the perspective of somebody who can fend for himself, but it disregards what happens to people who are not so fortunate.

TAKEAWAYS

DAVID On one or two issues we were on opposite sides of the fence, but that didn't mean we were enemies. That would be a hopeless way of living.

STIJN While Ukip is one of the most horrible vehicles in this country in the last 10 years, he is still a dad, and a person. I think some of the ideas are horrible, and Nigel Farage is particularly horrible. But it's nice to sit in front of another human being and talk.

20 NOVEMBER

Are the 2020s really like living back in the 1970s? I wish ...

POLLY TOYNBEE

Queuing for petrol, I turn on the radio and there are Abba, singing their latest hit. Shortages on shop shelves are headline news, with warnings of a panic-buying Christmas. And national debt is sky high. But this isn't the 1970s; it's 2021. People who weren't born then have been calling this a return to that decade. There are similarities, of course: this retro-thought was sparked by the recent petrol queues, people as frantic to fill up to get to work as I remember back then. Elsewhere, flowing floral midi dresses are back, just like the ones I wore; Aldi is selling rattan hanging egg chairs and, as well as Abba, the charts have been topped by Elton John. But is this really a 1970s reprise?

No, nothing like it; not history repeated, not even as farce – just a stylist's pastiche. Folk memory preserves only the 1974 three-day week; the miners' strike blackouts, with no streetlights and candle shortages; the embargo that quadrupled the price of oil. True, I did queue at the coal merchant's to fire up an ancient stove for lack of any other heat or light. But the decade shouldn't be defined by this, or by 1978-79's 'winter of discontent' strikes, a brief but pungent time of rubbish uncollected and (a very few) bodies unburied by council gravediggers.

Most 70s imagery is a deliberately manufactured caricature, with its garish wallpaper and avocado suites, an ignored time zone between the swinging 60s and glitzy, greed-is-good, big bang, big hair 80s. It's an image that obscures the radical social changes and great progressive leaps forward that took place then. True, we all construct our own pick'n'mix memorabilia and there's a risk anyone my age will pine for the decade when they were in their twenties. But that's not why I reject any comparison to Boris Johnson's Brexit-stricken regressive and corrupt era.

So why does history record the 70s as nothing but a time of strife, shortages, hyper-inflation and decline? Well, it's because history is written by the victor. And that victor was Margaret Thatcher, whose 1979 election conquest sought to uproot, marketise and diminish the role of the postwar state. Her political tribe used all their media power to expunge inconvenient 70s memories that didn't fit her narrative, as surely as Stalin purged Trotsky from the photographic record. It was a goodbye to John Maynard Keynes's generous social democratic state and hello to Friedrich Hayek's desire to let the market rip; Thatcher kept his book *The Road to Serfdom* in her handbag to waggle at her cabinet.

In 1970, I was travelling the country researching my book *A Working Life*. I took jobs at Unilever's soap factory in Port Sunlight, Merseyside; in a cake factory; as a hospital ward orderly; and I joined the Women's Royal Army Corps for a while. Working as a switch-cable operator in one of the 11 Lucas car-parts factories in Birmingham (all now closed), I watched a strike by our foremen and charge hands, who were trying to restore their differentials – the extra pay they received above those they supervised. By the second day, 19,000 car workers were laid off, so just-in-time supply chains were fragile even then. However, unions were simply striving not to fall behind a rate of inflation that later soared to nearly 30 per cent; the reality I saw was unrecognisable from the 'grasping workers' vilified in the anti-union Tory press (Rupert Murdoch had bought the *Sun* the year before). Union membership peaked at 13 million by 1979. Now less than half as many belong. Strong, 70s-style unions would never have let this current zero hours gig economy destroy rights that had been hard-earned back then.

Here's another crucial contrast. Look at the relative ease with which Edward Heath's Conservative government took the country into Europe in 1973, a move confirmed in Labour's referendum two years later on a 67 per cent to 33 per cent vote. Yet now we're out, a country adrift and wrenched apart by an acrimonious Brexit.

For all the turmoil, Britain's democratic institutions never buckled. Now they come under greater threat from the prime minister himself, who assails the powers of regulators, judges, scrutiny committees and all the checks and balances of our unwritten constitution. He sends in his culture warriors to spearhead 'a war on woke'. But for my friends and me, 'woke' began in 1970 with Germaine Greer's *The Female Eunuch*, an electric shock of awakening. *Spare Rib* and *Gay News* heralded liberation for millions more. Each new iteration of activism rolls those freedoms forwards, as #MeToo energises a new generation to break silence on sexual harassment by bosses. Back then, I'm afraid, we wearily fended off beware-the-stationery-cupboard lecherous gropings, regarding them as part of women's working life.

I joined the *Guardian*'s women's page in 1977 when the great and funny writer Jill Tweedie broke every mould, challenging every assumption, including those of SCUM, the Society for Cutting Up Men, pretty much a one-woman crusade by Valerie Solanas. Jill never dodged the dilemma of 'liberation' from men we loved and lived with: she had lost two children; stolen abroad by an abusive husband. Her influence sometimes shocked her: a woman called her in the *Guardian* office one day from a public phone box, saying: 'Right, I've left my husband. I'm in a caravan with my children, what do I do now?' Feminism was always plagued by rifts: Jill and I were locked in at an angry meeting by radical feminists threatening not to release us until the *Guardian* backed abortion of all male foetuses. Now, I tear my hair out over the latest feminist arguments over trans issues.

How far have we come? Never far enough. Of demands drawn up at the first National Women's Liberation Conference in 1970, there is still no equal pay or opportunity, no abortion on demand, or free 24-hour nurseries. Despite some state aid, Britain still has some of the most expensive childcare in the developed world, costing parents more than their rent or mortgage, often for poorly trained staff paid a pittance.

The first women's refuge opened in 1971 – but 80 women a year are still murdered by a partner or ex-partner in England and Wales. When I worked in a Wimpy bar half a century ago, no single women were allowed in after midnight: those who were unaccompanied were presumed to be prostitutes. It could be hard to get served in a pub. Some things slide backwards: as I

buy presents for my newest granddaughter, I find the pinkifica-
tion of 'girls' toys has got worse since my daughters were small:
there were no pink space hoppers. Children are more shut in
now, parents too afraid to let them roam, more anxious about
threats of every kind, from strangers to impure food. There were
always a thousand ways to make mothers miserable: in 1975, only
57 per cent of women worked, with rightwing papers running a
drumbeat of spurious research on the damage done to children
to make working mothers guilty, often wheeling out John Bowl-
by's 'attachment theory'. Now women's employment stands at 78
per cent, but with the absolute necessity of two incomes to keep
an insanely expensive roof over the family, full-time work and
lack of childcare feels less like liberation for many.

Newly married in 1970, aged 23 with a full-time job, when
I bought a washing machine I needed my husband's signature
on the hire purchase agreement. The rampant misogyny and
racism of 'jokes' in 70s TV comedy has made some of those
programmes unrepeatable. The 'political-correctness-gone-mad'
brigade should be made to watch the revolting Benny Hill
chasing bikini-clad young girls, or the sitcom *Mind Your Language*,
with its riot of immigrant jokes in a night school class, to appreciate how Labour's Equal Opportunities Commission and Race
Relations Board in 1976 began the long, slow culture change.
For all the Enoch Powellite anti-immigrant racism, it was a
decade that saw more people emigrate than immigrate. As feminists, we thought Barbara Castle's 1970 Equal Pay Act and the
Sex Discrimination Act would fix everything, but here we are,
still fighting old battles. Three-quarters of mothers say they face
discrimination at work for being pregnant, with shocking cases
of sackings and demotions from the Pregnant Then Screwed
campaign. Some glass ceilings shattered through that decade:
the Old Bailey got its first woman judge in 1972 and now there

are equal numbers, but still only 28 per cent of university professors are women.

By the 70s, the worst brutalities of childbirth were ending: Sheila Kitzinger had rebelled against enforced pubic hair shaving and giving birth with legs strapped up in stirrups. I had my first two children in the 70s, and I worked as a ward orderly in a maternity ward in a run-down hospital, and it's striking that women had kinder care and attention then. A full week in hospital was a blessing for many, and health visitors were closer at hand for everyone. My daughters were turfed out within hours of their children being born and, compared with 2015, there are a third fewer health visitors, leaving them to struggle with impossible caseloads.

A great landmark of the decade was Harold Wilson's Open University. With its first students starting in 1971, it offered second chances, especially to women, and is now Britain's biggest university by far. Women's new freedom and opportunity helped triple divorce rates in the 70s: better child benefits made escape easier. But the penalty for single parenthood is higher now, with 49 per cent of children in lone-parent families living below the poverty line, according to the Child Poverty Action Group. We have more things now, but many more children are left outside the consumer society.

Now, civilisation is on a climate knife-edge, but then world-ending fear focused on nuclear war. Alarm at extinct species and environmental pollution was rife, but concern could be gently laughed at in the Surbiton of 70s sitcom *The Good Life*. I was keenly aware, because my father, a millenarian by nature, founded an ill-fated agricultural commune in Monmouthshire in the 70s, designed to be self-sustaining. He used to wag a finger at me and my city ways, warning I'd come crawling to their door begging for cabbages when my unsustainable lifestyle caught up with me. The venture collapsed in 1979.

For a family on the left, with a relaxed attitude to sex, I don't think there was any greater gap between my parents and me than between me and my children and they and my grandchildren. I went on an anti-Vietnam war demo with my father, and pro-EU membership and climate protests with my grandchildren. But I see how each generation has a greater sensitivity on race, gender and privilege, which I find encouraging. Here's the greatest generational difference: we boomers had it all in the 70s – free university, plentiful good jobs with pensions, cheap homes to buy, but none of those are there for millennials.

Don't be tricked by false parallels between the 70s and now. Look at the hard economic facts: in the 70s, Britain reached its most equal point ever in pay and wealth. In a century-long trajectory, super-taxes and inheritance taxes had gradually eroded the mega-incomes of the rich to pay for a growing welfare state with pensions, benefits and the NHS. That's how my generation was taught O-level social history: as a story of unstoppable progress from reforming factory acts, working and voting rights to a social security safety net. To understand the 70s, remember that the unions' struggle was about holding on to that progress against a tidal wave of inflation.

In 1979, that battle was lost and everything went into reverse. The slump of 1980-81 caused by an extreme austerity budget tipped millions, especially the young, into unemployment, which rose above 11 per cent. Later, deregulating the City blew the lid off top earnings, so the income and wealth gap widened astronomically. The victors' history tells a story of militant strikers making outrageous demands, designed to justify Thatcher's crushing of the unions and the deep inequality that has endured ever since as a result.

As I write, the number of people falling into poverty is growing rapidly, after universal credit cuts. Last month's budget cemented the fact that pay – stagnant for the past decade – will continue to be so through the next.

I can see why some look back now, imagining the 2020s – full of political, economic and environmental doom – as a reprise of those times. Look how many of that era's icons retain their cultural clout. I've just read John le Carré's posthumous bestseller *Silverview*, and I urge his 1974 classic *Tinker Tailor Soldier Spy* on my older grandchildren as the best evocation of a cold war that framed our thinking and fears. Debbie Harry, still magnificent when she goes to Glastonbury, Led Zeppelin's Robert Plant back in the charts, ditto Nile Rodgers of Chic – 70s icons have been revived or never went away. Back then, the UK could win Eurovision song contests, too, but a repeat of that feat seems unlikely now that everyone hates us.

Style? The flowery dresses back in vogue remind me of Laura Ashley in her heyday, though her clothes strove to be more authentic Victorian country print copies, with mutton chop shoulders, and I even had one with a bustle. Yes, I had an egg chair, but – as Aldi shoppers will find – they're more for posing than comfort. And I did have one room with wallpaper that looked like fried eggs. Are these lurids really back in vogue? Not with me.

But do reject the rightwing trashing of the 70s as a time of 'decline' and 'failure', the Austin Allegro of decades. Thatcherites needed to invent that history to disguise their social vandalism and promote the myth of her glittering capitalist renaissance. Take it from me, and from all the social statistics: the 70s were a good time to be alive.

26 NOVEMBER

'He didn't come back': the grim camps from where refugees set off for the UK

LUKE HARDING AND DAN SABBAGH

For four days this week Karwan Tahir shared a tent in the woods around Dunkirk with a young man named Karim. In the early hours of Wednesday morning Karim set off for the UK – a journey in darkness to the nearby beach, and from there into the vast and uncertain Channel in a flimsy dinghy.

'I don't know if he made it or if he drowned,' Tahir said on Friday, showing off the living space he and Karim had briefly shared. 'He didn't come back. I only knew he came from [Iraqi] Kurdistan, like me. We met at the camp. He knew I spoke English and so he invited me to share his tent.

'Now it's mine,' he added.

Karim's last known location was a sprawling encampment of shelters on the outskirts of Grande-Synthe, next to a bridge and a canal. The camp is home to several hundred people, almost all Kurds from Iraq. Most probably the 27 people who died in the icy waters on Wednesday had lived and slept here before they set off on their final journey.

Precise information, however, is hard to come by. In this makeshift community, people look out for each other, but apart from family or buddy groups, relations are temporary and transient. Although everybody has a mobile phone to be in touch with family and friends, firm information about the dead is hard to ascertain.

Grieving relatives will probably be back at home.

It does not pay to ask too many questions. The atmosphere changes after dark, when deals are struck and the Kurdish mafia who run smuggling operations are present.

According to local aid workers, a 23-year-old Iraqi Kurd was shot twice in the leg on Wednesday after an argument, and was taken by ambulance to hospital. A smuggler is said to have opened fire after the man refused to get on a boat, hours after news spread that 27 people had died. He had paid £1,500 – half his fee – with the other £1,500 promised once he had landed in the UK.

It is not clear if Karim was among the 17 men who drowned, together with seven women – one of them pregnant – and three children, or if he made it to Dover. Tahir showed off the lifejacket he had bought in anticipation of his own crossing – 'it cost me 35 [about £30]', he said – as well as a cuddly tiger left by a newly departed family.

Tahir described the tortuous journey that had taken him to the north coast of France. He said he had left the Kurdish city of Sulaymaniyah a month ago and then flew from Dubai to the Belarus capital, Minsk. He reached the EU border with help from Belarusian border guards who showed him where to cross, he said. From Poland he travelled by car to northern France. The trip so far had cost £12,000, he said, including £3,000 paid to smugglers upfront for his forthcoming boat trip.

Most of those camping out in the rain and mud are young, unaccompanied men but there are a few families, too. One small boy, Muhammad, was playing with a plastic helicopter under a tarpaulin, next to an open log fire built by his father, Adil. Adil's wife, Sarah, and baby son, Malik, sheltered in a tent. The camp is grim and rubbish-strewn, with no toilets or running water. Charities provide clothes and food.

Despite Wednesday's tragedy, many of those camping here said they were still determined to reach the UK. Sokar Mawlud, 20, from the Iraqi city of Kirkuk, admitted the bad weather made the journey even more perilous and he was 'stuck'. He was intending to go to London with his brother Sarhand, 13, and their mother, Shawbo, 42.

Mawlud's odyssey has been a long one. He said he left Iraq in 2015 and spent six years in the German city of Nuremberg, going to school, before he was forced to leave and put on a flight to Turkey. From there he tracked back to France. Why the UK? 'My sister lives there. She's a hairdresser,' he said. He thought he knew one of the people who had drowned, but was not sure.

On Thursday Mawlud and his family headed for Loon-Plage, the beach west of Dunkirk from where the 27 victims are believed to have set off. A boat was waiting. They turned back, Mawlud said, after spotting a French police patrol on the sands. 'It's dangerous, actually. The smugglers buy a dinghy meant for 20 people and then cram 50 people on board.'

On Loon-Plage there were haunting signs of the migrants who had left. A collapsed dinghy lay amid the dunes; further along, against a backdrop of Dunkirk's busy port with its cranes and smoke, was another abandoned dinghy, made by the German firm MaRe Boote. Nearby was a red lifejacket and a left shoe, half filled with sand. Its owner's fate was unknown.

Most of those camped around Calais and Dunkirk have some family connection with Britain – uncles, siblings, friends. Others said they had learned from social media that it was easy to get a job. Tahir said he had lived in Bury St Edmunds for seven years, working in Pizza Express, and had gone home to Iraq in 2006, thinking his country was safe. 'A mistake,' he said.

Nationalities tend to clump together in different camps along the Nord-Pas de Calais coast. Akhmed Wikky, 21, was one of a handful of

Afghans who had ended up in Grande-Synthe, a suburb of Dunkirk. He said he left Afghanistan five months ago on foot from his home in the city of Mazar-i-Sharif. By the time he reached Turkey in August, the Taliban had seized his hometown and the capital, Kabul.

What would he do now?

'My brother lives in Luton. I'll try and join him there. If I can't, my plan B is to stay and learn French,' he said.

The bigger politics of the migrant crisis, he said, had passed him by. 'I'm not a drug dealer, or a terrorist, or a bad man. I just want my human rights,' he said. 'My ambition is to study in the UK. I would like to be a town planner.'

29 NOVEMBER

The English turned Barbados into a slave society. Now, after 396 years, we're free

SULEIMAN BULBULIA

On 20 October, in a joint sitting of parliament, Mia Mottley, the prime minister of Barbados, described the removal of Queen Elizabeth as the head of state and the decision to become a republic as a 'seminal moment' in our country's history. We have reached the day that this becomes a reality, as Barbados embarks on its new path, cutting the umbilical cord that bound it to its former colonial master, the United Kingdom.

It began yesterday, when Dame Sandra Mason was installed as the first president of Barbados. That event – at which public participation was extremely limited due to Covid protocols – had the Prince of Wales in attendance as representative of the Queen.

That decision itself stirred emotions. Some Barbadians were not happy with his presence. Others suggest that now may be a good time to raise the issue of reparations with Charles. In any case, this day has been a long time coming. It was on 14 May 1625 that the first English ship reached the island under the command of Captain John Powell, who claimed it on behalf of James I. It was from that time, 396 years ago, that 'Los Barbados' (the bearded ones) became an English colony. It acquired its name from the Portuguese – earlier visitors who some claim were struck by the abundant fig trees, which have a beard-like appearance. Others surmised it was down to the presence of bearded people.

From 1627, the English settled on the island, wiping away any traces of the original inhabitants, the Arawaks, who had lived here for centuries. People with good financial backgrounds and social connections with England were allocated land in this new colony; Barbados's strong connection and staunchly British attitude earned it the title of 'Little England'. The English turned Barbados into a slave society, a slave economy, which would be replicated in several parts of the 'new world'. It was known as the 'jewel in the crown' of the Caribbean. It is a history that we can never be proud of, but one that we must understand.

Professor Hilary Beckles, a Barbadian historian, the current vice-chancellor of the University of the West Indies and a leading figure in the push by Caribbean islands to secure reparations, sums it up best. 'Barbados was the birthplace of British slave society and the most ruthlessly colonised by Britain's ruling elites,' he writes. 'They made their fortunes from sugar produced by an enslaved, "disposable" workforce, and this great wealth secured Britain's place as an imperial superpower and caused untold suffering.'

We see it as a journey: 30 November – when we become a republic – is another stop on our journey. It's a date with resonance, as 30 November 1966 was our independence day. It is a sign of this journey continuing that at 55 we are confident to say to the UK and the world that, despite our size and our limited resources, we can be our own shepherds, our own stewards.

Of course, our transition may not find favour among those who still believe that the 'sun will never set on the British empire'. Older folks here remember the days when British royalty would visit. They would stand in the sun waving the union flag, hoping to catch a glimpse of the Queen or her representatives. But Little England has grown up, it has matured, it should no longer be loitering in its 'master's castle'.

As part of the transition, there will be official activities in National Heroes Square in the capital city, Bridgetown, but one notable absence will be Lord Nelson. For 208 years his statue stood there, but in 2020 it was ceremoniously removed – a result of the Black Lives Matter movement here and the reawakening of our consciousness.

There are no plans to change our national symbols: the flag, the coat of arms, the national pledge, the national anthem. However, the terms 'royal' and 'crown' will be removed from official terminology. The Royal Barbados Police Force will become the Barbados Police Service; 'crown lands' will become 'state lands'. Independence day will still be 30 November, and the focus will stay on the birth of the modern nation. The day will belong, as it always has, to our national hero, our first prime minister, the father of independence, the Right Excellent Errol Walton Barrow.

Of course, Barbados will maintain a strong relationship with the UK. Our main source for tourists is from there; Brits love Barbados. But this is a new era, in which all Barbadians must take pride and take ownership. As for Little England, these times may call for a new term of endearment.

Suleiman Bulbulia was a member of the republican status transition advisory committee in Barbados and is a columnist for Barbados Today.

10 DECEMBER

Tories, look in the mirror: hasn't the price of being humiliated by Johnson become too high?

GABY HINSLIFF

Thinking of throwing a boozy office party, a potential super-spreader event in the teeth of a Covid storm? Then knock yourself out, is the official advice from a government accused of being only too willing to open a celebratory bottle itself. Just don't, whatever you do, enter the office to actually do some work.

The Omicron variant has prodded Boris Johnson into adopting his fallback plan B, and what a classically Johnsonian plan it is: contradictory, rushed and shrouded in murky allegations. From Monday, everyone who can should work from home, but he wants office bashes and school nativity plays to go ahead. There will be vaccine passes for entering big venues, but no masks in pubs and restaurants.

If these compromises were meant to placate freedom-loving Tories, they failed: backbenchers threatening to rebel en masse were only further incensed when Johnson hinted he was considering making vaccination compulsory. That his own health secretary, Sajid Javid, promptly said this would be unethical indicates how carefully that idea had been debated before being tossed out, seemingly on the hoof.

The kindest explanation for the chaos is that Johnson was distracted by his wife, Carrie, going into labour, as he careered from parliamentary showdown to Covid press conference on Wednesday. But even some of his own backbenchers are no longer willing to be so charitable, publicly accusing him of playing games with public health to distract attention from the now notorious Christmas party allegedly held in Downing Street during last year's lockdown – just one of around half a dozen assorted soirees alleged to have taken place when socialising was banned last year.

Downing Street has repeatedly denied any rules were broken on its premises but only 9 per cent of voters believe it, according to a poll for Sky News; meanwhile, genuinely necessary public health measures are unfortunately tarnished by association with the prime minister. Most people will rightly still obey the new rules, as they always have. But the corrosive suspicion lingers that, as Michael Kill, the dismayed chief executive of the Night Time Industries Association, suggested, hospitality might have been thrown under a bus 'for the prime minister to save his own skin'. Just as his magic rubbed off on Conservatives in the good times, now the muck splatters across everything he touches.

Watching a distraught Allegra Stratton gulp her way through her resignation statement this week, you could see this effect unfolding in plain sight. A little over a year ago, she was best known as the aide responsible for artfully polishing the halo of the squeaky-clean Rishi Sunak. Then she was poached by No 10 to do something similar for Johnson, hosting the televised briefings he considered holding but ditched shortly after she arrived. It was while rehearsing for this job that Stratton was filmed giggling through questions about a party she says she never attended. On Wednesday, she looked genuinely broken, as if realising for the first time what had become of her.

Whether he knew about the parties or not, the charge against Johnson is that he's responsible for creating a louche and reckless culture in which anything seemingly goes but all too often those who follow his lead get burned. Former Treasury permanent secretary Nick Macpherson this week tweeted the lines from *The Great Gatsby* that have been echoing in my mind, about a gilded set who 'smashed up things and creatures and then retreated back into their money or their vast carelessness', leaving others to pick up the pieces. The question is whether Johnson's apparent willingness to throw his own team under the bus finally encourages some of those helpful others to cut their losses.

Why do Tories keep metaphorically jumping into bed with him, knowing how it invariably ends? Some assume they can control him, as Dominic Cummings seemingly did, calculating that he would get Brexit done and could then be ousted. A few imagine that they can change him. Others are under no illusions but consider the trade-offs worth it, for now: a briskly transactional category covering many MPs who voted for him as leader. And it's on their constantly shifting calculations that much depends.

If No 10 had given straight answers from the start, Christmas parties might be ancient history. But the focus would have merely shifted to the Electoral Commission fining the Tory party over its role in trying to get donors to fund a makeover of the Johnsons' private flat, and a discrepancy between that report and what Johnson previously told Lord Geidt, the independent adviser on ministerial interests, about the renovations. If not that, it would have been fresh allegations that during the chaotic British evacuation of Afghanistan either Boris or Carrie Johnson controversially intervened to help get the animal rescuer Pen Farthing and his menagerie out of Kabul, which Downing Street had also previously denied.

It's no longer just about whether voters care, but whether MPs sent out to defend the line can look themselves in the mirror. The Conservative party must ask itself whether it is content to keep being humiliated by its own leader or whether, like a long-suffering mistress tired of spending weekends alone, it can finally summon the self-respect to break free.

17 DECEMBER

'A toxic cocktail of issues': how North Shropshire turned against the Tories

JESSICA MURRAY

Marching alongside her fellow Liberal Democrats through Oswestry, their orange placards thrust triumphantly in the air, North Shropshire's newest MP insisted her sensational byelection win was about more than voters aghast at recent headlines.

'It was moving towards us even before the Christmas party stuff last week,' said Helen Morgan. 'People felt they'd been taken for granted. When we told them they could have an MP who would listen, that message really resonated.'

Something certainly resonated. Morgan's win counts as one of the biggest byelection shocks ever, turning a near-23,000 Tory majority in the 2019 election to a Lib Dem victory margin of just under 6,000.

'When did we know we were going to win it?' said Morgan. 'Well, you never know until the day. But we were starting to feel more confident as the campaign progressed. People here really wanted change, and they wanted to send a message to Boris Johnson.'

The victory was not without effort. 'The Lib Dems have worked so hard here, the volume of literature and the number of calls, and the overall visibility of their campaign has been fantastic,' said Jessie Miller, who works at an organic food shop in the town and voted for the party for the first time.

Others certainly noticed the all-out Lib Dem campaign, likened by one weary rival to 'carpet bombing', with households reporting they had been sent up to 15 leaflets. This was seen as the only way to stand a chance in what one Lib Dem campaigner called 'the truest of blue Tory seats', which has had a Conservative MP for all but two of the last 189 years.

John Biffen, who held a series of cabinet posts under Margaret Thatcher, was the local MP for 35 years. He was followed by Owen Paterson, born and bred in the area, who served for 24 years until his resignation after breaching lobbying rules in November.

In the end, Paterson's name came up fairly little. But it was still a 'toxic cocktail of local and national issues', as one Lib Dem campaigner described it, that conspired to overturn the Tory majority. Access to healthcare and ambulance waiting times are a huge issue in the seat, with many voters saying this was one of their main priorities when deciding how to vote. All four of Shropshire's community ambulance stations, including in Oswestry and Market Drayton, closed in October to much local outcry.

According to a West Midlands ambulance service boss, the county 'ran out' of vehicles on a day in November when they were all queuing outside hospitals.

A Lib Dem tally of the wording used on the many campaign leaflets said that while sleaze was mentioned 13 times, ambulances were raised 72 times, and farming on 41 occasions. But nine days before polls opened, the party was handed the extra ammunition of the reports of parties at Downing Street. 'It was like Barnard Castle on steroids,' one Lib Dem campaigner said.

The party went full throttle, promoting a photograph of a Conservative HQ Christmas party, complete with buffet, to North Shropshire voters on Facebook within an hour and a half of it emerging. 'Tell them the party is over' quickly became their tagline.

After his defeat, the Tory candidate Neil Shastri-Hurst said the party would need to 'reflect upon the result' and some local campaigners have been quick to blame 'partygate' for the loss.

But a number of voters also said they were frustrated the Tories hadn't chosen a local candidate and felt Shastri-Hurst, a lawyer living in Birmingham, had little in common with the community.

Tactical voting also played a major role in a seat where the Lib Dems, with Morgan also standing, came third in 2019, with just 10 per cent of the vote. In a speech on Friday morning, the former Lib Dem leader Tim Farron thanked 'people who support Labour and the Greens who chose to lend us their vote'.

Considering Labour have been the runners-up in every general election in the constituency bar one for the past two decades, the local Labour campaign was irked at the Lib Dems' unilateral declaration that only they could challenge.

But there was no doubt the Labour candidate, Ben Wood, faced a lack of party HQ support. His campaign team say their chances were hampered all the more when one of the party's MPs, Yasmin Qureshi, said in an interview: 'Labour are never going to win North Shropshire. The Lib Dems do have an opportunity to do so.'

Jessie Miller was among those who switched: 'I always voted Labour, so this is the first time I felt like my vote has counted.'

The Lib Dems were pushing the message that the shock result had burst the 'Boris bubble'. 'If we can win North Shropshire we can win anywhere,' Morgan said. But questions remain whether the result shows a genuine shift in UK politics, or if it is itself a product of a byelection bubble.

No party could be worth the hangover Boris Johnson is now suffering

MARINA HYDE

Like me, you probably cannot BELIEVE that after hubris comes nemesis. If only there'd been some clue to this in all that Ancient Greek stuff Boris Johnson is forever wanging on about. Anyway. The prime minister woke yesterday morning in a pre-title sequence set in an eerily silent bedroom. Suddenly, ambulance sirens rend the air outside, while in the bedroom, multiple phones start ringing. Somewhere in the house, a baby begins screaming, while the frozen expression on the prime minister's face simply says: 'What just happened?!'

Cut to black. CAPTION: '45 DAYS EARLIER ...' On 2 November, bubbly British premier Boris Johnson was flying back from Cop26 on a private plane, laughing off world-beatingly high Covid transmission rates at a time when light interventions would have reduced them, and nicely set for dinner with mid-Mesozoic influencer Charles Moore at the all-male Garrick Club. At this fateful repast with his former boss, the newspaper columnist who runs Britain cemented a plot to stop Owen Paterson – rule-breaking MP for ultra-safe North Shropshire – from having to serve a mere

30-day suspension from parliament, apparently on the basis that Johnson's people can do whatever they like.

Yesterday morning, North Shropshire fell to the Liberal Democrats, with the many, many rule-breaking Christmas parties held last year by Johnson's people turning out to be a nuclear issue on the doorstep.

Unable to pass legislation on the biggest issue of his premiership and the era without Labour support, Johnson has lost control of the voters who voted to take back control, to say nothing of his batshit backbenchers. His Downing Street lectern reads 'Get boosted now', but might as well say 'BEHOLD YOUR WEAKLING KING'. At a Downing Street briefing this week, the chief medical officer explained: 'What we've got is two epidemics on top of each other.' Yeah, and two press conferences on top of each other. One is being held by Chris Whitty; the other is being gibbered through by a knock-off Richard II, surrounded by useless cronies. 'Don't mix with people you don't have to,' advised Whitty, who agonisingly has to mix with Boris Johnson.

As for the aforementioned backbenchers, of COURSE all the Tory free-speech nuts are now demanding Whitty be silenced, at the same time as refusing to believe that the NHS is under the sort of meaningful pressure that might require even plan B. When they become the last to know about the mind-bending Omicron numbers, and cancer services and so on get even further screwed for the coming year, do remember to thank the likes of Steve Baker for their endless fricking 'vision'. The rest of us will mildly observe that the Conservative party is yet again under the control of its 'bastards'. Aside from the New Labour interregnum, the Tory party has been chained to these lunatics and their political ancestors since the early 90s. And so, by extension, has the country.

But listen: don't worry. Because of course – OF COURSE – there is renewed chatter about a leadership contest. A standout report for me this week had Rishi Sunak 'quietly letting it be known to Tory MPs that he argued against the introduction of plan B at this stage'. Presumably he let this be known from California, where the chancellor is twatting about while the hospitality trade collapses. Meanwhile, foreign secretary Liz Truss is 'hosting drinks receptions for potential supporters at a discreet private members' club in Mayfair'.

What's not to love about this traditional moment in the Conservative snuff movie cycle? All you have to remember is that no matter how terrible the horrors raining down on the nation, the party will always find time for homicidal self-pleasure, in the form of a mooted leadership contest. We could be standing in the post-apocalyptic ruins of our country, with said apocalypse even caused by the last leader they decided had 'special sauce', and the likes of Liz Truss would still be hosting receptions for supporters at discreet clearings in the rubble. 'If you want a drink, you'll have to distil your own urine – and all I'll say about the canapés is that you need to catch them first. Anyway: MY VISION.'

Speaking of canapés, the prime minister was this week still standing by his allegedly rule-breaking staff, defending them on the basis that they 'have worked blindingly hard for a very long time in cooperation with people around the government and across the whole of the public services to do our very best to keep people safe'.

What self-pitying bollocks. Is there anything more pathetic than this idea that desk johnnies in Westminster work harder than anyone else in this country? Do me a favour. It's not going down a mine, is it? It's not evacuating people from Afghanistan. More to the point, it's hardly working in an intensive care unit. You don't actually have to wash public service down with cheese and wine when no one else is allowed to. Honestly, they all want to be in the room where it happens, and when they are, they moan about the hours. So as we seemingly stare down the barrel of another grim and restrictive winter – in which no one has done more to undermine their own public health message than they themselves – Downing Street staff, from the prime minister downwards, are reminded that there is a very easy solution to all this. Other jobs are available – why not start looking around?

20 DECEMBER

Strictly exclusive! Winner Rose Ayling-Ellis on the glitterball, Giovanni and the joy of being deaf

EMINE SANER

When she was a small child – too young to remember, though her mother has told her this story – Rose Ayling-Ellis was once so delighted to be at the park, she excitedly climbed on to a bench and started dancing. People stopped and, unable to resist her infectious happiness, clapped and cheered along.

Two decades later, millions more were clapping and cheering (and, I suspect, sobbing at times) as Ayling-Ellis and her partner, Giovanni Pernice, became 2021 *Strictly Come Dancing* champions in the most emotional and joyous finale I can ever remember.

Yet, for once, it felt as if there were no losers: the runners-up, John Whaite and his partner Johannes Radebe, would have been easy winners any other year, as would AJ Odudu, who had to pull out of the final after an injury, but Ayling-Ellis had something extra

– the show's first deaf contestant, she had to work harder than anyone else, although the effort never seemed laboured. She is a beautiful dancer, light and agile and emotive. She radiates pure joy.

'I was so shocked,' says Ayling-Ellis of the moment her name was announced, when we spoke briefly by Zoom, joined by a sign-language interpreter the morning after the final. 'It was really weird – it felt like I was out of my body for a moment.' She is tired and happy – 'We celebrated last night. There was a bit of prosecco, and dancing' – but she says it hasn't really sunk in yet.

It was emotional behind the scenes; she says she had to get her makeup redone at least twice before the trophy announcement. But this probably helped when it came to being crowned champion: 'I was crying so much beforehand that I ran out of tears,' she says – though as soon as she hugged her mum – who was sitting in the audience with Ayling-Ellis's boyfriend – she 'burst into tears and couldn't stop'.

Despite a strong series, with some of the best couples the show has ever seen, Ayling-Ellis, 27, was always a favourite. She was the first to get the perfect score of 40, which she did in week six. Her acting skills – she's in *EastEnders* – are a given, but the expressiveness in her body (or 'musicality' as the judges would put it), when she cannot really hear the music, is extraordinary. One dance, Ayling-Ellis and Pernice's 'couple's choice', was a powerful, celebratory routine that featured a silent section halfway through, in tribute to the deaf community. When they performed it again for the final, it lost none of its power – I watched it with goosebumps.

'I love it so much,' she says of the show, when we spoke a couple of weeks earlier, after a long day in which she had been trying to perfect the American Smooth. 'I love all the ballroom,' she says. 'It's the Latin I'm terrified of – it's fast, there's a lot of counting, it's a bit more solo, you're not really [dancing close] together. With ballroom, I don't have to think as much.'

She doesn't 'feel the vibrations' of the music, as has been claimed, but instead commits each step to muscle memory and counts them out in her head. 'If I had to start thinking about vibration, it would distract me.' Also, she points out, there is a big difference in sound between the live band on the night and the recorded music played in rehearsals. Ayling-Ellis can hear some aspects of music, using her phone to Bluetooth it directly to her hearing aids (when, one day, she forgot to bring spare batteries, she and Pernice couldn't rehearse).

Part of the pleasure of watching the pair dance was Ayling-Ellis and Pernice's affectionate partnership. 'Giovanni has been incredible,' she says. 'He really supports every single step – and I mean every single step: even when I'm doing stuff on my own he, off-camera, is giving me timing.' Learning the choreography is difficult for a hearing person; for Ayling-Ellis, it must have been a giant task. There have been days, she says, when she has struggled. 'There are a lot of ups and downs and some dances are harder than others. But Giovanni is such a good teacher, and he's really adapted to the way I learn, rather than making me learn it in his way.'

Being on the show, she says, has 'been life-changing. I try not to think about it ending too much because it makes me feel really sad.' How has it changed her? 'I feel more confident. On the first week, I was really shy, but now I can be myself. The first week, I was like, "Everyone's going to be expecting a deaf person to dance really badly."' She smiles. 'But I definitely proved a lot of people wrong.' When we speak before her eventual triumph, she says while winning would be great, 'what is more important is breaking the barrier, proving that deaf people can do anything. I feel that I've achieved that, so even if I don't win, I still feel like I've won.'

Since Ayling-Ellis has been on *Strictly*, online searches for British sign language courses have gone up by 300 per cent, and one training company told the BBC that the number of people enrolling had gone up by 2,000 per cent. She has had lots of messages from deaf people, and parents of deaf children, who have said how much watching her has meant to them. 'That's made me quite emotional,' she says. 'It's 2021, and, finally, they've got something like that. It's really good that it's happening – but why has it taken this long? I didn't have that growing up, and a lot of deaf people didn't have that. So it's really nice that we've got somebody out there.' She smiles, and adds: 'I can't believe it's me.'

She is thrilled that appearing on *Strictly* has challenged perceptions. 'Hopefully, it will change the way people look at deaf people. That if they come for a job interview, they won't freak out and will be more excited. I'm glad that it's happening. We've been fighting for so long.'

Were there people who were surprised she was going on a dance show? 'Yes, because I think a lot of people probably ...' She pauses. 'I think, for deaf people, the thing we have to live with is that people have such low expectations of us. So when you do things that are normal, it's like, "Wow!" So I knew that me being on *Strictly*, a lot of people were probably thinking, "How's she going to hear music, how is she going to dance?" I always felt like I have to give 120 per cent,' she says, 'so that I can seem capable of doing the same as everyone else.'

Ayling-Ellis grew up in Hythe, Kent, and has an older brother; after her parents' divorce, she lived with her mother. She had ballet lessons when she was a child, but not for long – and that was about the extent of her dance training. 'In a home video, you can see all the kids with perfect timing and I'm trotting along behind trying to copy what they were doing,' she says. 'I remember my first day with Giovanni, he was really shocked at my posture. He still tells me off for it.'

She was, however, a very creative child, 'always in my own bubble. I love art and making things, and I communicated a lot with my family through drawing.' She wanted to be an artist. At school, she says, it was the popular kids who did drama. 'And I wasn't very popular, so I never thought about doing drama.'

At Ayling-Ellis's school, there were only a handful of deaf students. 'I didn't get bullied, I still had a good time at school but I had to fight for my education,' she says. 'They only had three notetakers, and [the deaf children] were in different classes, so most of them went to a classroom with no interpreter, no note-taker. My mum really fought to make sure I had a notetaker and interpreter with me at all times. I was lucky, but it was ridiculous. Unfortunately, that's a normal life for many deaf children – they are in mainstream schools with no access.'

The hard work was a real test, she says, 'because that's what life is going to be. You always have to fight for your access.' Not having to struggle for this made all the difference on *Strictly*. 'I have an interpreter with me so I can understand what's going on all the time. If I didn't have an interpreter there, and I was trying to concentrate, trying to understand what everyone's saying, I can't be me, I can't be myself.'

Ayling-Ellis remembers realising for the first time she was different from others around her, when she was around four. 'In nursery, we had this special deaf unit. I remember playing with other deaf kids, and looking out the window and it was all the hearing children outside. I thought, "Why am I not over there? Why am I in here?" I thought everyone was deaf.

'I feel really glad that I knew who I was from a very early age. I never ever once thought: "I wish I could hear." Because if I was hearing, I'd be a completely different person. I wouldn't have the life experience that I have. I'd just be really normal.' She laughs. 'I don't want to be normal – that's boring.'

Being part of the deaf community 'is very special', she says. 'It is the one place I can be where I fully understand everything. In the hearing world, I'm constantly having to lip-read and trying to understand what's going on. Sign language is so beautiful. It gives you a strong identity, something to be very proud of – the community, the culture. I love the deaf community.'

Ayling-Ellis's family became involved with the deaf community quite early on, and her mother learned sign language. 'They're really supportive, and I love my family to bits, but I did feel, growing up, that I would love to have a deaf brother or sister, or someone deaf in my family. I was very lucky I had deaf friends and deaf people around me. But I wish I'd had a deaf role model.'

One weekend, as a teenager, Ayling-Ellis went away on a film-making course with other deaf children. She was interested in animation, but tried it and didn't like it. 'They said I should try acting,' she says. 'It was such a safe space, so you felt really safe to be yourself.'

She fell in love with acting. She had been a confident child, but had become self-conscious as a teen. With acting, 'I felt a lot of freedom. And I realised I was not bad at it.' The director who was running the weekend, Ted Evans, asked Ayling-Ellis to be in his short film. But, she says, 'I didn't think it was something that I could do full-time – I didn't see any other deaf actors out there.' Instead, she went to university to study fashion design, but kept acting with the Deafinitely Youth Theatre, and her career grew.

Ayling-Ellis did theatre work, and had roles in *Casualty* and the Stephen Poliakoff drama *Summer of Rockets* before joining *EastEnders* last year, playing Frankie Lewis. Up to this point, she says being deaf has given her an advantage as an actor, because she is usually always considered whenever a casting director is looking for a deaf actor. 'The problem is when it's not a deaf role – that's where I've found it really hard,' she says. 'I've gone for auditions and they've said, "I really liked you, but we're going to find a smaller role for you somewhere." But why can't I play that role, a character who just happens to be deaf? *EastEnders* works really well, because the storyline isn't about me being deaf – she's just a character.'

The conversation about diversity on television isn't always that inclusive. 'You see so many different races and sexualities – and it's brilliant, it's what it should be – but where are the disabled people? It is changing, but very slowly, and in very small ways.'

What would it have meant to see a Rose Ayling-Ellis on mainstream TV – in two of the BBC's biggest shows – when she was growing up? 'A lot. It's not just for me, but also for my parents. When they first had a deaf child, they had never met anybody deaf before.' For parents who may be anxious about a baby's diagnosis, or not know what it could mean for them, seeing Ayling-Ellis might make them think, she says, 'that "my child can do whatever they want to do, because she can do that".'

Did she grow up thinking there was anything she couldn't do? 'I grew up knowing there's always a way around things,' she says, smiling. 'I just always knew that other people think I can't do it, and that was a bigger barrier for me.' She has, with each joyous step, proved what she's capable of. 'It's so much more than the glitterball,' she says with the immensity of her win still sinking in. 'It feels like acceptance for a deaf person to achieve something like that. It means so much, and I know it means a lot for the deaf community, and for anybody who feels a bit different – to never think that you can't do it, because it is achievable when you are given the opportunity.'

26 December

South Africa set for battle over legacy of 'moral compass' Desmond Tutu

JASON BURKE

From the moment when he resigned from his post as a school-teacher rather than comply with the orders of the racist, repressive apartheid regime in South Africa in 1958, Desmond Tutu never deviated from his principles, fighting for tolerance, equality and justice at home and abroad. This brought him love, influence and a moral authority equalled by few others on the African continent or further afield.

Tutu was not just outspoken in support of the causes he knew to be right, such as LGBT rights; he was also a fierce and impla-cable opponent of what he felt to be wrong. Criticism was often tempered with humour. On occasion it was delivered straight. This earned him enemies, and still does.

Tutu's first and most famous enemy was the apartheid system that prevailed in his homeland from 1948. Fully engaged in the freedom struggle from the late 1970s, Tutu was a key figure in telling the rest of the world about the grievances of South Afri-ca's exploited majority communities. Branded a 'rabble-rouser' by authorities, he did not pull his punches. Apartheid was as bad as Nazism, he told the UN in 1984, adding that those politicians in the West who failed to support sanctions campaigns against the regime in Pretoria were racists.

'We don't want to drive the white people into the sea, we don't want to destroy white people,' said Tutu, who won the Nobel peace prize that year for his nonviolent efforts to end apartheid and avoid devastating conflict in South Africa. 'But is it too much to ask that in the land of our birth, we walk tall as human beings made in the image of God? ... To say we want to be free?'

In a letter, Tutu, then head of the South African Council of Churches, informed Margaret Thatcher that a British invitation to the then South African prime minister to visit the UK was 'a slap in the face of millions of black South Africans who are the daily victims of one of the most vicious policies in the world'.

He did not spare those in power in the 'rainbow nation' that emerged after South Africa's first free election in 1994. The phrase was his own, and set up aspirations that were never fulfilled.

A decade later, Tutu gave a high-profile lecture in which he listed the many achievements of his countrymen under democracy but implied that many came despite their new political rulers who sought their own advancement before that of the poor.

'What is black empowerment when it seems to benefit not the vast majority but a small elite that tends to be recycled? Are we not building up much resentment that we may rue later? We are sitting on a powder keg,' Tutu said.

His criticism of the ruling African National Congress became even harsher during the tenure of Jacob Zuma, which ended in 2018 amid allegations of corruption and maladministration. Relations between the ANC and Tutu improved slightly after Cyril Ramaphosa, a former labour activist who has sought to bring in moderate reforms, took power.

Ramaphosa's tribute yesterday – with its reference to the passing of 'a generation of outstanding South Africans who have bequeathed us a liberated South Africa' – underlines the general sense of disillusionment.

Even now, some Zuma loyalists have distanced themselves from the tributes. One reason is the memory of Tutu's rigorous and harrowing leadership of South Africa's truth and reconciliation commission, which probed apartheid-era crimes. Tutu's commitment and determination did not just anger supporters of the white officials made to disclose the depredations of the apartheid regime; the council's investigation of Winnie Madikizela-Mandela, Nelson Mandela's former wife, for the abduction and eventual murder of a teenager, still rankles. On social media yesterday, some branded Tutu a 'stooge for white people'.

In reality, Tutu took aim at exploiters and autocrats anywhere he found them. Justly lauded as an icon of nonviolent activism, he enraged those who prefer less pacific means to effect change or hold on to power. Robert Mugabe, the former dictatorial leader of Zimbabwe, resorted to insults to counter Tutu's cutting words, calling their author 'an angry, evil and embittered little bishop'.

Such sentiments did not bother the smiling, chuckling, charismatic cleric – though Tutu confessed to one interviewer that he 'loved to be loved'. Even in the Anglican church, an institution to which he dedicated much of his life, Tutu's liberal understanding of faith riled many. No one doubted his faith or commitment to the institution but not every cleric enjoyed hearing about a God who had a 'soft spot for sinners' and fewer still on a continent riven by visceral homophobia appreciated his vocal, consistent support for LGBT rights.

'I would not worship a God who is homophobic and that is how deeply I feel about this,' he said in 2013. 'I would refuse to go to a homophobic heaven. No, I would say, "Sorry, I would much rather go to the other place."' He also supported the right to assisted death, another controversial position within the church. Other interventions argued for urgent action against climate change and a change in US policy on Israel.

Right to the end Tutu was 'on the side of the angels', as one resident of a township not far from where the archbishop lived and died said on Sunday.

In one of his last public appearances, aged 89, he received a Covid vaccine, an important statement in a country that has lost up to 250,000 lives to the pandemic out of a population of 59 million, according to excess mortality figures, and suffers from widespread vaccine hesitancy.

Analysts predict a battle over Tutu's legacy as South African political factions jostle to claim they are the true heirs of 'the Arch', as he was familiarly known. For the moment, though, there is profound grief at the loss of the country's 'moral compass' and a genuine sense of bereavement.

'South Africa and the world has lost one of its greatest parents and role models. [Tutu] was abnormally imbued with a sense of pastoral duty to serve the best interests of his species – the human family – and planet,' a statement from the office of the archbishop of Cape Town said. 'To do the right thing. To make people feel part. To advance justice, humanness, peace and joy ... His work is not done; it is in our hands now.'

Winter

Watching *Don't Look Up* made me see my whole life of campaigning flash before me

GEORGE MONBIOT

No wonder journalists have slated it. They've produced a hundred excuses not to watch the climate breakdown satire *Don't Look Up*: it's 'blunt', it's 'shrill', it's 'smug'. But they will not name the real problem: it's about them. The movie is, in my view, a powerful demolition of the grotesque failures of public life. And the sector whose failures are most brutally exposed is the media.

While the film is fast and funny, for me, as for many environmental activists and climate scientists, it seemed all too real. I felt as if I were watching my adult life flash past me. As the scientists in the film, trying to draw attention to the approach of a planet-killing comet, bashed their heads against the Great Wall of Denial erected by the media, and sought to reach politicians with 10-second attention spans, all the anger and frustration and desperation I've felt over the years boiled over.

Above all, when the scientist who had discovered the comet was pushed to the bottom of the schedule by fatuous celebrity gossip on a morning TV show and erupted in fury, I was reminded of my own mortifying loss of control on *Good Morning Britain* in November. It was soon after the Cop26 climate conference in Glasgow, where we had seen the least serious of all governments (the UK was hosting the talks) failing to rise to the most serious of all issues. I tried, for the thousandth time, to explain what we are facing, and suddenly couldn't hold it in any longer. I burst into tears on live TV.

I still feel deeply embarrassed about it. The response on social media, like the response to the scientist in the film, was vitupera-tive and vicious. I was faking. I was hysterical. I was mentally ill. But, knowing where we are and what we face, seeing the indiffer-ence of those who wield power, seeing how our existential crisis has been marginalised in favour of trivia and frivolity, I now realise that there would be something wrong with me if I hadn't lost it.

In fighting any great harm, in any age, we find ourselves confronting the same forces: distraction, denial and delusion. Those seeking to sound the alarm about the gathering collapse of our life-support systems soon hit the barrier that stands between us and the people we are trying to reach, a barrier called the media. With a few notable exceptions, the sector that should facilitate communication thwarts it.

It's not just its individual stupidities that have become inexcus-able, such as the platforms repeatedly given to climate deniers. It is the structural stupidity to which the media are committed. It's the anti-intellectualism, the hostility to new ideas and aversion to complexity. It's the absence of moral seriousness. It's the vacuous gossip about celebrities and consumables that takes precedence over the survival of life on Earth.

It's the obsession with generating noise, regardless of signal. It's the reflexive alignment with the status quo, whatever it may be. It's the endless promotion of the views of the most selfish and antisocial people, and the exclusion of those who are trying to defend us from catastrophe, on the grounds that they are 'worthy', 'extreme' or 'mad' (I hear from friends in the BBC that these terms are still used there to describe environmental activists).

Even when these merchants of distraction do address the issue, they tend to shut out the experts and interview actors, singers and other celebs instead. The media's obsession with actors vindicates Guy Debord's predictions in his book *The Society of the Spectacle*, published in 1967. Substance is replaced by semblance, as even the most serious issues must now be articulated by people whose work involves adopting someone else's persona and speaking someone else's words.

Then the same media, having turned them into spokespeople, attack these actors as hypocrites for leading a profligate lifestyle.

Similarly, it's not just the individual failures by governments at Glasgow and elsewhere that have become inexcusable, but the entire framework of negotiations. As crucial Earth systems might be approaching their tipping point, governments still propose to address the issue with tiny increments of action, across decades.

It's as if in 2008, when Lehman Brothers collapsed and the global financial system began to sway, governments had announced that they would bail out the banks at the rate of a few million pounds a day between then and 2050. The system would have collapsed 40 years before their programme was complete. Our central, civilisational question, I believe, is this: why do nations scramble to rescue the banks but not the planet?

So, as we race towards Earth-system collapse, trying to raise the alarm feels like being trapped behind a thick plate of glass. People can see our mouths opening and closing but they struggle to hear what we are saying. As we frantically bang the glass, we look ever crazier. And feel it.

The situation is genuinely maddening. I've been working on these issues since I was 22, and full of confidence and hope. I'm about to turn 59, and the confidence is turning to cold fear, the hope to horror. As manufactured indifference ensures that we remain unheard, it becomes ever harder to know how to hold it together. I cry most days now.

Britain's shameful slavery history matters – that's why a jury acquitted the Colston Four

DAVID OLUSOGA

There were cheers from the public gallery of Bristol crown court when the verdicts of not guilty were returned. Eighteen months after Bristol's now infamous statue of the slave trader Edward Colston was sent crashing to the pavement, the four young people who had been charged with criminal damage were acquitted.

The strategy that the prosecution appears to have adopted – in a case that some now argue should never have been brought to trial – seemed to centre on asking that the jury be blind to history. Who the statue venerated, it argued, was irrelevant. This, it claimed, was an open-and-shut case of criminal damage, one in which the defendants did not even deny their role in the toppling of the statue or, in one case, helping to roll it to Bristol harbourside, from where it was cast into the water.

The contention of the prosecution was that the crimes of Colston, shareholder and ultimately deputy governor of the Royal African Company, the most prolific slave-trading entity in British history, should simply be set aside. That the statue depicted a man whose wealth was based on the enslavement of 84,000 men, women and children was immaterial. As was the fact that he was complicit in the deaths of 19,000 of them, who died, squirming in agony, chained to the decks of the Royal African Company's slave ships.

That should be of no concern to the jury. Their suffering, their deaths, their very existence was irrelevant to the issue at hand. In adopting such a strategy the prosecution was merely asking the jury to occupy the same stance of wilful, moral blindness that Colston's defenders have occupied for decades.

That strategy failed because the lawyers defending the so-called Colston Four were able, through their own legal arguments and the striking eloquence of the four young defendants, to place history at the centre of this trial.

In this I played a small part, appearing as an expert witness for the defence. They successfully demonstrated that the real offenders were not the Colston Four, but the city of Bristol and those who have done everything in their power to burnish the reputation of a mass murderer.

The keepers of Colston's legacy had rendered his historic crimes live and present through the erection of a statue to him. By allowing that edifice to stand for 125 years, even as Bristol became home to thousands of black people whose ancestors had been victims of the trade that the Royal African Company had pioneered, they had, so argued the defence, permitted the statue to become an 'indecent display'.

Having established these arguments Liam Walker QC, representing Sage Willoughby, the youngest of the defendants, argued that the Colston Four 'were on the right side of history'. Jurors were invited to join them there.

In the aftermath of this verdict those who now have questions to answer are Colston's defenders. In particular, the Society of Merchant Venturers, a grouping that for decades dismissed and discounted appeals for the statue to be removed or contextualised. Its strategy of muddying waters and maintaining the status quo fostered indecision and inaction. Decades of inertia were brought to an end in just under three hours – the time it took for the jury to arrive at its verdict.

The merchant elite of late Victorian Bristol who erected the statue of Colston, many of them members of the Merchant Venturers, did so in the full knowledge that the man they sought to elevate to civic sainthood had been a trader in human flesh. The details of his grim career had been obscured but not obliterated.

Despite what they knew they expanded the bizarre cult of rituals, religious services and exclusive dinners that had been built around him, but their most public triumph was the erection of the statue. To validate the imposition of the cult of Colston on to the wider city, they falsely implied that the statue had been paid for through popular, public subscription.

They did all of this confident in the belief that no one would ever question their decisions, as no one would ever come to care about Colston's crimes or his victims. Their confidence sprang from their collective inability to envisage a future moment in which the Africans who had perished in the bellies of the Royal African Company's ships, or on the plantations of Barbados or Jamaica, would matter to anyone in Bristol or beyond.

The moment they were unable to conceive of is now. The generation for whom the lives of Colston's victims matter deeply is the generation from whom the four defendants in this case were drawn.

In the months since the murder of George Floyd millions of people across the world have examined their nations' official histories, and the history lessons they were taught at school. They have discovered missing chapters, half-truths and lost connections between the crimes of then and the inequalities of now.

As Rhian Graham, one of the Colston Four, noted in the impromptu speech she made from the pavement outside court, the dethronement of Colston was not a stand-alone event, but part of a global movement.

I am writing this from Covid isolation in a hotel on the southern coast of Barbados. From my window I can see the approaches to the island, the sea lanes along which the ships of the Atlantic slave trade once passed, before docking to unload their human cargoes. To the north of me is a place called Speightstown, its nickname in the 18th century was 'Little Bristol', so firmly was it connected to the slave traders and sugar merchants of that English city 4,000 miles away.

The global shift of consciousness that inspired the toppling of Colston was also a factor in the decision made by the people of this island to break decisively away from that history and become a republic.

This shift in consciousness, translated into action across the world by young people, will be strengthened by this verdict and by the very fact that, when made aware of long-obscured historical and moral truths, an English jury chose to place itself – and the city of Bristol – on the right side of history.

12 JANUARY

Boris Johnson's best party excuse is he's even dimmer than we feared

JOHN CRACE

Finally we got some kind of explanation from the prime minister for his boozy parties at Downing Street. It turns out that Boris

Johnson wants us to believe that Boris Johnson thinks that Boris Johnson is catatonically stupid. And that the British public are equally half-witted enough to believe any old lies he happens to come up with. There's just one problem with this. Johnson may be dim, but he's not that dim. And the rest of us have long since learned to see through his mendacity.

This was the prime minister's questions at which Johnson finally ran out of road. An outright denial that he had been at the party on 20 May 2020 would no longer keep him out of trouble. So all that was left to him was to come up with the best possible excuse and hope it would buy off a few of the more gullible Tory MPs. Except the best possible excuse turned out to be a crock of total shit.

Here's how it was, said Johnson, as he made a short statement to the Commons. He recognised the sacrifices the country had made and he wanted to apologise for having got pissed with No 10 staff in his own back garden. The thing was that he had just not realised the party was a party. When the email inviting everyone to enjoy the sunshine and bring your own booze was sent – and which he definitely had not read – the last thing he had imagined was that a party was about to take place. Even though 60 staffers had made that assumption, realised it was against the law and decided to stay away.

So anyway, he and his then fiancée – Carrie always came along to work meetings – coincidentally turned up, even though they hadn't seen the invite, and stayed for 25 minutes because it seemed rude not to. He discussed a few work matters before going back to his flat and remembered thinking how brilliant it was so many people were staying late to work over a few bevvies.

And he hadn't even thought the party was a party when he saw the staff clearing up the empties from the flowerbed the following morning. Indeed it was only when Dominic Cummings had mentioned last week that the party might have actually been a party that it occurred to him the party could have been a party after all. He now bitterly regretted everything – most of all, getting caught – and all he was asking was that people gave him a bit of wriggle room before Sue Gray submitted the findings of her investigation.

None of this cut any ice with Keir Starmer. This PMQs may have seemed like the most open of goals for the Labour leader but he still needed to stick the ball in the net in front of a packed chamber. Which he did six times. Johnson was pathetic: after months of denial, was this the best he could come up with? A dog-ate-my-homework excuse would be less insulting. The prime minister had attended the party. He had broken lockdown rules. He had misled parliament when he had said how sickened he was about other No 10 parties. The country thought he was a pathological liar. He needed to resign.

Johnson visibly crumpled. Unlike Prince Andrew, he knew what it was like to sweat.

The king of bullshitters was all out of ideas. Even he could see how abject his lies were. Just wait for Sue Gray. Hope that she dematerialises.

Rishi Sunak had made himself scarce in Devon. 'I'm right behind you, prime minister. Two hundred miles behind you.' The rest of the cabinet stared impassively at the floor; their expressions hidden behind their masks. They too would rather have been anywhere but the Commons. This was also their humiliation. They were the ones who had put a man transparently unfit to be prime minister into No 10. They knew what Boris was like but hadn't cared. His incompetence and corruption was also theirs.

The Tory backbenchers were also out of sorts. No one could bring themselves to actually defend their leader; but neither did they dare attack him. His immorality cast a toxic pall over proceedings. Boris was the turd that would not flush and which no one dared mention. So instead they asked him about irrelevant details of constituency business. A county motto. It was all somewhat surreal.

It was left to Labour's Chris Bryant to get the last word. How stupid did he think we all were? Did he really imagine even a 10-year-old thinking he would get away with lines like that? And would it yet again be people, like Allegra Stratton, who had worked for Boris that would end up losing their jobs? Johnson shrugged, still a semi-absentee observer of his own downfall. Needs must. If that's what it took for him to survive. It was a fight to the death. Whose exactly would soon become clear.

12 JANUARY

On the day of No 10's lockdown party, I buried my sister

RORY KINNEAR

Without wishing to sound like an episode of *Poirot*, I remember well what I was doing on the evening of 20 May 2020, when more than 100 people were invited to a BYOB party in the prime minister's garden, 'to make the most of the lovely weather'. While they recovered from an 'exceptionally busy period' with, it might be presumed, laughter, companionship and their own bottles of wine, I was at my house.

Like them, I, too, had a glass of wine, although I had drunk it by myself. I had then gone for a short walk around my block where I had bumped into a friend out on his 'daily permitted exercise'. We spoke a little, at a distance of more than two metres. He offered his condolences. I thanked him and returned home, alone. 20 May 2020 was the day I buried my sister.

Like those assembled with their bottles in Downing Street, I, too, had broken the government's existing guidelines, implemented to mitigate the spread of Covid-19, in a familiar garden. After my sister Karina's funeral, I had gone to my mother's house. It was a baking hot day and, while the circumstances didn't really allow me to 'make the most of the lovely weather', the sunshine did permit me and my other sister, Kirsty, to sit in our mum's garden, at the state-appointed distance from each other, and recall the many joys, as well as strains, that Karina's life had brought. There were three of us in the garden, from three separate households, one more than was permitted. It might not have been exactly to the letter of the law, but we reckoned it was the least our grief would permit.

Luckily we could remain physically, if not emotionally, distanced from each other. Karina had died of Covid and we felt we should take the best precautions possible to prevent the disease's spread. We didn't hug, didn't allow ourselves any of the consolation of physical touch: we thought it would be safer that way. Physical contact was, after all, what they had instructed us to avoid. For 48 years my mother had fought to keep her disabled daughter happy and alive. For 48 years, whenever Karina had been ill, my mother had slept in hospital chairs for weeks on end, gone days without sleep, sacrificed her own health for Karina's wellbeing, driven by a love that only a parent can know. And now Karina was dead. And we couldn't hug each other. It was bleak, yes, but then it was a time of incomparable global uncertainty. An unparalleled, unifying swathe of sadness had devoured us all. Pain like ours was tearing through families the world over. So, in some ways, it felt like we were all in it together.

A couple of hours earlier, we had driven in separate cars to the cemetery in which my father is buried. Two gravediggers stood by a fence as we watched six strangers, wearing masks and latex gloves, lower Karina's coffin into a freshly dug plot adjacent to his. A priest, somewhat concealed behind another gravestone, invited me to speak. I attempted to hold back tears as I gave thanks for the extraordinary role Karina had played in our family. A tinny speaker played Abba's 'Thank You for the Music', the lyrics a little drowned out by the rustle of the willow tree above. We threw some earth on her coffin, got back in our separate cars and went back to my mum's for a slice of chocolate cake on disposable plates. I had brought my own. Ours was just one of thousands of similar stories happening across the country. We were, we consoled ourselves again, all in it together.

That evening, as I walked alone, the streets were piercingly quiet. How sad it all is, I thought, how devastatingly sad. And yet, what consolation there is in seeing and hearing these manifest absences; silences that speak of self-denial and mutual respect. The sepulchral pallor that my corner of London had been bathed in was the result of a shared commitment to rules, designed by *them*, to keep us, our loved ones and our wider society safe. I walked past my neighbours' houses; friends numbed by screen time and family dynamics, unsure how long this would all last, no access to society beyond their phones, windows open to mitigate against that lovely, lovely weather. I couldn't help but feel grateful that my community was taking the deaths of people such as my sister as seriously and profoundly as I was. Their confinement spoke of a silent but wholehearted sympathy for families such as mine. They knew, they felt too, that we were all in it together.

Well, not *all* of us, it turns out. Not *them*.

Just under two miles separates my corner of London from the garden of Downing Street. I am, today, haunted by the tinkling of those glasses there on that sun-drenched night, the echoing of their thin laughter, the stifled chuckles as they practised their imagined denials and, most perniciously, the leadership that encouraged it to happen. Their actions feel like direct assaults in the face of my family's, and all of our shared national, tragedy. To me, and I'm sure many others, the revelations of the manifest and repeated failures of those in power to understand, empathise or show solidarity with what the people of this country experienced during that time have released from the body politic a stench so toxic that I can't see how they will be able to put it back in the bottle, no matter how desperately they try. They can't point the finger anywhere else this time, can they? After all, they brought the bottle themselves.

14 JANUARY

Novak Djokovic v Australia is a grudge match for our polarised age

BARNEY RONAY

First they came for the multimillionaire tennis players with pictures of border form infractions on their Instagram page. And I did not speak out.

Actually, no, it's not quite that. The decision to re-cancel Novak Djokovic's visa, thereby imperilling his ability to compete at next week's Australian Open, is not an act of war on the Serbian people, or an executive order from the lizard-lords of Project Deplete The

Sheeple. Or indeed anything to be celebrated with any real relish, unless the spectacle of enforced deportations rings your bell.

Perhaps the people most directly concerned by the intervention of the Australian government yesterday are those detained in the kind of migrant hostel from which Djokovic escaped last week. Those same harsh border policies will remain once the current celebrity edition has faded out of the news cycle. And none of those unfortunates still resident in Melbourne's Park Hotel will be cheering with any great warmth.

For now it is worth noting that the court decision on the procedural fairness of Djokovic's summary visa-justice at Melbourne airport has not been overturned. Immigration minister Alex Hawke has used a separate statutory power to rule that Djokovic is not entitled to stay, whether on grounds of the public good or for reasons of bad character and bad conduct. That decision will be reviewed on appeal over the weekend.

And so we go again. For all the noise, the scarcely credible cut-through as a global news event of one Serbian tennis player's weirdness about mainstream medicine, there was something reassuring yesterday in the sight of this inferno coming to rest on the agreeably furrowed brow of Judge Anthony Kelly of the Melbourne federal court.

Slumped in his high-backed chair, tie askew, Judge Kelly had the look of a man who finds himself routinely appalled, without favour or exception, by every single object in his eyeline. As petitions were made and timings wrangled over he listened with an expression of weary suffering, as though doggedly sitting out a violent bout of sciatica. At one point he batted away an interruption from Djokovic's lawyer with the words 'I will finish because it's the last thing I wish to say', and one wondered, what, like ... ever? The end result was not the one Djokovic's lawyers had been seeking, the re-inflicting of their case on Judge Kelly's court over the weekend. Instead it has been referred to the next step up the judicial ladder. And whatever the ultimate outcome, this has been another bewilderingly strange step in a bewilderingly strange interlude.

Here we have the intersection of humanity's polarised response to a global plague, and the irreconcilable career ambitions of the world's best male tennis player and the prime minister of Australia. But a few things have at least become a little clearer.

First, it is all excellent news for Scott Morrison, who is no doubt hugely grateful to have been granted this lever on public opinion during an election year. No, don't look over there at the inferno of Covid cases. Watch instead while I windmill Novak Djokovic around my head like a super-healthy vegan celery juice Action Man.

Is it possible to trim away the emotive edges here? Djokovic may be a maddening figure. He may deserve it all for the basic shithousery of entering the country via a medical loophole while ticking the wrong box on his border forms. But he is still basically being deported for the crime of making the prime minister look bad, for holding weird views, for giving out an unpleasant vibe.

The word binary was thrown around the courtroom. And it is perhaps the most interesting point to arise because, if Australia v Djokovic tells us anything, it is that this is our world now. At one extreme the Australian people can be invited to focus their anxiety on a single, slightly ludicrous hate figure. On the other Djokovic has already been enthroned as a hero by people who think #Australiahasfallen – to melts, wokies, Bill Gates, whatever – while Djokovic Sr tells us his son, who is undoubtedly very good at tennis, is 'a Spartacus of the new world' here to fight against injustice, hypocrisy and (for some reason) colonialism.

In the shadow of all this there are two things worth remembering. Djokovic is a highly unusual person, out there in his sealed bubble of celebrity sport entitlement, surrounded by acolytes and supplicants. And Australia is also a pretty weird place right now, a vast, dusty, atomised island nation, two years in isolation, gruellingly dutiful, fatigued by outbreak-anxiety.

Just as Covid really does start to let rip, it finds itself presented with this absurd, dunderheaded Djoker, skating in through customs with his wonky forms and his belief in detoxifying mind-power. Take a step back and the arrival of Djokovic is the most absurdly provocative single event imaginable on those shores right now, something that might have been staged just to press Australia's already quivering buttons.

What were we expecting? It is hard to see how Djokovic gets to play in Melbourne or, indeed, to picture any kind of happy ending – apart from the obvious one. Frankly the only sensible option would be to fold and leave now, to offer that rarest of things, a hand across the net-divide. No? Me neither. See you back in court.

23 JANUARY

Christ and cocaine: Rio's gangs of God blend faith and violence

TOM PHILLIPS

'Pastor, do you think we could hold a service at my house next Thursday?' the young gangster wondered, cradling an AK-47 in his lap as he took a seat beside the man of God.

He had just bought his first home with the fruits of his illegal work for one of Rio de Janeiro's drug factions. Now, he wanted to give thanks for the blessings he believed he had received from above.

'I've dodged death so many times. It was He who delivered me from evil,' the 23-year-old drug trafficker reflected as he began another 12-hour night shift on the frontline of the Brazilian city's drug conflict.

That Christian conviction was echoed all around him, on walls adorned with frescoes of the Old City of Jerusalem and an extract from the Epistle to the Galatians: 'Walk by the Spirit, and ye shall not fulfil the lust of the flesh.'

He had a tattoo of a cross and the words 'Jesus lives' on one wrist and 'May my courage be greater than my fear and my strength as great as my faith' on the other.

'They know theirs is a cut-throat world so they seek something to believe in,' said Elias Santana, a favela-based preacher who has made it his mission to save the souls of Rio's ever more evangelical gangsters.

When Rio's drug conflict exploded in the 1980s, Brazil's evangelical revolution was still gathering pace and many gangsters looked to Afro-Brazilian deities such as Ogum, god of war, for protection. Drug bosses built shrines to Orixás and showed their devotion to the Umbanda and Candomblé faiths.

Four decades later, there are sculptures of Bibles and murals of the Last Supper as a new generation of born-again criminals takes power, influenced by a brotherhood of Pentecostal preachers.

The sway those pastors hold over Rio's 'narco-Pentecostals' is unmissable in the hundreds of favelas controlled by gunmen from its three main gangs: the Red Command (CV), the Friends of Friends (ADA) and, perhaps the most evangelical of all, the Pure Third Command (TCP).

Drug lords, some regular churchgoers, have incorporated Christian symbols into their violent trade. Packets of cocaine, handguns and uniforms are emblazoned with the Star of David

– a reference to the Pentecostal belief that the return of Jews to Israel represents progress towards the second coming.

A senior trafficker recently wandered into a service in suburban Rio, unarmed and unannounced. Surrounded by local children and their smartly dressed parents, the gangster took a white plastic chair in the corner, bowed his head and began to pray.

Nowhere is the evangelisation of Rio's underworld more visible than the Complexo de Israel, a cluster of five favelas near the international airport governed by Peixão ('Big Fish'), a preacher turned drug peddler who takes his nickname from the Christian ichthys fish symbol. (His second-in-command is named after the prophet Jeremiah, and their troops are known as the Army of the Living God). A mural of the cartoon character Fishtronaut adorns one entrance, framed by a line from Psalm 33: 'Blessed is the nation whose God is the Lord.'

A neon Star of David, visible for miles at night, sits on a water tower. Nearby, on an outcrop looking south towards Rio's Christ the Redeemer statue, a Bible sits in a display case. 'Rescue me, O Lord, from evil men,' reads its inscription, from Psalm 140. 'Protect me from men of violence who devise evil plans in their hearts and stir up war every day.'

Peixão is wanted for crimes including torture and murder. Police say he is one of Rio's most iron-handed villains, whose fast-growing criminal empire makes a mockery of his purported Christian faith. In 2019 he was accused of leading the Bonde de Jesus (Jesus Crew), a gang of rifle-toting extremists who allegedly ransacked Afro-Brazilian temples.

But some residents say the bling-averse gangster's Bible-in-fused 'doctrine' – which includes keeping streets tidy and lit, acts of charity to impoverished locals, discouraging swearing and drug use among gang members, and a military-style focus on discipline – has improved life in the ghetto.

'There's order in the favela,' said Juju Rude, a local rapper whose songs describe life in a community ruled by God-fearing gangsters. Overall, she thought life had improved under the current church-going boss, but she is troubled by the surge in faith-related bigotry and violence. 'It's not cool to see people prevented from practising their faith in the place where they live.'

Rio's narco-Pentecostals admit their work clashes with the scripture they profess to follow. A trafficker in another gang-run part of town, lounging on a motorbike surrounded by armed bodyguards, acknowledged the drug trade was an 'evil' business that sometimes entailed horrific violence.

But he claimed his faith inspired him to minimise the barbarity. 'Those I can save, I save,' he said, remembering how he once persuaded a colleague not to murder a trafficker who defected to a rival group. Instead, the traitor was forced to clasp his hands as if in prayer, and they were shot through at close range, shattering his bones but preserving his life.

In another favela, a foot soldier with a Bible tattooed on his chest said he enjoyed services at the God is Love Pentecostal church, which has temples across the US and Europe. 'It makes me feel lighter,' he said, before racing away on his motorbike with his AR-15 rifle.

Christina Vital, an academic who has spent nearly 30 years studying evangelism's advance into gangland Rio, said it was inevitable traffickers had embraced Christianity, given the evangelical tsunami that has swept over Brazilian society during that time. Evangelicals now occupied key positions in the world of crime, just as they did in the media, politics, judiciary and culture, she said.

Nor was it surprising that marginalised young men sought guidance and compassion from the preachers searching Rio's favelas for souls: 'It's such an awful, fragile life. They live in fear.'

Vital said the consequences of the improbable fusion were unclear. There was 'a certain containment' of bloodshed, she said, but the blending of religious intolerance with 'staggering' gang violence was disturbing.

A week after being invited to bless the foot soldier's first home, Pastor Elias set off down winding, muddy passageways to the modest first-floor abode. He says he respects all faiths and believes he is helping pacify a city where hundreds of mostly young, black lives are lost each year. 'This is Christianity's duty: to save.'

He squeezed inside the home for which the criminal had paid 8,000 reais (£1,000), accompanied by half a dozen Bible-carrying helpers, and the group began to sing 'Oh! Jesus Loves Me'. A female church member then clutched their host's arm. 'God has chosen you. God is here right now!' she told him. 'Just look at my goosebumps! God is here!' she said, her voice trembling as she summoned an angel to watch over the trafficker's life.

After 20 minutes of prayer and a reading from Psalm 23, the trafficker thanked his visitors over hotdogs, visibly moved. 'It's a life of loneliness,' said the pastor, 'and Christ has come to free them.'

A warm breeze coursed through the favela and briefly the world seemed at peace – but the calm did not last. Shortly after midnight the crackle of gunfire woke residents, as traffickers stormed a nearby neighbourhood. Another night of chaos and heartbreak in a city crying out to be saved.

Brands are moving from fast to 'forever fashion' – but are new clothes ever sustainable?

JESS CARTNER-MORLEY

Fashion has a new look this spring. Well, of course it does – that's how fashion works. Except this time round, the trend isn't crimson or corduroy, or Peter Pan collars or platform shoes. The hot look for spring 2022 is the 'forever wardrobe'. The key pieces of the season are clothes that come with the promise that they will never go out of style: think crisp white shirts and well-cut blazers; classic knitwear and timeless little black dresses. Throwaway fashion is so last season. This spring, chic comes with a lifetime guarantee.

The irony is that the forever wardrobe never went away, it just went out of style. The fast fashion industry, which has exploded during the past 30 years, turbocharged the trend cycle, abandoning the principles of enduring elegance in favour of a rollercoaster of plot twists (woah, jumpsuits!), comebacks (Crocs) and about-turns (black is back, again) designed to keep an audience hooked. Bored of your jeans? Why not try leather trousers! Throw out your neutrals, it's the season for neon!

Many stylish people ignored this all along, of course – even inside the fashion industry, where the front row cheerleads for apple green one season and salmon pink the next, while continuing to mostly wear navy. Now, an urgent need for sustainability has brought investment dressing back into the spotlight.

But can fashion ever really come without an expiry date? Or is forever fashion just a feelgood label to make us feel less guilty about buying new clothes?

On an emotional level, the change of heart in the world of fashion is real, among both the people who buy clothes and the people who design and make them. Fashion is about the future; without a future for the planet, there is no fashion. Everybody gets that now. But on an economic level, things are not so easy. The fashion industry generates about 2 per cent of global GDP, and employs about 400 million people. It has grown to this size specifically through selling us more clothes than we need. And the thrill of transformation has always been part of the power of clothes. From *Cinderella* to *My Fair Lady*, *Grease* to *Pretty Woman*, the magic of a radical new look is ingrained in our culture.

At the height of its imperial pomp, around the beginning of this century, fashion leaned hard into the lure of newness. During the 1970s and 1980s, teenagers tuned in to the radio every Sunday to find out what pop song was at No 1 that week; in the 1990s and 2000s, they gravitated to Topshop every weekend to find out what look was new for Saturday night. But that was a more innocent age, before we all understood that we were running up a carbon tab that we would never be able to pay off.

Forever fashion is an easy sell for those lucky enough to be in a position to pivot from buying several new outfits in Zara at the beginning of a season to buying one designer dress. But for those shoppers who are at the 'value' end of the market, where jeans can cost as little as £10, there is no Chanel tweed suit (ballpark cost: £8,000) or Hermes Birkin handbag (around £10,000) at the end of the rainbow. Fashion has become a cheap payday treat, with a new blouse often costing less than a takeaway pizza. High-street price wars have dragged down the quality of the clothes on sale in many shops.

Shoppers have become accustomed to cheap, thin fabric that tears easily, to loose and irregular stitching that makes for seams that don't hold, to buttons that snap or fall off. If your budget is tight and your experience of fashion is shoes with soles that come unstuck and sweaters that lose shape after the first wash, it is entirely rational to resist spending more than the bare minimum on clothes. Right now, investment dressing is an elite sport, like polo or skiing, a luxe pursuit for those with spare cash. At the lower price points, the trust level between shop and shopper has been eroded, and that will take some fixing. Forever fashion is not just about timeless classics over quick turnover trends, but about making clothes that last.

The forever wardrobe really does exist, if it's well designed and properly made. A crisp white cotton shirt, a striped Breton, a simple black one-piece swimsuit, a camel trench coat, loafers: these were here all along, and they look as modern now as ever. It may be that we will come to look back on the breakneck-speed version of the industry we have known over the past two or three decades as an aberration, and fashion will return to being about beautiful clothes that are made to be treasured.

In a perfect world, the label of a 'forever wardrobe' would not be weaponised as a hard sell by retailers to entice consumers with already bulging wardrobes to buy yet more clothes. But the last train to a perfect world left the station some time ago. To use the phrase du jour, we cannot shop our way to sustainability, but neither can we make an industry that employs one in eight of the world's workforce disappear overnight. Clothes we want to wear for ever and ever might seem like the opposite of what fashion represents. But from where I'm standing, they look like the last word in chic.

11 FEBRUARY

I've started, so I'll panic: what it's really like to go on *Mastermind*

SIRIN KALE

In all honesty, I have no idea why I decided to go on *Mastermind*. I love pub quizzes, sure, and I'm good at them. Pre-Covid, I was part of a crack team called Quizlamic State, who regularly took home first prize in our local one. As team coordinator, I developed a reputation for ruthlessness, brutally ejecting friends and, on one occasion, my boyfriend, if I thought they were underperforming. At university, I was picked for our college's *University Challenge* team, though we didn't get on the show: too boring, apparently. (The producers picked a team of historical re-enactors and archers from a different college.)

All of this stuff is what I say when people ask why I went on the show. But if I'm being honest, I don't know why I did it. I don't know why I do most things. I'm an incredibly impulsive person; always have been. To paraphrase Kim Kardashian West's reply when asked why she filmed the sex tape that made her famous: because I was bored, and I felt like it.

I guess if I'm honest, I thought it would be a win-win situation. Nail *Mastermind*, in which case I have lifelong bragging rights; or don't, in which case I'll have a funny story I can write about.

Here's the funny story.

Another confession: when I apply for *Mastermind*, I haven't watched it for years. How hard can it be? I think, with the breezy optimism of a rookie journalist thumbing a lift into a war zone.

In late May, I fill out an online form and, to my surprise, get a call the following day. The first round is a Zoom interview and quiz with a friendly Northern Irish casting researcher. (*Mastermind* is produced for the BBC by Hat Trick Productions, which has offices in Belfast.) 'You did great!' he says when I correctly name Virginia Woolf's artist sister. (Vanessa Bell.) I feel a childish jolt of self-satisfaction.

The email comes through the following day: 'Well done on being shortlisted for this series of *Mastermind*!' I'm told that hardly anyone gets picked for the show, which inflates my confidence. 'Your score in the trial was very impressive,' says a producer in a congratulatory phone call.

Next, to pick my specialist subject. The answer comes quickly: the Kardashians. I know everything about that wretched family: their plastic surgeon (Raj Kanodia), the high school they went to (Marymount High), the designer of Kim's house (Axel Vervoordt). The opportunity to scrape some utility from this knowledge, like penicillin from mould, is too good to pass up. But alas, I'm not allowed to. ('We can't accommodate the Kardashians this series,' says a cryptic email from the producers.) Nor am I allowed my second choice (Spice Girls), or my third, the novels of Jane Austen – there are only six major ones, so I figure revision will be easy – as both subjects have featured too recently.

I'm floundering. There's nothing else I want to do. I consider the novels of Hilary Mantel, but they're so long, and I've only read them once. At this point, I go dark on the producers, but they keep calling me from unknown numbers, asking if I've got another specialist subject. Flailing, I cast out the TV show I've been binge-watching during lockdown: *ER*. Yes, they say. That could work. *ER* it is.

I realise my insane folly a week later, when it becomes clear that I've got to rewatch all 331 hour-long episodes of *ER* in under six weeks, before the show is filmed in early July. I send a panicked email. Please, I beg yet again: can't I just do the Kardashians? They are unmoving but, after some horse trading, the producers and I settle on an inspired compromise: I will focus only on the character of Dr Doug Ross in ER, who handily exits the show as a recurring character in season 5, and, even more handily, is played by George Clooney, in a career-defining role.

For the next six weeks, I eat, sleep, and breathe Clooney, which, in all honesty, makes for the most fulfilling and erotic revision experience of my life. I listen to *Setting the Tone*, an ER podcast, when I'm brushing my teeth in the morning and getting ready for bed at night. I cancel my plans and instead stay in and watch ER every evening, watching Clooney save a boy from drowning in a storm drain while wearing a tuxedo, punch child abusers, and do that classic Clooney shtick of tilting his head down then looking up with those hangdog puppy eyes. It is rough going.

As July rolls around, I'm feeling good. In the park a month before filming, a friend tests me on my general knowledge. I get two questions right out of 20. 'I think the questions are easier than that,' I say breezily. He looks doubtful. 'That's ... the official *Mastermind* quiz,' he says.

I touch down in Belfast for filming, carrying a selection of wardrobe options at the producers' request, and three pages of revision notes. The hotel is full of *Mastermind* contestants, which makes for a surreal dinner, each of us sitting alone, all of us side-eyeing each other, assessing who has the most bountiful general knowledge of them all.

By the following morning, a small animal is doing yoga in my stomach. I return to my room for last-minute revision and begin to unravel. Part of the problem is that I've seen the other contestants' revision folders, which are the Gutenberg Bible to my SparkNotes. But there's nothing to be done and, before I know it, a researcher is walking me and three other contestants to the studio for our heat.

A lovely makeup artist does her best to calm my nerves – really, she is so kind and, more importantly, my makeup looks great – and then it's time to face the chair. The chair. How best to describe the *Mastermind* chair? It is spotlit, well worn, imposing. Its leather has been burnished by the arses of minds far greater than mine, minds capable of retaining all manner of trivia while staying cool under pressure and not panic-sweating profusely via their bum cheeks on to the seat; cellulite-free grey matter, crammed full of general knowledge like a suitcase you have to sit on to close. My mind, by comparison, is a duffel bag containing a single pair of socks.

A floor manager instructs us to stare into a camera while the *Mastermind* music thunders. *Da da da da ... DA DUH*. The floor lights are raised. *DA DUH*. What am I doing here?

Clive Myrie, the host, nods me into the chair. I'm first. He asks me my name and specialist subject, then we're away. I get a couple wrong, a couple right. At the end of my specialist subject round, I've scored eight points, which is a respectable though not particularly impressive score. I definitely would have done better if I'd had more time to revise, as many of the questions were on minor plot points for episodes I'd only watched once, but lots of them I'd predicted, and did get right. In all honesty, it was fun. I enjoyed it. After everyone else has had their turn, I'm in joint third place for the specialist subject. Which is fine; I didn't seriously expect to win.

When Myrie beckons me to the chair again, I realise that, for all my cramming about dishy Dr Ross, I've completely omitted to even think about the general knowledge round. All my energy and focus has been on not tanking my specialist subject. Walking back to the chair, I think: should I have prepared for this? Could I have prepared for this?

I fumble the first question, which is maddeningly easy – a question about tennis that I know, but wasn't listening to properly – and, just like that, it all falls apart. I can't seem to hear the questions properly, like I'm in an aeroplane and my ears won't pop. The only sensation I can compare it to is the time I jumped off a waterfall in South America and, while freefalling through the air, realised I had badly misjudged the angle and was about to land on a rock. *Uh oh*, I think, as Myrie pummels me with question after question I have no answer for. *This is going to hurt.* I emerge, dazed and metaphorically bloody, with a paltry four points, leaving me with an overall score of 12.

To my eternal shame, I spend the next five minutes actively wishing for all the other contestants to do worse than me. Annoyingly, they do not.

The final scores are 17, 16, 16 and 12. Reader, I came last.

Back at the hotel, I call my boyfriend and deliver the news. After a pause, he says: 'Probably not worth it in retrospect. All that effort and you came last.' I consider never telling anyone about this ever, but I'd stupidly posted on social media about applying for the show, and my editor saw it and asked me to write this piece, and it felt wormlike to weasel out – even though writing this has, at times, felt like acupuncture with a drill bit, or watching every embarrassing thing I've ever done on an Imax screen.

(Besides, I tell myself, as I lie awake at 2am, it's not like I got the lowest-ever score on the show. That honour goes to athlete Kadeena Cox, who scored just three points on her specialist subject of Arsenal on the celebrity edition, and none on general knowledge. I wonder how she's doing.)

What lessons can I learn from my tale of televised quizzing mediocrity? That *Mastermind* is harder – I would go as far as to say considerably harder – than a pub quiz. That next time I feel like doing something dumb and impulsive, I should get another piercing. That the best way to transcend shame is to lean all the way into it, make it a funny story, and come out the other side: because the only thing worse than a person who flubbed *Mastermind* is a person who can't laugh at themselves.

Oddly enough, I actually don't regret it that much. I still love quizzes. I definitely didn't do well, but I did go for the grandfather of all quiz shows as a complete newbie with barely any revision, like scaling K2 without supplemental oxygen, in winter, on my first attempt at climbing. Next time, I'll try a gentle walk up Ben Nevis first. Something straightforward, like *The Weakest Link* or *Pointless*. Until that day, I'll return to the comfortable camaraderie of my Quizlamic State teammates. Some games are better played in the pub, after all.

16 FEBRUARY

The *Guardian* view on Prince Andrew: closure with no prospect of redemption

GUARDIAN EDITORIAL

In the end there was nowhere left to hide, and there were no good options remaining. Since 2015, Prince Andrew has sought to discredit allegations of sexual abuse made against him by Virginia Giuffre, who claims that as a teenager she was repeatedly forced to sleep with him by the sex trafficker Jeffrey Epstein. The prince has repeatedly denied this and, in a car-crash interview with *BBC Newsnight*, said he had no recollection of ever meeting her. As the screws tightened and Ms Giuffre filed a civil damages claim last year, his lawyers accused her of seeking a 'payday', questioned her mental health and tried to have the lawsuit thrown out on technical grounds.

All in vain. But it was only when the Duke of York's back was against the wall, and cross-examination under oath before a jury loomed, that he threw in the towel on Tuesday and settled. The amount to be paid by the prince remains undisclosed, but Ms Giuffre's lawyers have previously suggested that it would need to be large enough to represent 'a vindication' of her claim. The accompanying statement by both parties contains no admission of wrongdoing on Prince Andrew's part, but the formerly dismissive prince recognises his accuser's bravery in standing up for herself and her status as a victim of sexual abuse. He states that he never intended to malign her character. This was anything but a legal score-draw. The settlement represents a major victory for an abused young woman from a modest background. Ms Giuffre's determination to hold the wealthy, powerful and connected to account for their actions has been spectacularly validated.

For Prince Andrew, on the other hand, it seems unlikely that this deal will deliver the kind of closure he must crave. Ms Giuffre's lawsuit will not now cast a shadow over the Queen's forthcoming platinum jubilee celebrations – a consideration which appears to have been a significant factor in the decision to settle. Future criminal charges are also rendered extremely unlikely. But the reputational damage to the monarch's favourite son has been done. The damning verdict already delivered in the court of public opinion will only have been confirmed by Prince Andrew's decision not to fight in an actual one.

From the sustained nature of the friendship with Epstein – which continued even after a warrant was issued for his arrest over trafficking allegations – to the initial haughty indifference to Ms Giuffre's claims, the prince's behaviour has been that of a man who believed himself too powerful and too protected to be brought down. In that he was mistaken, and this misplaced, tin-eared hauteur contributed to his fall. The royal family has, in effect, cut him loose; the military titles and royal patronages have already gone and will not be restored. A campaign is under way to remove the title of Duke of York. Rightly, there is no comeback to public life in prospect.

Prince Andrew's future thus looks likely to play itself out in a purgatorial twilight, haunted by the grave allegations he chose not to refute in court. The terms of the settlement submitted to the New York judge, Lewis Kaplan, state that he will show his regret for his friendship with Epstein by supporting the fight against sex trafficking. But while the prince's substantial donation to the charity set up by Ms Giuffre to support victims' rights will be welcome, a more personal route to atonement is complicated by the fact that he has not admitted to any wrongdoing. The existential price of this settlement – more costly than the millions to be paid out to shut the case down – is a permanently stained reputation and a blocked path to public rehabilitation. It is a fate that Prince Andrew has brought upon himself.

17 FEBRUARY

My five-letter reaction to the *New York Times* taking over Wordle? I quit

EMMA BROCKES

There is something very satisfying about going, in the space of a few months, from neophyte to expert to outraged dissenter, and enjoying that journey alongside thousands of others. I'm talking about Wordle, obviously, the five stages of which, after its invention in October last year, might usefully be delineated as indifference, confusion, enjoyment, obsession and resolution to cancel the *New York Times*. Here we are in February and it's a new world, teetering for some of us on the brink of post-Wordle. I'm not quite ready to jump. But after a week of scandalous decisions by the NYT, the puzzle's new owners, it's only a matter of time.

This is a sad outcome, given the ancillary pleasures that come with the game. As in all things, I was not an early adopter, only giving in and trying a Wordle when friends with even less interest in puzzles than me got sucked in and triggered my competitive machinery. For five weeks, I have patiently and conscientiously done a puzzle a day, while enjoying all the benefits of my new hobby. I have made judgments about people who post their results. I have made judgments about myself, primarily how brilliant I am. During a bout of insomnia, I've shared my grid at 3am. with someone who has sent me their middle-of-the-night results, an action I have understood, obliquely, to be both a boast and a small cry for help. I've texted the word 'genius' to people when they've solved the puzzle in two, and received the same validation in return. I've wondered if I'm rescuing myself from dementia.

And of course, in the last week or so, I have given much thought as to whether, under new management, the words are getting harder. All of which experience is probably very quaint and familiar to veterans of these kinds of games. Here's another discovery that we, the interlopers – the people who only like football during the World Cup but with puzzles – have made: a land in which the inhabitants couldn't have been nicer. Who are these lovely people, with their tolerance for our amazement that word games can be fun? For my entire life, I've been operating under the delusion that other people are my people, when in fact, these people might be my true people. It's a wild ride.

'Is it an indication of smartness?' asks the friend with whom I trade scores. 'Definitely,' I say, but when I click on the millionth Wordle story of the day, I discover that it's ability in maths, not words, that's considered the key (I am not good at maths). This makes sense, given my history with word games. I've always hated Scrabble and had no time for crosswords. Boggle didn't take. It has been a source of small but nevertheless real sorrow to me that if I had been alive during the Second World War, I wouldn't have been picked to code-break at Bletchley. But Wordle, for some reason, is different.

For me, the fact that it's on a device definitely helps, allowing me to stare at a screen and still feel virtuous. It's to the advantage of Wordle that it takes so little time to complete – if you haven't nailed it within 20 minutes, it's a lost cause – making it seem like a manageable addiction. Like slow-release drugs, you can't binge Wordle, all of which adds up to an experience that we don't seem to have had for a long time, of having to wait for something for 24 hours, with no possibility of cheating.

Which brings us to the *NYT*, effortless ruiner of all things. This week, the kerfuffle was about two answers being generated on the same day, but that was an administrative error. The main thing is the choice of words. I'm not sure the puzzle is getting harder – I'm still thinking about the word 'tapir', which appeared in one of the early games. But there is something different now it's under Big Puzzle management. On Wednesday, I got 'caulk' – a word I associate with 'spackle', and is annoyingly obscure – but this morning, for the first time, I bombed out and didn't get the word. This wasn't because it was hard but because it was easy, and I'd wasted two tries on obscure words that I thought were more likely to come out of the *NYT*'s puzzle desk. It's not going to be 'cakes', is it, I thought; it's going to be something aggravating like 'slake' (it wasn't either).

Take it from a puzzles veteran of five weeks, once you stop trusting the puzzle master, it's all over, and I can feel my interest curdling, a withdrawal helped along by my seven-year-old. 'Oh,' she said flatly, when I showed her a Wordle this week. 'It's hangman.'

24 FEBRUARY

Stay or flee? Kyiv comes to terms with disaster of Russian invasion

LUKE HARDING

It began in darkness soon after 4.30am local time. There were distant explosions in the Ukrainian capital, Kyiv. A nation shook itself awake. What had been foretold by Western governments, by experts, and – late in the day – by the country's president, Volodymyr Zelenskiy, was actually happening. Russia was attacking and invading.

Vladimir Putin's apparent goal: the subjugation of a nation, a culture, a people. It was unthinkable in the 21st century. And yet, with imperial swagger, Russian troops, tanks and planes were on the move.

The disaster unfurled on a grey, ordinary Thursday, sprinkled by rain. By 5am friends and loved ones were ringing each other, peering into their phones, making life and death decisions.

Stay or flee? Some packed and got ready to leave; others took refuge in basements. An underground garage began to fill up in Yaroslaviv Val, close to Kyiv's historic golden gate, dating back to the 11th century and to Kyivan Rus, a pre-Moscow dynasty. A family arrived. A mother shepherded her two bleary-eyed children to safety. The children were carrying colouring books, scant defence against Russian missiles.

By breakfast, the scale of Russia's multitudinous military assault was clear. Putin's ambitions, it turned out, went well beyond the Donbas region, whose separatist territories he recognised earlier this week. They included practically the entire country: east, south, north and even west. The port city of Mariupol on the Sea of Azov; the city of Kharkiv, home to 1.4 million people; Odesa on the Black Sea and Kherson; Ukrainian-controlled towns and villages on the Donbas frontline – all were being bombed.

Russia was clinically targeting Ukraine's defences: aerodromes, bases, ammunition dumps. It was shock and awe, done with ruthless indifference to the human cost.

Amid this grandiose onslaught there were moments of normality. A few Kyiv residents emerged to walk their dogs. Queues formed outside cash machines. Most cafes were closed but Aroma Coffee had opened as usual, selling croissants and takeaways.

The mood was one of shock, fear and quiet disgust that Putin – without reason or rational pretext – had decided to unleash war. 'Russia is 100 per cent wrong,' said Viktor Alexeyevich, speaking in the capital's Maidan Nezalezhnosti square. Behind him was the city's independence monument, a marble column once topped with a statue of Vladimir Lenin. Perched on top – at least for now – was a woman with a rose branch in her arms, symbolising Ukraine's independence.

What would he do now? 'I'm going to take my grandson out of the city. And then I will come back,' he said. 'I don't have any weapons but I'm ready to defend my country. Maybe the national guard will help.' Alexeyevich said he had rung his son when he heard the first explosions, and turned on the TV. He had watched Zelenskiy address the nation, introduce martial law, and urge citizens to be calm, he said. 'Putin is the aggressor here. He's invaded Ukraine because we don't want to live under his strictures, his model.' The square, normally full of tourists and shoppers, was quieter than usual. A few people waited in the rain for a trolleybus.

For months, Kyiv's pro-Western government has said Ukraine will resist Russian attack and occupation. It says the country's armed forces are in better shape than in 2014, when they wilted under superior Russian firepower. On paper, this is true: Ukraine has 220,000 troops, 400,000 veterans with combat experience and modern weapons recently supplied by the US, UK and other allies.

Ukraine's operational command reported some early successes in beating back attacks from the rebel-held cities of Donetsk and Luhansk, run for the past eight years by Moscow's loyal proxies.

And yet the cars streaming out of Kyiv told their own story. From early in the day, the streets were jammed as civilians sought a way out – to Zhytomyr, west of the city, and from there to Lviv and the Polish border. Traffic on the boulevards moved slowly. There was no panic as such, but an awareness that the window to leave was beginning to close.

Reports suggested Russian formations were advancing to the capital from Belarus and the north, two hours' drive away.

They had broken through the international checkpoint and – seemingly – were trundling towards Kyiv through a primordial landscape of pine trees and swamp. It seemed Belarus was facilitating war on Kyiv too.

Oleg Olegovich, a 30-year-old officer in the army, said he had been summoned at 4am to come in for work. His office was in the centre of Kyiv. 'Civilians are leaving. But we will stay,' he said. Could Ukraine defeat mighty Russia, with its vast air power and Black Sea navy? 'We will smash them,' he said. 'The military is in good shape; our communications are working.'

Lyudmila – a young city police officer who had popped out for coffee – said she would carry on. 'I didn't sleep last night,' she said. 'I tried to sleep before work but I couldn't manage it.

'Cheerio,' she said with a smile.

Nearby, the trade union building overlooking the Maidan played the national anthem on a loudspeaker. Few were around to hear it. It played a key role in the Euromaidan protests in 2013 and 2014 against the country's pro-Russian president Viktor Yanukovych. The uprising saw Yanukovych flee to Russia. After that, the country moved in an emphatically pro-EU and pro-NATO direction. Putin responded in 2014 by annexing Crimea and kickstarting a pro-Russian revolt in the east. Eight years on, he seems determined to stop Ukraine's westward integration forever.

Zelenskiy – a TV star and comedian before he turned to politics – was still in Kyiv and at work, his press service said. Historians may rebuke him for failing to prepare Ukraine for an inevitable Kremlin attack. But in a speech on Wednesday evening – the eve of invasion as it turned out – Zelenskiy addressed the Russian people directly. He reminded them of Ukraine and Russia's joint ties – of family, friendship and of love – telling them that the portrait painted by Russian state TV of a fascist Ukraine bore no resemblance to its vibrant, modern and tolerant reality.

Zelenskiy's personal fate and that of the country he leads remains unclear. It seems likely Russia will demand his capitulation and replacement with a pro-Russian puppet administration. For the moment he is in power – just.

Meanwhile, Kyiv's familiar rhythms continued. The bells of St Michael's domed monastery tolled the hour, as they have for centuries. The baroque building sits across the square from St Sophia cathedral, an 11th-century building done in vivid turquoise. Locals protesting outside the now-empty Russian embassy pointed out wryly that when it was constructed Moscow was a mere forest.

The square's playground was empty, home now to a few jackdaws and a stray dog. Europe was at war. The world – two decades into the century – had reached a crisis that was likely to reverberate well beyond the early overcast hours of invasion.

It was Mikhail Bulgakov in his masterful novel *The White Guard*, written almost a century ago, who dubbed Kyiv 'the City', with an uppercase C. The City will endure. But it seems only a matter of time before it has new, harsher masters.

24 FEBRUARY

The *Guardian* view on Putin's war in Ukraine: a bleak new beginning

GUARDIAN EDITORIAL

There is no shock today, only profound horror at what Russia has already unleashed upon Ukraine, and at what is to come.

The invasion launched in the early hours of this morning is illegal, immoral and outrageous. It is, above all, a catastrophe for Ukraine: a massive assault by an aggressor with a well-documented ruthlessness and disdain for civilian lives.

But as the country's president, Volodymyr Zelenskiy, warned: 'The fate of not only our state is being decided, but also what Europe will be like.' A country that endured so many 20th-century traumas is now experiencing the continent's biggest attack by one state on another since the Second World War.

The unprovoked assault does not merely destroy the hopes of 1991. It is also a terrible blow to the broader international system. Vladimir Putin launched this attack even as the UN security council made its last desperate attempts to stave it off, and as the secretary general, António Guterres, pleaded with him publicly to call off his troops. It is true that the rules which prevailed after 1945 have been honoured perhaps as often in the breach as the observance. But the Russian president has spelt out his utter contempt for the teetering rules-based international order at its very heart.

Russia claimed for months that it would not invade; its assurances that it will not occupy Ukraine are worth nothing. Even on its own supposed logic, the request for military help from the breakaway 'republics' in the east cannot explain why troops are advancing from the north and south, and bombarding targets across the country. Mr Putin says that he wants to 'demilitarise' and 'de-nazify' a democratic country that freely chose its Jewish president. Kyiv believes his aim is to topple the government and install a puppet regime.

How far the Russian president goes may be determined in large part by the Ukrainian response, and the costs its military can inflict. Mr Putin warned against other countries 'meddling', with the chilling warning that otherwise there would be 'consequences you have never encountered in your history' – a barely coded nuclear threat – though Ukraine has long known it will fight alone, albeit strengthened by the recent influx of arms and advice.

A brave minority in Russia have publicly decried this war. Even allowing for his work to insulate his country – amassing foreign currency, reducing Western imports and increasing links with China and others – it is likely to pay for this assault with a weakened economy, increasing isolation, a reinvigorated NATO and a bitterly anti-Russian Ukraine. Though state media is pumping out propaganda, and internet censors threatened others with fines if they used non-official sources in their reporting, Mr Putin has done strikingly little to prepare the public for the invasion, or its costs. Yet a president who has twinned aggression abroad with repression at home seems indifferent not only to those costs, but also to the public response to them.

Ukrainians now need and deserve the staunchest support. Those who flee must be given a true welcome by western Europe as well as neighbouring countries. But the big question is what price Ukraine's backers are willing to pay. The UK and EU promised 'massive' sanctions, but hours after the invasion, states were still bickering over how far to go. A further hike in energy prices could tip countries into rampant inflation and potentially recession, with the danger of political destabilisation and further division as citizens struggle to get by.

Mr Putin has reason to believe that he can weather the reaction. Nord Stream 2 is now on hold; yet its construction began just one year after Russia annexed Crimea. Ukraine's friends must make clear that this time is different, with a sustained as well as large-scale response. Serious attempts to counter Moscow's aggression must start now, but will be the work of years. It will take years, too, to understand the new era on which we are all now embarking.

What's going on inside Putin's mind? His own words give us a disturbing clue

MICHEL ELTCHANINOFF

'They have only one objective: to prevent the development of Russia. They are going to do it in the same way as they did it before, without furnishing even a single pretext, doing it just because we exist.'

These were Vladimir Putin's words on 21 February, in his now notorious speech on Ukraine. They repeat the argument already formulated in his speech on Crimea in March 2014: 'The politics of the containment of Russia, which continued throughout the 18th, 19th and 20th centuries, continues today. There is a constant attempt to push us back into a corner because we have an independent position, because we stand up for ourselves.' Putin's vision of Russian history is one of an emergence continually blocked by enemies.

The contemporary 'West', in this vision, battles to contain Russia out of jealousy. Europe has collapsed into decadence, crushed by the weight of its humanism and political liberalism: tired, divided, at the mercy of every passing wind. The United States, mired in an instrumental, materialist culture and the contradictions of its own history, is in the process of losing its pre-eminence. Russia, by contrast, like its emerging ally, China, is on the rise in civilisational terms.

Putin leans here on a strange theory advanced by the 20th-century historian and ethnographer Lev Gumilev. The son of two of Russia's most famous poets, Nikolai Gumilev and Anna Akhmatova, Gumilev maintains that every people possesses a distinct life force: a 'bio-cosmic' inner energy or passionate substance that he calls *passionarnost*. Putin may have known Gumilev in St Petersburg at the start of the 1990s. At any rate, he has embraced his ideas and never misses an opportunity to refer to them. In February last year, he said: 'I believe in *passionarnost*. In nature, as in society, there is development, climax and decline. Russia has not yet attained its highest point. We are on the way.' According to him, Russia carries the power and potential of a young people. 'We possess an infinite genetic code,' he has said.

In addition to Gumilev, Putin relies on another thinker – a minor figure in the history of Russian thought. Last October, he spoke of regularly consulting a collection of political essays titled *Our Tasks*, the major work of Ivan Ilyin, who died in 1954. In one of the president's preferred essays, 'What does the world seek from the dismemberment of Russia?', Ilyin denounces the country's 'imperialist neighbours', these 'Western peoples who neither understand nor accept Russian originality'. In the future, he suggests, these countries will inevitably attempt to seize territories such as the Baltic countries, the Caucasus, central Asia and, especially, Ukraine. The method, according to Ilyin, will be the hypocritical promotion of values such as 'freedom' in order to transform Russia into 'a gigantic Balkans'. The final object is to 'dismember Russia, to subject her to Western control, to dismantle her and in the end make her disappear'.

It is necessary, then, to understand that what is actually happening in Ukraine is the result of a vision of Russia that is deeply embedded in the mind of Putin. In 2008, he punished Georgia for its desire to leave the orbit of the old imperial power. In 2014, he annexed Crimea and prevented Ukraine from joining NATO by starting the Donbas conflict. But that is not enough for him. He wants a confrontation with – and a victory over – a West that he holds responsible for the fall of the Soviet Union, for the weakness of Russia in the 1990s, and for the autonomous tendencies of the old Soviet republics.

Why now? In the years following his re-election in 2018, the patriotic exaltation that followed the annexation of Crimea faded. Everyday problems for ordinary people – declining living standards, increased poverty, inflation, a healthcare crisis – have become worse year by year. Meanwhile the US has become more preoccupied with China than Russia. So in July 2021, Putin published the infamous article in which he proclaimed the unity of the Russian and Ukrainian people. The Ukrainians, he maintained, could not be left to suffer indefinitely under an illegitimate government, which came to power in what he described as a coup d'etat in 2014. Putin massed his troops on his neighbours' borders from the spring. He intensified military preparations in the autumn and issued his ultimatum to NATO and Washington. He set a carefully laid trap for the West, knowing it was impossible to accept his demands. Everything was ready for what followed.

As in 2008, Russian state media echoes Putin in evoking the risk of a genocide. In place of the Ossetians, supposedly menaced by the then Georgian president, Mikheil Saakashvili, this time the victims to be defended are in Donetsk and Luhansk. The manufacture of this humanitarian crisis may, for Putin, carry a pleasing element of irony. He has never forgotten NATO's bombing of Belgrade in the spring of 1999, a few months before he became prime minister. By parodying the language of ethnic cleansing and genocide (the Russian-speakers of Donbas this time, rather than the Kosovars), Putin wishes to cancel out the affront caused by that episode in the darkest way imaginable.

What should we think of this perpetual sense of victimhood that allows the Russian president to artificially create situations in which Russia appears humiliated and insulted? Are these the actions of a rational leader? The answer is both simple and worrying. Putin has developed, over decades, a vision of the world that is paranoid but coherent. According to this vision, Russia has for centuries been the victim of an attempt to contain and dismember it. These attempts must be resisted. The logic of this is based on a belief that Russia's *passionarnost* must not be constrained.

For Putin – in stark contrast to the tired Westerner, lost in the search for profit and material comfort, 'the Russian man thinks first of all ... in relation to a superior moral principle'. And he is prepared to die for it. Putin often cites a well-known Russian saying: for Russians, 'even death is beautiful'. There may, therefore, be no limits to the quest to avenge perceived humiliation. The president's worldview paves the way to extremism.

1 MARCH

'It might be the last chance to get out': citizens flee Kyiv as assault intensifies

SHAUN WALKER

The piercing screams of children mingled with the barking of traumatised dogs and the shouts of soldiers desperately trying to maintain order, as the 14.07 to Ivano-Frankivsk pulled into Kyiv's central station.

There was a crowd of thousands on platform one, surging towards the blue carriages and desperate to secure a prized place on a ride west out of the Ukrainian capital. Most people would not be able to board.

'Look at these faces around us, they are exactly the same as in the photographs from the Second World War, and it's just five days. Can you imagine what will happen in a month?' asked Tanya Novgorodskaya, 48, an art historian who arrived at the station with her 15-year-old daughter.

She had bought tickets for six different trains, but soon realised they counted for nothing. Instead, there was a boarding algorithm: first mothers with children, then women, then old people. Others were kept away by the police and soldiers standing guard.

Quickly, the train was crammed full. Families had to make split-second decisions, as mothers and children were allowed to board but grandparents told to wait behind. This was the sixth day of Vladimir Putin's war on Ukraine, and by now fear had taken over.

In the first days, there was a sense of shock and disbelief. Then came pride and inspiration at the surprisingly resilient Ukrainian response and the unity of society.

But the success at repelling the initial Russian assault comes with a terrifying caveat. With Putin's plan A failing, will his plan B involve turning Kyiv into Aleppo or Grozny?

The missile strike on a residential block in Ukraine's second-largest city of Kharkiv on Monday, followed by another strike that hit the city's central square yesterday morning, led many in Kyiv to realise what the capital could be dealing with in just a few days.

Today there was another reminder of the sheer power that Ukraine is up against, when a missile strike hit Kyiv's television tower, reportedly killing at least five people. The tower is close to the memorial site that commemorates the victims of Babyn Yar, the ravine where Nazi soldiers massacred up to 150,000 people during the Second World War – including more than 30,000 Jews.

The Russian defence ministry warned residents of the capital to flee, according to the Russian state news agency Tass, promising airstrikes against various targets.

Like many, Novgorodskaya had underestimated the ferocity of the invasion, and ignored those who told her she should leave. Even when the missiles started falling, she decided to stay and tough it out. Yesterday, though, she changed her mind, having seen footage of the missile attacks on civilian areas of Kharkiv.

'We realised it might be the last chance to get out. Personally, I would stay and try to fight, but I think if you have children, you should leave,' she said.

She and her daughter had taken only a small grey hand-luggage case between them, for a trip that could end up being indefinite.

The crush to board the 14.07 was too intense for many to even attempt, and as pleading wails emanated from the scrums around each carriage door, a middle-aged couple stood nervously some metres back, carrying a suitcase and a five-litre bottle of water, their brown boxer dog standing alongside them, panting nervously.

The man, Yuri, said his children lived in Munich and had been pleading with him for weeks to leave Ukraine, but like most people here, he had simply not believed Putin was capable of launching the kind of war that is now under way.

On the first night of the assault, he and his wife slept in the basement of their apartment block. Since then, they had been sleeping in the bathroom of their ninth-floor apartment and hoping for the best. When they saw images of the missile attacks on Kharkiv on Monday, they made the decision to flee. 'I am scared for what's coming and I really want to get out of here,' he said. But Yuri and his wife were far too low down the priority list, and far too polite, to have any chance of boarding the train.

His wife tried to make the case that he had high blood pressure, but he shushed her out of embarrassment, and nobody was listening anyway.

Finally, with a grinding of wheels and a hiss of smoke, the train pulled out of the station, a huddle of humans visible through the grimy windows and the faces of children squashed against the glass.

On arrival in western Ukraine, many will have a further gruelling journey to get to the border with Poland, Slovakia or Hungary, where people have reported waiting times of several days this week.

Yuri and his wife were left behind on the platform along with thousands of others, hoping they might be luckier next time.

An elderly man with an amputated leg stumbled on crutches, as his wife tried to raise his spirits to wait another few hours and try for a spot on the next train west. A young couple hugged each other in support, both of them crying. A woman leaned against a pillar, dejected, tears falling on the cat she was cradling in her arms.

Adebayo Babatunde, a Nigerian management student who has been studying in Kyiv for the past six months, appeared to have little chance of being allowed to board, and no real idea of where he might go if he did. He was speaking via WhatsApp to his sister, a British citizen who lives in London.

He had applied for a UK visa in Ukraine weeks ago, she said, but had no response, and she could not get through to the Home Office or the British embassy. 'Please help my brother to get on a train,' implored the voice from the phone. The train station is one of the few hubs of activity in Kyiv, which a week ago was a fully functioning, lively European capital city.

Khreshchatyk, the city's broad central thoroughfare, was almost deserted yesterday. Most shops are closed, with the only signs of life the queues outside pharmacies. On the edge of the city, more and more checkpoints spring up each day. Yesterday, army cranes were lifting concrete blocks into the road to form barricades.

Digital billboards on the outskirts of town announce 'Putin has lost! The world is with Ukraine', while the information tableaux at the side of the highway announce: 'Air temperature +1, road temperature +2, Russians, fuck off!'

The threat from the Russian defence ministry appeared to justify the fears of Yuri, voiced on the platform earlier as he explained his decision to leave. 'It was hard to believe Russia could strike Kharkiv, but now it's clear what the plan is. They're going to do here what they did in Chechnya.'

2 MARCH

Unravelling of Roman Abramovich era leaves doubts at Chelsea and beyond

BARNEY RONAY

Stop all the clocks. Stow the faux-fur hats. Delete the Russian folk music from the pre-match playlist. Roman Abramovich is now officially looking for a buyer. Indeed, if we are to believe the reports, Chelsea Football Club could even be sold within the week.

It is an impossibly narrow timeframe for such a complex transaction, made credible only by the fact that, frankly, right now anything seems possible.

Perhaps even – who knows? – a little honest reflection on Chelsea's departing owner, the single most lavish individual investor in the history of European football but even now a strangely opaque and mysterious year-zero billionaire.

As Abramovich's benevolent Chelsea dictatorship draws to an end, as even the lavish London houses are rushed to market, all against a backdrop of war, sanctions and the denial of Kremlin ties, perhaps the most extraordinary aspect right now is the memory of those early days when this bashful, oddly sullen-looking suitor emerged blinking into the Stamford Bridge light and began the process of complete and irreversible transformation.

It is 19 years since Abramovich bought Chelsea from Ken Bates for £140 million. Looking back now at the late summer sunshine of 2003, it feels like an oddly gauche and guileless world.

In the stands the fans threw mock paper roubles. The newspapers goggled over £200,000 cars, the failed attempt to buy an entire ski resort, the high-end super-divorce. Chelsea spent so much money they had to invent Financial Fair Play. And three years into Vladimir Putin's version of Russia, Abramovich looked at that moment like a vanguard of some new human category, the billionaire uber-lad, with his yacht-flash, his Riviera tan, his endless no-strings spending.

For Chelsea the years since have brought on-field glory at unrecoupable expense, all of it overseen with an air of gloomy command by that sphinx-like arm's-length presence. Over time there has been an enduring singularity, too. Abramovich leaves the stage as he entered it: a club of one, the only disinterested, endlessly benevolent single-person owner of any football club anywhere. The man with the suit and the face is leaving the building. And still the most obvious question remains. Who was this person exactly? And what, exactly, have we just been party to? Perhaps in the months to come it will be possible to have an open discussion about the meaning of Roman; and to examine forensically sport's role in the wider culture. Even, who knows, to learn some lessons about protecting these valuable assets.

There has certainly been some concern about Abramovich's motives. In January of this year David Davis MP spoke in the House of Commons about the use of the English legal system to control, as he saw it, the reporting of the activities of wealthy Russians. Davis expressed his views on Abramovich too.

'It is worth reminding people of Mr Abramovich's background and the character of the man. We are speaking here of the man who manages President Putin's private economic affairs, according to the Spanish national intelligence committee. This is a man who was refused a Swiss residency permit, due to suspected involvement in money laundering and contacts with criminal organisations. Abramovich was also deemed a danger to public security and a reputational risk to Switzerland.'

A little later Davis added: 'When he bought Chelsea FC, Abramovich was the governor of the Chukotka region of Russia. It was alleged by associates of his that the purchase was done at the behest of the Kremlin. As a result of the purchase, he now has enormous soft power and influence in the UK. I ask the house to come to its own conclusion about whether this man is acting at the behest of the Kremlin or Putin's government.' It is important to note that Abramovich has vehemently and repeatedly denied having access to, favour with or any special relationship with Putin or the Kremlin. Abramovich also denies that he was motivated in any way by Putin to buy Chelsea FC. He denies that his ownership of the club has anything to do with soft power or political ends.

It is also worth noting that Davis has been an MP for 35 years in the same ruling Conservative party that has overseen the flow of Russian money and influence into the heart of London's financial industry, legal system and its politics (the same Conservative party that is funded to a startling degree by donations from Russian-born patrons).

What is most striking here is that, whatever the truth of Davis's statements, it has still taken this long, to the point where the world has begun to burn, before anyone in a position of power has felt alarmed enough to investigate.

If this is what David Davis thinks, if his colleagues in the house are similarly alarmed, why has no one, from government to the Premier League, felt moved to show some concern for the fate of Chelsea Football Club? Why, given the scenario Davis describes, has this same government refused to apply statutory force to the suggestions for a football regulator? Instead of which Abramov-ich's time at Chelsea has coincided with the embrace of an unfettered global market, with an apolitical, ideological, amoral approach to club ownership. Don't ask. Don't regulate. Just check the bottom line.

This outlook seems increasingly blind to the way big sport works. Football is the popular culture now, Premier League clubs powerful engines for public relations and soft power, so much so that the term sportswashing already seems a little wet and outmoded. If the iconography of Putin and sport tells us anything, it is that there can be hard edges here, a direction of travel that goes beyond simply promoting the tourist industry.

Two English Premier League clubs are owned by nation state governments, one via a private equity fund run by the crown prince himself. Why do these politicians want to own English sporting clubs? There can surely be no doubt this is, on some level, foreign policy. Saudi Arabia in particular is on a charm offensive, building alliances and establishing itself as a state that no longer needs to have its security guaranteed by the US.

Mohammed bin Salman, chair of Newcastle's fund, could be seen high-fiving Putin at the G20 summit not so long ago. This is not to impute hostile motives, merely to be aware that a larger game is in train, that football is a part of the surrounding noise, and that clubs are fragile pawns in this stagecraft, the loyalties of supporters and surrounding media piggybacked with surprising ease.

Right up until the point the world moves on. For Chelsea the future looks uncertain. Even if a buyer can be found to act quickly enough, the club has been reliant on the owner's deep pockets to function at its current level. The £187 million wage bill, the grandiose new stadium plans (now discontinued), the high-priced signings: none of this would have been possible without £1.5 billion in personal loans.

The good times will have to roll in some other, more metered fashion from here. That era is now gone, wrenched out at the roots with startling haste.

For the rest of English football, and indeed all sport, there is a lesson to be learned in its unravelling.

17 MARCH

Debt, sanctions and a cold Westminster tent: how the Iranian hostages were freed

PATRICK WINTOUR

The long, necessarily cloak-and-dagger struggle to secure the release of Nazanin Zaghari-Ratcliffe and Anoosheh Ashoori is a story that started in New York and – via the Sultan's palace in

Activists at Cop26 in Glasgow, November 2021. Anger over the state of Britain's rivers and coastal waters became a recurring theme of the following year.

A queue of lorries makes its way to Dover in March 2022, after P&O abruptly sacked 800 crew members, causing widespread disruption.

A convoy of Russian military vehicles heads towards the border of Ukraine on 23 February 2022, signalling the start of Putin's 'military operation' in the region.

A woman stands outside a burning home in the town of Irpin, near Kyiv, which was heavily bombarded in the early weeks of the war.

Families fleeing Kramatorsk in the Donbas region in April. Five months after the invasion, some 12 million Ukrainians were thought to have been displaced.

Ukrainian troops in Donbas fire at Russian positions on 15 June. By the summer it was clear that Putin's attack was not going to plan.

A protestor attends a rally in front of the US Supreme Court in June, after the shock decision to overturn the constitutional right to abortion in the US.

On a day when temperatures in the UK reached a record-breaking 40°C, a firefighter tackles a wildfire in Sheffield in July.

After weeks of political turmoil, Boris Johnson announces his resignation on 7 July, triggering a Conservative leadership election that dominated the summer.

The Queen invites Liz Truss to become prime minister at Balmoral on 6 September. Just two days later, the Queen died at the age of 96.

Rose Ayling-Ellis with partner Giovanni Pernice, on her way to winning *Strictly* in December 2021. Deaf since birth, she kept time by counting beats.

Lib Dem leader Ed Davey has little success canvassing Mikee the cat in Watford in April, though his party went on to make considerable gains in local elections this year.

A model peers out from her hat at Richard Quinn's show at London Fashion Week in February.

Fans prepare for the Women's Euro 2022 final at Wembley on 31 July. England were crowned the winners after defeating Germany 2–1.

Grenadier Guards bear the Queen's coffin as they leave Westminster Abbey on 19 September. The funeral was watched by a peak of 29 million people in the UK.

Providing a welcome sense of perspective in a year of tumultuous news, NASA released this stunning image of the Carina Nebula on 12 July, taken by the James Webb telescope.

Muscat and a cold pavement in London's King Charles Street – ended with nail-biting delays in Tehran international airport.

After the two British-Iranians were finally freed yesterday, the foreign secretary, Liz Truss, and her team received plaudits in the House of Commons for her role and quiet determination in overseeing this extraordinary endeavour.

Others will say it should never have taken so long, and in a moment of triumph she has resorted to some brutal realpolitik, leaving behind other British citizens, such as Morad Tahbaz, in Iran – ostensibly released from prison on 'furlough' but in reality still under armed guard.

It is true that Truss happened to be in office – the fifth foreign secretary to have the file – when the moment for a deal finally became ripe. But she did invest significant personal effort in the negotiations with Iran, with no guarantee of success. She was on the phone to Richard Ratcliffe, Zaghari-Ratcliffe's husband, within days of taking office and made a point of meeting Iran's new foreign minister, Hossein Amir-Abdollahian, in New York on the fringes of the UN general assembly in September, the first person-to-person meeting between the two countries since Jeremy Hunt returned empty-handed from a meeting in Tehran three years earlier. Most of the meeting was taken up with the discussion of how the issue of the £400 million debt and the dual-national detainees could be progressed after two false starts earlier in the year.

But Truss was also galvanised by an unexpectedly successful 21-day hunger strike by Ratcliffe outside the Foreign Office on King Charles Street in freezing November. With his small tent pitched so close to parliament, Ratcliffe's cause became Westminster's as MPs struck by his personal integrity developed a cross-party respect for him. The political momentum must have left the Foreign Office reeling. One meeting in Westminster Hall overflowed with MPs who had seen Ratcliffe on hunger strike and were now demanding the debt be paid.

By then it had become clear to Truss, as to previous foreign secretaries, that no British detainee in an Iranian jail was going to be walking free until the £400 million debt to the country was repaid. In her own mind the first issue – one of moral hazard – could be overcome: this was payment of a debt, not succumbing to a ransom demand.

The second issue increasingly became how to make the payment, which had been an obstacle for years, since US sanctions imposed after the collapse of the Iran nuclear deal in 2018 closed off many avenues, such as payment to the Iranian Central Bank, the country's preferred method. The evolving attitude of the Biden administration in the US became critical.

At the turn of the year Truss turned to a trusted intermediary – Oman's foreign minister, Sayyid Badr Albusaidi, whom she met at a Gulf Cooperation Council meeting on 20 December at her grace-and-favour residence, Chevening. Oman over the decades has acted as a home for discreet diplomatic back channels. Her own officials, including Laura Hickey, the head of the Iraq desk, then travelled to Oman to finalise the details in Muscat.

Much of this was done in anticipation of talks on reviving the Iran nuclear deal coming to a successful conclusion in Vienna – a potential turning point in British-Iranian relations, and indeed relations between the West and Iran.

In Oman there were detailed exchanges between British and Iranian officials on how the debt would be paid. Iran argued it was payable to its Ministry of Defence. The UK ruled that out and said paying it to the Iranian Central Bank or in cash, an idea once advanced by Boris Johnson, was not possible since it would be 'fungible' – it would seep into other parts of the Iranian financial system, and possibly become subject to sanctions.

Instead the actual conduit used was via the Bank of Oman. Another route examined by the Foreign Office was that the money be paid first as a UK credit to the US, and the money then transferred to the Saman Bank using the Swiss Humanitarian Trade Arrangement, a channel set up in 2020 by the Trump administration to allow for humanitarian trade to flow into Iran.

The precise sum, and the issue of interest, had already been settled in earlier court cases that saw the UK's high court rule that due to sanctions, no interest was payable to Iran on the debt, which was outstanding from the collapsed sale of Chieftain tanks to Iran in the 1970s.

The third issue was 'the third man': Tahbaz, a conservationist with British, American and Iranian citizenship, accused of espionage after tracking endangered species with cameras. A previous UK attempt to settle the debt had collapsed partly over Tahbaz. In the interim, between Biden's election as US president and Donald Trump's departure in January 2021, Dominic Raab, the then foreign secretary, proposed a deal to Tahbaz in jail whereby he would be left in Iran on furlough – out of jail but not free – while Zaghari-Ratcliffe and Anoosheh would come home. The Iranians regard Tahbaz as American and so did not see him as a legitimate part of any bilateral British trade-off.

Tahbaz, from prison, according to his family, rejected the Raab deal, and so did the US. At the time the outgoing Trump administration was not eager to see £400 million flood into the Iranian coffers. As a result the UK backed off, leaving Anoosheh and Zaghari-Ratcliffe in detention.

But reviewing the issue last month, the Foreign Office evidently decided to change tactics. By then a former British Council employee, Aras Amiri, had been released. The reasoning became: if the UK could get its two most high-profile detainees home, they should accept the offer, even if it was tough on Tahbaz and his wife who is also trapped in Iran. The Tahbaz family only heard of the imminent Zaghari-Ratcliffe release through the British press on Tuesday, and battled to find anyone in the Foreign Office to admit to them that this time he had become expendable. The nail-biting delay before Zaghari-Ratcliffe left the Islamic Revolutionary Guard Corps' hands was fruitless last-minute haggling over the terms of Tahbaz's furlough.

It feels like a dreadful betrayal for the conservationist, even if he is no longer in jail. He is the only British-born among the three high-profile hostages and his family in the US and UK have been left wondering if they took the right course in not campaigning in public as much as other families.

When it comes to the deal struck this week, there remain points of factual difference. Iran says it received the money – nearly £394 million – from the British on Monday. The UK says the money did not touch the Iranians until wheels up, with Zaghari-Ratcliffe and Ashoori safely off Iranian soil. Iran maintains the story that the two were spies. The UK says they are innocent. Iran claims an Iranian prisoner has been released by the British as part of the deal. The UK says that is untrue.

But the bigger truth after the celebratory homecomings and hugs is that the Foreign Office needs to reflect on whether this release needed to have taken so long, to have been so painful. Equally, the families of those who have waited so long for their loved ones' return will one day deserve frank answers from the diplomats and shadowy figures in the defence industry.

It can hardly be a matter of celebration that British nationals were held in jail for so long when the solution – the payment of an outstanding and long-acknowledged debt – was self-evidently at hand. The Foreign Office reply remains to this day that the two issues – the debt and detentions – are separate, but this partition is a diplomatic fiction demonstrated by the fact that the detainees were put on a small plane to Oman only once the £394 million had finally landed in an Iranian bank account.

It should not have taken the personal courage and persistence of two ordinary citizens, Richard Ratcliffe and Sherry Izadi, the wife of Ashoori, to force the British state finally to do the right thing.

18 MARCH

When a bomb falls, its impact is felt for generations. I know that from my own family's trauma

JONATHAN FREEDLAND

Every time I look at the pictures of Mariupol or Kharkiv, I see a corner of Whitechapel in east London. I reacted the same way to images of Aleppo and, before that, Falluja, and, before that, Grozny, because buildings crushed to rubble have a sad habit of looking the same. It brings back a memory – or rather something fainter: an inherited memory, one that was passed to me.

Its origin is 27 March 1945. Early that morning, at 7.21am, a V2 rocket landed on Hughes Mansions, a block of flats on Vallance Road in the East End. It killed 134 people more or less instantly. Among them were two sisters, Rivvi and Feige (pronounced fay-ghee). Feige Hocherman was 33 and she left behind two children, a son not yet 11 and a daughter aged eight and a quarter. The little girl was my mother, Sara.

The war was in its final weeks and the bomb that fell that morning would be the very last V2 to land on London. It wasn't a targeted missile, though if it had been it could hardly have delighted its masters more. For of the 134 people killed by that Nazi rocket, 120 were Jews.

It meant that, as a very young child, I somehow thought 'Vallance Road' belonged alongside Belsen or Auschwitz in the small lexicon of words to be spoken only in whispers, each of them bywords for terror and grief. I was well into my thirties before I ever went close to that place. And yet, though I did not witness it and though I only ever saw the physical destruction that bomb wreaked through grainy archive photographs, I can honestly say that event shaped my life. Because it shaped my mother's life. It made her who she was.

There were the direct legacies, of course. For many decades, my mother was implacable in her anger towards the Germans, because it was a German rocket that had killed her mother. There would be no German products in our house; no German car. She was no less unbending on the necessity of Israel. For the Nazis, the identity of the victims of Hughes Mansions was no more than a lucky accident; but the fact remained that my mother had lost her mother to a Nazi operation that killed Jews en masse: she had felt the breath of the Shoah on her neck. Like many others, she would never lose the conviction that Jews would always need a place they could call their own and a means to defend themselves.

The experience of such intense hurt so young had another, perhaps less predictable, consequence: it opened up deep reservoirs of empathy for the suffering of others. 'I feel your pain,' has become a joke phrase. But my mother really did feel your pain, even if you were someone she had only just met and whose life she had only glimpsed.

Why do I say all this now, nearly 80 years later? Because, as I look at the terrible destruction of Mariupol and the burning ruins of Kharkiv, I remember that the damage done by a rocket or artillery shell cannot be measured in the stark numbers of a death toll or, still less, the impact on infrastructure – though I saw this week that the cost of rebuilding Ukraine after Vladimir Putin has rained fire on that country is estimated at $100 billion (£76 billion) and it is rising every day.

Instead the cost is measured in the aftershocks felt by those who survive the blast: the injured and the maimed, those whose homes are smashed, those children who once had a mother or father but who, in the briefest of moments, had them taken away by a bolt from the sky. That kind of bomb damage cannot be repaired with concrete. It lives on in the children of the dead, and in their children. I know, because it lives on in me.

And yet the conclusion I draw from this is not the pacifist's resolve that no bullet must ever be fired, no missile must ever be launched. For this, too, I learned from my mother: that while war is evil, the greater evil is murderous aggression that goes unchecked. No one would dare say 'stop the war' to Volodymyr Zelenskiy and the people he leads, because that would be to demand that Ukrainians allow their children to keep being killed, their bodies tossed into mass graves at speed because it's too dangerous to linger in the open, even when one of those bodies belongs to a six-year-old girl, buried in the pyjamas she wore when she was hit, patterned with cartoon unicorns.

When a killer has his hands around your neck, choking the life out of you, what you need is the strength in your arms to get him off. This is what the Ukrainians are demanding the West give them.

It is the right not to make war, but to repel aggression. It is the right to defend oneself against missiles that flatten an apartment building or destroy a theatre, whose basement shields up to 1,500 people, most of them old or very young. It is the right to protect a city where the last inhabitants melt snow to drink, and burn furniture to ward off the icy cold or cook what scraps of food they can find. Given that the West won't do it, for fear of tangling with a nuclear state, Ukrainians want the equipment – above all the aircraft – to do it for themselves.

It's such an elemental need, and yet many struggle to comprehend it. There are plenty in western Europe and the US who took, or perhaps still take, a dim view of NATO, regarding it as a cold-war throwback or an arm of Western imperialism and militarism. But Ukrainians saw it differently: for them NATO was the body that might protect them from the neighbourhood bully who had already proved, just eight years ago, his determination to hurt them and take what was theirs. Most Ukrainians saw the European Union in the same way.

Those in Britain who so casually disdained our membership of the EU or NATO betray an unwitting but unappealing strain of privilege, akin to the trust-fund millionaire who insists they never think about money. It's easy to dismiss something precious when you have lots of it. That goes for individuals with wealth, but also for those countries or peoples who have only ever known the security of having a state of their own, whose borders are stable and where the notion of an enemy attack is all but unimaginable (or forgotten).

My mother took none of those things for granted, and because she didn't neither do I. In eight decades' time, there will be Ukrainians in middle age who feel the same way, because of events happening right now. The reverberations will keep sounding, through the generations. That is why even short wars last so long. I am the son of that terrified little girl and I always will be.

Don't mention the slap!
Why no one was talking about
Will Smith and Chris Rock
at the Oscars afterparty

HADLEY FREEMAN

So that was Oscars 2022, or, as the Academy possibly refers to it: 'The Oscars where absolutely nothing strange happened, and how was the play, Mrs Lincoln?' Apparently some broadcasters bleeped out the Slap Heard Around the World. Well, if it's any consolation, TV viewers, even inside the Dolby Theater it wasn't much clearer what the hell had happened, mainly because of the Oscars' discombobulating determination to carry on – with the palpably strained smile of a Ziegfeld girl who has fallen down and broken her leg in several places, but is determined to get to the end of the routine with a grin, dammit.

Instead, everyone acted as if everything was totally normal, with Chris Rock having to present an award 10 seconds after Will Smith slapped him on stage. It was the weirdest instance of gaslighting I had ever experienced – until half an hour later, when Smith won the best actor Oscar, and implied in his speech that his attack was all part of God's plan and he had merely been 'protecting' his family. Shame he didn't bother to tell Rock what God's plan had been about how to protect his face.

It's almost enough to make you feel sorry for the Academy: it spends decades trying to find ways to make the Oscars inter-esting, only for them to become interesting in a way it really didn't want them to be. The Oscars' producer, Will Packer, had decided the right way to make the Oscars interesting was to cut some of the technical awards from the live TV broadcast in the hope it would stop people from going on too much about politics. Turns out he could have let all those sound and editing folks have their moment on TV after all. 'Too many awards' was never going to be the takeaway of the night.

Even before the ceremony, this Oscars was shaping up to be the most ridiculous yet, thanks to celebrities who continue to prove that Team America underplayed its satire. One of this year's hosts, Amy Schumer, announced that she was fighting the bravest battle currently being waged in the West: trying to get more political content into the Oscars. And to this end, she wanted to give a boost to the latest sexy starlet, the content-provider everyone's talking about, Volodymyr Zelenskiy, the president of Ukraine.

'I wanted to find a way to have Zelenskiy satellite in or make a tape or something, just because there are so many eyes on the Oscars,' she said. Yes, so true. Unlike that silly war, which no one knows about, because it's, like, super far away and not even on the front of *Variety*. 'I am not afraid to go there,' Schumer carried on bravely, 'but it's not me producing the Oscars.'

Sean Penn then issued what was described by some journalists as 'an ultimatum' and by this journalist as 'a parp' when he announced on Saturday that he would 'smelt' his Oscar in public unless someone from the Academy would 'check in with the leadership in Ukraine'.

It's always the celebrities who are the most keen to prove how deep and un-Hollywood they are who reveal themselves to be the most shallow and Hollywood-centric of all. Only a brain that has been severely corroded with too much Botox or narcissism would think that a politician in the middle of a literal actual war is waiting for a call from the Academy. 'Oh please, Amy Schumer,' Zelenskiy is no doubt thinking right now, in between walking through bombed-out hospitals and asking for more foreign aid, 'please make me a star at the Oscars! Can I send in my audition tape?'

Spoiler: Zelenskiy was a no-show, and the references to Ukraine were notably limited. But there was a mid-show 'moment of silence' (and hashtag) for Ukraine, which, by a remarkable coincidence, lasted exactly the same amount of time as was needed for the stagehands to change the set. So convenient! I love it when resolving international conflicts can be multitasked with the housekeeping. Like doing the ironing while catching up on your podcasts: two birds, one hashtag.

It was shortly after the moment of silence that The Incident happened. Now, I am sure there will be much commentary over the coming days about why Smith slapped Rock and who was more in the wrong (answer: Smith). But as I was in the theatre when it happened, and not a million miles away from Rock, I would like to point out a few oddities about the whole thing.

1. It's quite weird that Smith and Jada Pinkett Smith were fine with the host Regina Hall joking about their open marriage early in the evening, but not with Rock joking about Pinkett Smith's hair, no?

2. To all the people saying Rock's jokes were dickish, it's a good thing you didn't hear Schumer completely roasting everyone else in the room earlier in the evening, and none of them slugged her in the face.

3. No one in the auditorium knew at first whether this was all a joke or not, and nor, it seemed, did Smith. I watched his reaction to Rock's joke and at first he laughed. Then he saw how annoyed his wife was, then he realised the whole audience saw that because the camera was on her, then he got angry and got up to slap Rock. However anyone wants to spin it, he went on quite an emotional journey.

4. When Smith then claimed in his, um, let's just call it his acceptance speech that he had been 'protecting' his family, just as he 'protected Aunjanue' Ellis during the making of *King Richard*, Ellis did not look best pleased. And who could blame her?

5. Judging by Smith's general demeanour, I would say Geoffrey the butler needs to give him a good talking-to.

Lots to cogitate on, but not for the Oscars, which dealt with the incident in a single terse tweet, and not with any of the celebrities at the event. Usually at the Governors Ball, directly after the ceremony, the celebrities are happy to talk about anything. But for the first time in my decade of covering the Oscars, not only would they not talk about anything, but many brought their PRs with them as protection. Any journalist who dared to get too close to Oscar winners Billie Eilish and her brother Finneas was quickly shooed away by an anxious PR, and same for Francis Ford Coppola. Steven Spielberg was happy to pose for selfies with everyone and their mother, but when I asked if he had enjoyed the evening, he replied, very politely, that he wouldn't be answering questions.

Happily, you can always rely on a Canadian to laugh at the ridiculous Americans, and Denis Villeneuve did not disappoint. I asked what he made of the evening. 'It was unpredictable,' he laughed. 'Although last time I was here was when they mixed up the envelopes with *Moonlight* and *La La Land*, so my wife and I were like: "What happens when we come to the Oscars? Is it us?"'

I tried to ask Jane Campion what she made of the evening, but at that point the DJ started playing 'Satisfaction' by the Rolling Stones and she, Benedict Cumberbatch and Kodi Smit-McPhee broke into some extremely enthusiastic dancing, and I worried she might clobber me with her Oscar. So I headed over to the *Vanity Fair* party, thinking maybe people would be sufficiently relaxed (drunk) there to talk. But no. The first people I saw were the Williams sisters, who are far too godlike to approach.

So instead I went up to Mr Serena, AKA Alexis Ohanian, the co-founder of Reddit. What Reddit threads was he expecting to see on tonight's awards?

'Ummm, I didn't know they let press in here?' he said with faux-but-actually-a-bit-genuine nervousness, while looking around for security. Only the best press are let in, Alexis. So what did he think of the ceremony? 'Look, I'm just a plus-one here. I'll just say I'm very happy for the family and that's it,' he said.

The whole party was a heaving mass of suppressed hysteria. In one corner, James Corden chatted intensely with Adrien Brody and Georgina Chapman, AKA Harvey Weinstein's ex-wife; in another, Kourtney Kardashian stalked past Trevor Noah. It was hellish and hyper-real, and everyone seemed giddy and anxious at the same time, excited to be out, but not sure what was allowed. 'This is the first time I've been out in two years – and without a mask! It feels naughty but nice,' said Michael B Jordan. So what did he make of the Oscars ceremony? 'Oh, I'm not talking about that,' he said. Even Larry David – a man whose whole shtick is being rude about everything – declined to speak about the evening, as did Jake Gyllenhaal, Lady Gaga and Wanda Sykes.

Maybe none of them could figure out what the right opinion is about Rock and Smith. After all, to have an opinion you need principles, and those aren't included in the Oscars gift bag. Or maybe they just didn't want to be bothered with boring questions on their first night out in two years. Just as I was about to give up and go home, I spotted Jesse Plemons, on whom I harbour a quiet and not entirely professional crush. So what did he make of the evening? He was sitting right behind Smith, wasn't he?

'Yeah, we were pretty close,' he said, referring to himself and his fiancée, fellow nominee Kirsten Dunst. 'At first I thought it was a joke ...' Me too, Jesse! 'Then when Smith was shouting all those swearwords, I thought: "Oh, maybe they'll bleep those out."'

That's exactly what I thought! We have so much in common! 'And then I realised it wasn't a joke, and yeah, it was pretty weird. But you know, all this,' he said, gesturing around the party, 'is pretty strange, and everyone's feeling so riled up and strange, and everything's kinda nuts. So maybe it kinda made sense, you know?' Oh, Jesse Plemons. So lovely and wise.

So maybe that's the right opinion: it's a weird time so it was a weird Oscars. That seemed like a nice gentle take to end the evening on. But just as I was leaving, I spotted Sean Combs. He always struck me as a man with little fear of expressing an opinion, so I asked him what he made of Smith whacking Rock. 'Best Oscars ever. Ever!' he shouted, walking off. Then came back, looked me square in the eye and said: 'Best. Oscars. Ever.'

Spring

'Cost of living crisis'?
No – this is a social emergency
that will define who we are

JOHN HARRIS

Lexie lives in rural north Wales. She is disabled, and her husband recently lost his job in the building trade. The heating and hot water in their council house is oil-fired, and the price of 500 litres of fuel has just gone up from £235 to £480. They have also just found out that their annual electricity costs are rising from £1,851 to £2,564. Their four sons are aged from eight to 18. They have not put their radiators on since last November.

I first wrote about Lexie – not her real name, but the one she has used to write diary entries for a research project called 'Covid Realities' – in January. Around 10 days ago, we had another conversation. She talked about squeezing multiple meals from the cheapest of ingredients (she had somehow managed to get five dinners out of a bag of 11 frozen chicken pieces), washing with hot water boiled on the stove, and the endless financial traps that she and her family now have to try to somehow avoid.

Lexie has a mobility vehicle provided as part of her disability benefits, but the soaring cost of diesel means it has to be mostly used for the school run. Visits to the supermarket have to be carefully rationed, but that means buying basic goods from the local convenience shop, which is more expensive. Lexie worries most, she says, about her youngest child, who has asthma. His coughing fits are sometimes so bad that he vomits. 'It's because he's cold,' she told me. 'I know it is. But there's nothing I can do. I can't pull heat out of the air.'

The kind of want and hurt Lexie's family are suffering may sound as if it places them on the edges of society. The truth is that there are millions of British people like them, and those numbers are increasing fast. A stark metric is the UK's level of absolute poverty, which is defined as being a household income less than 60 per cent of the median income level of 2010-11, adjusted for inflation – a measure that usually goes up only in times of recession. The Resolution Foundation forecasts that, over the next year, the fall in real incomes means another 1.3 million people in the UK – including 500,000 children – will be pushed into this category, taking the total number to 12.5 million.

Has the scale of this social emergency sunk in yet? Last Friday was the day when the costs of some of life's most basic elements – from gas and electricity to social housing rents – shot up, way beyond the 3.1 per cent increase in benefits. As the cost of food continues to rise, energy bills are set to go up again in the autumn. Abstractions such as 'the cost of living crisis' do not do enough justice to 2022's mounting sense of dread; neither does the clichéd view of people having to choose between heating and eating, when a lot of people will soon be unable to afford either.

Across the country this weekend there were protests against yet another economic calamity being loaded on to the poorest people, and there will be more to come. The government, meanwhile, seems split between indifference and paralysed panic. Though Rishi Sunak's spring statement offered no meaningful action, the backlash that followed saw speculation about help that may belatedly arrive as things get even worse. But Conservative politics is still largely locked into that grim narrative that splits people into workers and mere claimants, even though its twisted logic is being undermined by the sheer number of lives being turned upside down by rising living costs. Labour has good intentions, but it also tends to stick to a script centred on 'working families', presumably for fear of scaring swing voters it sees as being judgmental about so-called welfare.

One thing we rarely talk about is when and how basic hardship began to become so inescapable. In the much-maligned 1970s, when trade unions were strong and the welfare state was entering its last years as a dependable safety net, income and wealth inequality were at an all-time low – and though poverty was an issue, it was yet to be allowed to run rampant. Then came the reinvention of Conservatism under Margaret Thatcher. In 1979, about 13 per cent of children lived in relative poverty; by 1992, the figure was 29 per cent. It consistently declined under New Labour, before increasing again after 2010. Thanks to David Cameron and George Osborne, rhetoric about 'welfare' reached a nadir, and policy followed the same trajectory. At the same time, the kind of precarious work that locks people into poverty was allowed to hugely increase.

The basic story was plain enough: the UK was once again being pulled away from any lingering affinities with European-style social democracy towards the market-driven individualism of the US, and the idea that poverty is either best ignored, or thought of as a failure of character.

But there has always been a pull in the opposite direction, towards solidarity and collectivism rooted not so much in ideology as in basic morals. Beyond Westminster, that view is now evident in the wider culture, thanks to such voices as the footballer Marcus Rashford and the cook and anti-poverty campaigner Jack Monroe. Public opinion seems to have shifted, thanks partly to the pandemic having drawn attention to the benefits system and glaring inequalities. In the annual British Social Attitudes survey of 2011, 77 per cent agreed that benefits for the unemployed were 'too high and discouraged people from finding a job', as against the idea that they were 'too low and caused hardship'. But in the latest survey, that figure had dropped to 45 per cent – the first time since 2000 that it had been the less popular of the two views. This, perhaps, highlights why Sunak's indifference became a much bigger talking point than he had bargained for.

In the midst of yet another crisis, we are about to find out who we now are: either the mean, hard-faced country many politicians still believe in, or a society moving in a more compassionate direction. Who will decide? I wonder about Tory MPs who represent newly acquired seats in Labour's old heartlands, whose constituency caseloads must increasingly be full of real hardship; there must also be plenty of voters who have long thought of themselves as sitting well away from poorer parts of the population, but are now seeing such distinctions fall away.

Therein lies both a grim kind of hope and yet another injustice – because the people who should surely have the loudest voices are those who have been suffering for years, and are now facing a level of want that is almost beyond words.

4 APRIL

'Of course I like life!' Shane MacGowan on the Pogues, his 'death wish' and his sideline in erotic art

SIMON HATTENSTONE

To say I'm excited is an understatement. Shane MacGowan, the reclusive former Pogue, has agreed to an interview. MacGowan has not talked to a British newspaper for 10 years and there is so much to ask him, not least how is he still alive. MacGowan, a brilliant lyricist and songwriter at his peak, drank and drugged himself to the point of destruction 40-odd years ago. Fans have feared for news of the inevitable ever since. But amazingly he's still with us, living in Ireland with his journalist wife, Victoria Mary Clarke, and about to publish a gigantic book of his art, handwritten lyrics and school essays. Dublin, here I come!

A few days before the interview, I receive a message from Victoria. 'If you can be here for a few days, you will have more of a chance of getting him in a good mood!' Ah. MacGowan is almost as famous for his irascibility as for his music. A few days in Dublin sounds lovely, but impractical. I apologise to Victoria, and tell her I can only do the Friday as arranged.

On the Wednesday, I get another message from her. 'Just to warn you, he is very depressed and anxious.' MacGowan always gave the impression nothing bothered him – he would say what he liked when he liked to whom he liked. Anxiety was the last thing you associated with him. And yet he has said he had his first breakdown aged six and has suffered with depression through much of his life.

I get into Dublin about 10am. Victoria says Shane will be in bed till at least noon and agrees to meet me at the hotel close to their home. She drives up in their ancient battered green Merc. Victoria is a youthful 55-year-old with emerald green eyes. Everything is green in MacGowan's life. She and MacGowan, 64, have been together on and off (much more on than off) for 35 years. We go for a coffee and a walk along the beach close to their house. It's a beautiful day, and Victoria is as sunny as the weather. She grew up in the Irish countryside with hippy parents (an Irish mother and English stepfather), whereas MacGowan lived in London with his Irish parents and spent the school holidays on his maternal grandparents' family farm in Tipperary. Victoria first met him in a pub in Temple Fortune, north London, when she was 16 and he was 24. He was with fellow Pogue Spider Stacy and told her she had to buy Spider a drink because it was his birthday. She told him to fuck off. But she was mesmerised. Back then he was phenomenally creative, held a room as soon as he walked in, drank for fun rather than out of necessity, and was a sex symbol despite the rotting teeth and Jumbo ears.

When their friend Johnny Depp suggested that having children would be the making of them, she told him they were too irresponsible. 'I said the thing is, if we had children, Shane would probably set fire to them. I was terrified Shane was going to burn down the house because he was always dropping his cigarettes. He set fire to John Belushi's bungalow at Chateau Marmont.'

The young MacGowan was a proud contrarian – he could happily wear a union jack jacket and have IRA tattooed across his head at the same time. As for the Pogues, they created a unique brand of riotous punk-folk. MacGowan's songs were short stories that referenced literature, music, Gaelic mythology and the Bible. There were songs of yearning ('A Pair of Brown Eyes'), of exile ('Fairytale of New York'), of protest ('Streets of Sorrow/ Birmingham Six'), and covers that were even better than the originals ('Dirty Old Town'). For a few brief years in the 1980s, the Pogues (originally called Pogue Mahone, the anglicisation of the Gaelic *póg mo thóin*, meaning 'kiss my arse') were wonderful.

Victoria says he has changed hugely since then, as has their relationship. They are closer than ever, she still finds him funny and fascinating, but she is as much a carer as partner these days. MacGowan uses a wheelchair and has to be hoisted out of bed by the official carer. In 2016, he fell and broke his pelvis. Then he had a fall on his Zimmer frame and broke his right knee. And another fall, this time tearing the ligaments in his left knee. He has never recovered.

In some ways, Victoria says, she would have liked to have had a more normal life. 'More domestic. I'm someone who likes to keep the place quite clean.' MacGowan was known for living in filth and never bathing. 'He still doesn't have baths. He showers very occasionally.' How does he smell? 'He smells fine. But he wasn't into making the place look nice.'

Victoria is extraordinarily open. She talks about her relationship with MacGowan; relationships with other musicians whom she would rather I didn't mention who wanted to marry her; how she had longed to be famous then hated being the Wag of a pop star and realised she wouldn't have found fame much fun; how she suffered from addiction to drink and drugs just as much as MacGowan did but has come out of it healthier than he has.

She looks at her phone. It's almost 2.30pm. She sounds anxious. 'I said we'd be back at 2pm.' So we head to MacGowan Mansions, which is actually a flat on a modest gated estate. She gives him a kiss and apologises for being late. He is watching a Clint Eastwood film. He spends a lot of his time watching movies and TV.

In some ways, MacGowan looks better than he used to. His new teeth are perfect, his hair is in great nick and his waxy skin is flawless, even though it doesn't seem to have seen sunlight in years. In other ways he looks terrible – old, immobile, saggy. He sits on his green armchair, dressed in black and with a long silver crucifix hanging from his neck, as if auditioning for the priest in a *Dracula* movie. On the walls are pictures, some drawn by Victoria, some by him. Above the fireplace is a crowded pew of religious icons.

Victoria heads off to make a drink. I introduce myself, and ask how he is.

'I can't walk any more,' he says. Does he still use the wheel-chair? 'Yeah, that's how I travel about.'

'Did you have a pleasant chat around the hotel?' MacGowan somehow manages to make the question sound sinister.

It was never easy to understand his slur, but now his words are so slow and indistinct they merge into one. He still has a presence – though a rather sad one. Victoria returns with a mug of tea for me and a tall glass of gin and tonic for him. Mainly tonic – she says he doesn't drink so much since his accidents.

'We went for a walk,' I say. 'It was lovely.'

'Yeah,' she says. 'We went to the beach.'

'Oh, right,' he says.

'I didn't snog him,' she says out of nowhere. 'Or shag him.'

'I didn't accuse you,' he says.

'No, I know. I'm just saying,' she says.

'*Chhhhhhhhhhhhhh.*' His laugh sounds like a snore.

'I'm too old,' I say, unsure how to respond.

'How old are you?' he asks.

'Fifty-nine,' I say.

'I've done older!' she says. 'That's not very old.'

They both laugh. 'That's not very old,' he confirms.

'I was really old in my thirties, but I'm much younger now than I was,' Victoria says.

He starts singing 'My Back Pages'. 'I was so much older then / I'm younger than that now.' MacGowan can still hold a tune.

'What's that Bob Dylan one about being young?' she asks.

'That was a Bob Dylan song,' he says.

'What's the other one, then?'

'Well, he did a few, didn't he?' He sniffs.

'"Forever Young" – that one's also Bob Dylan.'

'Oh yeah,' he says, slurping his gin incredibly loudly.

Victoria brings in bound collections of his art, much of which is in the new book, *The Eternal Buzz and the Crock of Gold*. There is an introduction from the art critic Waldemar Januszczak, praising MacGowan's 'demented, wild, fascinating, scabrous kind of energy', particularly the Catholic and sexual imagery, and saying that he is one of the few pop star artists he admires. The pictures were mainly drawn, in ballpoint pen or felt tip, when he was on the road and off his head. They reflect his character – punky, spiky, rude, religious, funny, surreal, half-arsed, filthy. Many are so densely cross-hatched they are virtually scrubbed out. Victoria points out a picture of Bono as Lord Edward Fitzgerald, leader of the 1798 United Irish rebellion.

Why did you turn Bono into Fitzgerald, I ask.

'I don't remember.'

'You did these when you were totally wasted,' she says.

'Yeah.'

It's hard to get anything beyond a monosyllable from MacGowan. In between there are long silences. He makes it clear he doesn't want to talk.

'You've got lovely skin, Shane,' I say, randomly.

'Oh thanks, sweetie. *Chhhhhhhhhhhhhh.*' He snore-laughs.

'Let's see some of the filth, then,' I say.

'The *filth*!' he repeats, possibly affronted.

'Erotic art,' Victoria says.

'Well, filth is a better word. *Chhhhhhhhhhhhhh.*'

We look at various pictures – a woman with huge nipples smoking a cigar, an array of penises, penetration, fellatio, upside down S&M crucifixions, the works. Have you got a favourite, I ask. 'Not really, no.' His short stubby sentences sound so weak they could be dying breaths. They are quickly followed by robust slurps of gin.

One of my favourite pictures is a martini with an eye for the olive and a syringe for the stick. It reminds me of the Buñuel film, I say – what's it called? '*Un Chien Andalou*. There's one shot in it of an eyeball getting sliced with a razor. I would say this is more Dalí. *Schhhhhhlrrrrp.*'

I ask if he is still writing songs. 'No. I've got a block.' The truth is he has had a block since the late 1980s.

'You wrote one a few weeks ago, didn't you?' Victoria says encouragingly.

Silence.

Was it good, I ask? He has been recording with the Irish indie band Cronin.

He looks at her, despairingly, wishing the conversation, or me, away.

'I thought it was good,' she says. 'Shane, is there anything you'd like to talk about?'

'Not really, no. *Chhhhhhhhhhh.*'

I've always been fascinated by the mix of Irish and English influences on MacGowan. His father did a degree in economics, and had a successful career working in management for C&A in London. Shane was a bright kid, and excelled at English. His writing won him a scholarship to the top public school Westminster, though he was expelled at 14 for selling drugs. He suffered another breakdown and spent six months in psychiatric hospital, including his 18th birthday. When he was released he found a new purpose in punk. In 1976, he achieved a level of pre-fame fame when the *NME* featured a photo of him bleeding from his ear under 'the headline 'Cannibalism at Clash gig' after he was bitten by his friend Jane Crockford (later of the post-punk band Mo-dettes) at a concert at the ICA in London.

Did living in England make him feel more Irish? 'I didn't live in England,' he protests. OK, did living in England most of the time make you feel more Irish?

'Yes.'

Why? He looks at Victoria despairingly. 'God, these questions are fucking ...'

'There's nothing I can do,' she says to him gently. 'You're going to just have to say something about something. Do you want me to close the curtains? The sun seems to be bugging you.'

Victoria leaves the room to talk to the carer.

'Victoria said you had bad anxiety yesterday,' I say. 'How are you feeling now?'

'Yes, I had a sudden attack of horrible fear. Nameless fear.' He softens.

I've had that, I say – it's paralysing, and makes you loathe yourself because it's so pointless. 'Well, that's you. You're projecting.' He's got a point.

For all his cussedness, MacGowan is still fantastically sharp. Despite his hostility, he's got a lovely smile, which he occasionally lets me see.

Victoria told me you like the royal family and cried when Prince Philip died, I say. 'Noooo!' he says, outraged.

'You know you like the royal family,' she says.

'*She* likes the royal family.' And you? 'I've got nothing against them.'

'You watch *The Crown* a lot!' she says.

'I watched the first series.'

'You're lying now. You watched all of it.'

'I can't remember, you know.'

Does he miss being on the road? 'Not really, no. I miss the early days of the Pogues. That was a lot of fun.'

What are your best memories? He gives her another 'Oh God' look.

Were you aware of how creative you were back then? 'Yes.'

I remind him of something he once said – that in his song-writing he wanted to remind people of how rich Irish culture was, so they would return to the literature of the land and be proud of what such a small country had produced. Silence.

If *Waiting for Godot* was the play in which nothing happened twice, this is the interview in which nothing happened 200 times. And yet, weirdly, I feel I'm beginning to understand him.

Critics of the Pogues complained that they weren't properly Irish. But that was to miss the point. MacGowan was writing about the experience of being a London Irishman, a Paddy. He wrote about the discrimination the Irish faced in Britain, republican politics and miscarriages of justice. He made many young Irish people born in Britain to Irish parents feel proud of their Irishness for the first time. He reclaimed the racist Paddy stereotype and embraced it (even if he ultimately reinforced it). Many of the songs were about being drunk, and he said he was never going to fake it on stage, so he was pretty much permanently pissed. Then he discovered heroin. He only got clean in 2000 after Sinéad O'Connor dobbed him in to the police with the blessing of Victoria.

I ask how he feels about the Pogues' most famous song, 'Fairy-tale of New York', being voted the UK's most popular Christmas song in 2019.

'It pisses me off when people always talk about it,' he says.

Why? 'Cos. Cos it just pisses me off, all right?'

Have you got a favourite song? 'I've got a few, but that's not one of them.'

Which ones? 'I *said* I've got a few.'

'He said which ones?' Victoria says.

'Oh, stop.'

I love 'A Pair of Brown Eyes', I say. It's one of many that come to mind. '"White City" I like a lot. No, not "A Pair of Brown Eyes".' You don't like that? 'No.'

In 1991, the Pogues sacked MacGowan from the band even though he by and large *was* the band. He had become too unreliable. He formed the Popes, which was little more than a Pogues tribute band. The Pogues split up in 1996, reformed in 2001 with MacGowan and finally split up again in 2014. They didn't record any new music second time round.

I ask how he fills his days now. Are you listening to much? 'Not really, no.'

Are you reading? 'No, not really.'

The story, possibly apocryphal, is that, by the age of 10, MacGowan was reading James Joyce's *Ulysses*. Is it true? 'Ten, 11 or 12,' he says. 'It's the anniversary this year. My dad was very into that, and he got me into it. My mother read a lot as well.'

Were people right to refer to you as a genius? 'Probably, yeah.'

What made you a genius? 'God! Fucking *ridiculous* question!'

In the 2020 Julien Temple documentary *Crock of Gold*, the former Sinn Féin leader Gerry Adams visits MacGowan and they reminisce (well, Adams does) about their long friendship. On the eve of peace talks with then prime minister Tony Blair, MacGowan asked him to pass on the message: *Tiocfaidh ár lá* ('Our day will come'). Do you see much of Adams? 'No. He's been here a few times. He's a very easy person to talk to,' he says pointedly.

'The priest comes round,' Victoria says buoyantly. 'That happens regularly. He talks a lot.'

'Yeah, he talks a *hell* of a lot.'

I am staring at the icons on the mantelpiece. Have you always had faith? 'I was brought up with it, you know.' Have you ever lost it? 'Yes, a few times.' Because of stuff that has happened? 'I don't know.' Does your faith get stronger as you get older? Silence.

Victoria brings out some more art – cartoon characters called Bim and Dim. Did you like cartoons as a kid, I ask. Silence.

'You did like cartoons,' Victoria says, exasperated. 'You *did*!' Silence.

'Shane, you definitely liked cartoons. I know you did. You liked the Phantom.'

'Yeah,' he finally concedes.

'Shane, you're looking at him as if he's here to kill you or torture you, but he's not. He's here cos he's interested. And he's trying his best. Come on – you're not making it easy.'

Do you hate talking in general or just interviews, I ask. 'Just interviews.' Why? 'After the first album we were totally misinterpreted.' In what way? 'In what way was I misinterpreted?' He looks at Victoria. Now I'm beginning to feel sorry for him. He seems on the verge of despair.

'That's a fair question,' Victoria says.

'It wasn't just me – it was the group.' But they were only interested in you? 'Yes. It turned into that.'

And you didn't like that? 'Yes.' It was undemocratic? 'I just told you: I don't like it.' I'm just asking why, I say. 'I don't know why I don't like certain things. *Schhhhhhlrrrrp.*'

Did journalists misinterpret you when they said you had a death wish? He nods. 'I still don't.' Contrary to popular belief, you actually like life? 'Yes!' he explodes passionately. '*Of course* I like life.'

'That's not always a given,' Victoria says.

'Well, *I* like life!' he says adamantly.

'I don't always like life,' Victoria says.

Has she ever not wanted to live? 'Yes, quite a lot of the time. But Shane never seems to want not to live. That's what's weird.'

Is life good, I ask him. 'I'm working at it,' he says. I have a feeling it's fear of death more than love of life that keeps him going.

Pretend I'm not here; would you say you were in a good place? 'Yes. *Yes!*' Will you be happy when I've gone? 'Probably, yeah. *Chhh-hhhhhhhhhhh*. You've worn me out, Si.'

Victoria shows me what the book will look like when it's finished. It's huge and incredibly heavy. They are publishing 1,000 copies at £1,000 each. She told me earlier that they need money for his care.

I ask him if he worries about money. 'It's important when you haven't got it.' Did you not earn as much as you should have done in the first place or have you spent it all? Silence.

'That may be a personal question,' Victoria says. 'Sweet pea, are you going to say anything helpful for the book?' She looks at me. 'I'll probably have to go quite soon.' Silence.

'Look, it's a picture book,' he eventually says. 'That's all there is to it. People seem to like the pictures.' She goes to put on her coat.

'You've been pretty reckless with drink and drugs,' I say. 'Have you had any regrets about how you've lived your life before? '*Of course!*' Another passionate explosion.

'She's done a great job,' he says suddenly. He's talking about how Victoria has put the book together, but he could just as well be talking about everything else she's done for him. 'Put that in,' she says, delighted. 'Put that in.'

Does he think he would still be here without her? A heavy pause, even by his standards. 'She lights up my life,' he says, from the heart.

'I definitely want to help him to stay alive for as long as possible,' Victoria says. She heads towards the door, waiting to give me a lift back into town.

'Shane,' I say, 'I'd like to say it's been a pleasure, but it's not been the easiest.'

'*Chhhhhhhhhhhhhh*,' he snore-laughs in agreement.

'Why don't I take a picture of the two of you together?' Victoria says from the door.

'No thanks,' we both say simultaneously, smiling at each other.

It's impossible not to warm to him when he smiles like that – however horribly he has treated you.

'Take care,' I say.

'God bless,' he says.

5 APRIL

'Barbarians': Russian troops leave grisly mark on town of Trostianets

SHAUN WALKER

The tanks rolled into Trostianets, a sleepy town 20 miles from the Russia-Ukraine border, in the first hours of the invasion. Russian troops fanned out across the town, occupying a number of buildings: the forestry agency headquarters, the railway station and a chocolate factory.

Their top general set up his office in room 23 at the local administration building, where the council's accountants used to sit. His bottle of single malt is still on the desk, the butts of his slim cigarettes perched on the edge of an ashtray. He slept on a single bed stolen from a nearby hotel.

His men lived one floor below. They appear to have slept, eaten and defecated in the same rooms, and some of them may have died there too, judging by the bloodied Russian uniforms littering the floor.

Thirty days after they arrived, amid a fierce Ukrainian counter-offensive, the Russians left Trostianets in a convoy of tanks, other armour, trucks full of loot and numerous stolen vehicles they had daubed with Z signs, the symbol of their invading force.

The carnage they left behind will be remembered by the residents of this quaint, historic spa town of 20,000 residents for the rest of their lives, and is yet another indictment of the results of Russia's unwanted 'liberation' mission in Ukraine.

In the square outside the train station, there is now a grim panorama of several mangled tanks, the whitened carcass of a self-propelled howitzer and a shot-up yellow bus with blood smeared on the seats. Hundreds of green ammunition boxes and casings remain, evidence of the shells and Grad missiles the Russians fired from Trostianets into neighbouring towns. Surviving buildings have been daubed with pro-Russian slogans, and crude insults about the Ukrainian president, Volodymyr Zelenskiy.

On a two-day visit to the town, the *Guardian* found evidence of summary executions, torture and systematic looting during the month of occupation, but it will take a long time to catalogue all the crimes the Russians committed in places such as Trostianets.

For now, the long and difficult clean-up is under way. Ukrainian sappers have removed mines and tripwires from the cemetery, the train station and even the chocolate museum, housed in an elegant villa where the composer Pyotr Tchaikovsky once stayed. Electricity returned for the first time in weeks on

Sunday. The first passenger train since the invasion arrived at the wrecked station on Monday. But the streets are still littered with the twisted remains of Russian armoured vehicles, and there is nothing to buy because everything has been looted.

Over the weekend, residents wheeled bicycles to the points across town where parcels of food aid are available: cartons of eggs, jars of pickled cucumbers and plastic bags bulging with potatoes, sent by volunteer groups in other parts of Ukraine. In the orderly but irritable queue to receive them, people embraced acquaintances who they were happy to see still alive, and swapped horror stories from the past month.

Spotting a journalist, ever more people joined in, shouting over each other. 'They smashed my place up.' 'They stole everything, even my underwear.' 'They killed a guy on my street.' 'The fuckers stole my laptop and my aftershave.' A symphony of stories, some of them personal, some of them second-hand, all of them awful.

This is a place where a decade ago, people had mostly good things to say about Russia, which is just a short drive away and where many people have friends and family. Now they competed to heap insults on the neighbours that had brought misery upon them. 'Barbarians!' 'Pigs!' 'Bastards!'

Yuriy Bova, the mayor of Trostianets, said it was too early to give a reliable estimate of how many civilians had been killed by the Russians, saying it was 'definitely more than 50, but probably not hundreds'.

Bova now struts about town in fatigues, a pistol tucked into the front of his body armour. But at the time of the invasion, he cut a very different figure.

The idea of a Russian invasion had seemed fanciful to him, he admitted. Nonetheless, as the crescendo of US intelligence warnings continued, he called a meeting of those who would like to join a territorial defence force.

About 100 people turned up. There are no military installations in Trostianets, and between them, they had a few hunting rifles, a couple of pistols and a few policemen with Kalashnikovs. They agreed to ask Kyiv for weapons.

But it was already too late. Three nights later, the invasion began. By breakfast time, a huge column of Russian armour was already on the outskirts of Trostianets. Bova sent a group of foresters to cut down trees along the entrance road, which won the town a few hours, and in mid-morning he called another meeting of the territorial defence unit.

'Trying to fight against tanks with a few rifles would have meant certain death, so I took the decision that we would become partisans,' said Bova. People had a few minutes to decide whether they would stay or go. The mayor and his deputies left town, retreating to neighbouring villages.

When the Ukrainians blew up a bridge to the south of Trostianets, it stalled the Russian advance plans, and the town became a hub of Russian servicemen and armour.

Local residents retreated to their basements and waited to see what would happen. Some of the first interactions with the occupiers were relatively painless, residents reported.

'We were scared of them but after a while we started pitying them. They had dirty faces, they stank, and they looked completely lost,' said Yana Lugovets, who spent a month sleeping in the basement with her husband, daughter and friends.

She said a soldier who had come to search the house where they were staying left without completing the task, his eyes filled with shame as her daughter cried out in fear at the intruder.

Daria Sasina, 26, who ran a beauty salon near the train station, said when she went to check on it and found seven Russian soldiers had broken in and were sleeping there, they were initially apologetic.

'I started crying, I was in hysterics. There was a young soldier, and he calmed me down. He said, "Listen, I'm sorry. We didn't know it would be like this."'

Many people recalled similar polite interactions, or flickers of shame in the eyes of the intruders, but any interaction with the occupiers involved enduring a game of Russian roulette. A few days later, when Sasina, her husband and father went on a risky mission across town to deliver bread to a 96-year-old great-aunt, a group of Russian soldiers sprang on to the street behind them and pointed their weapons at them.

'There were 20 of them, and they started shouting, "Run, bitches!" We ran through the mud as fast as we could, our legs were freezing and soaked, and we were terrified. They started shooting in the air. We could hear them laughing, they thought it was hilarious.'

When Sasina went back to check on her small salon the day after the Russians left, she found they had stolen thousands of dollars' worth of expensive hair dyes, shampoos and nail polishes, the hairdryers, all the cutting equipment, a sofa, all the chairs, several lightbulbs and the art on the walls. An air-conditioning unit was left dangling down from the wall, its wires having proved stronger than the desire to steal it.

In return, the Russians had left clumps of their own shaved hair on the floor, and piles of shit in the neighbouring grocery shop. Somewhere in Russia, the wives and girlfriends of soldiers will presumably soon receive gifts of high-end beauty products. For Sasina, she does not know how she will afford to rebuild her salon.

'Everything I worked to build has been destroyed,' she said.

The mayor has been criticised by some for his decision to flee, but Bova now insists it was the only sensible option. Flicking through photographs on his phone from the occupation days, he showed how people had sent him information about Russian deployments, including from one brave local who managed to fly a drone over their positions.

'People told us where they're sleeping, where they're eating, where their hardware is,' said Bova.

As the Ukrainian army called in strikes on the Russian positions, the Russians became more and more angry.

An expletive-laden audio recording released by the Ukrainian security services purportedly shows a Russian general ordering a missile strike on civilian targets after receiving incoming fire from a nearby village.

'Wipe the whole place from the Earth from the eastern side to the west,' he says.

As they came under fire more frequently, the Russians cut mobile reception in the town, and went house to house, demanding to examine people's telephones for compromising information.

A handwritten note found amid the mess of the soldiers' quarters in the train station lists the names of possible enemies to hunt down, with extremely vague identifiers, such as 'drives a white off-road vehicle'.

In Bilka, a quiet, windswept hamlet just outside Trostianets, where the Russians based more than 200 vehicles, at least two people were executed. Alexander Kulybaba, a pig farmer who protested against the takeover of his barn, was shot on the spot on 2 March, the day the Russians arrived in the village.

Mykola Savchenko, a kindly electrician with a handlebar moustache, who together with his wife, Ludmyla, had six foster children, went out on the first morning to find somewhere to charge his and his wife's mobile phones, as the electricity was already down.

'I'm just popping out for five minutes,' he told Ludmyla. He never came back.

On Monday, Ludmyla stood outside her home weeping, holding a stamped death report from the police that explained in neat handwriting that her husband had been 'brutally tortured and then killed with a shot to the heart and one to the head'. An inspection found broken bones in his fingers and arms. 'I didn't say anything to the children, because they are small and they still don't understand everything. Every day they waited for their dad to come home, but he never did. Yesterday, I said to them, "Sit down, I will explain everything,"' she said.

The youngest of her six children is four years old, the eldest 11. They stood alongside her, lined up like nesting dolls, silent and confused.

The boiling fury felt towards the Russians in villages such as Bilka, where people speak a mishmash of Ukrainian and Russian and previously felt far removed from geopolitical concerns, will be a lasting consequence of Vladimir Putin's grim decision to invade.

Along with this anger, there is confusion and disappointment about the attitudes of ordinary Russians. Nadezhda Bakran, a 73-year-old nurse in the local hospital, cowered in the hospital's basement together with her patients, as a Russian tank took pot-shots at the building, which is now empty and wrecked. Her nearby apartment block has also been reduced to a skeleton, with all the windows blown out and serious structural damage.

But when she called her best friend in Moscow, with whom she has holidayed together almost every year since they met in Crimea 43 years ago, she heard only sceptical derision and accusations.

'I tried to explain it to her, but she doesn't believe me, she believes her television. I said, "Your people are destroying my town." She said, "You caused this war yourself"... We were friends, what we had was even closer than just friendship. And she doesn't believe me. I don't understand.'

For many, this sense of betrayal from their friends and family has hit almost as hard as the material losses.

When Sasina, the beauty salon owner, called her aunt, who lives outside Moscow and had visited her in Trostianets most summers, to inform her of the horrors unfolding, her aunt told her she was talking nonsense. 'She said it's not possible, she said probably the soldiers are Ukrainians dressed up as Russians. She has stopped speaking to me now,' said Sasina, shaking her head in disbelief.

The Russian soldiers who made it out of Trostianets alive may never speak about the anger they witnessed and the carnage they caused, as they return to a country where their operation in Ukraine has been referred to by state propaganda as a heroic mission to save their neighbour from the clutches of radicals and neo-Nazis.

Russian television viewers may never see the ugly truth of the cost of their army's unwanted intervention, although many Russian families will now be mourning sons and brothers. The yellowed bodies of three Russian soldiers lie unclaimed and unrefrigerated in the Trostianets hospital morgue; a Ukrainian soldier involved in retaking the town estimated that up to 300 may have died here.

In the basement of the train station, weak torchlight revealed an improvised field hospital where the Russians treated their wounded. Silver padding had been placed over two desks to create makeshift operating tables. The floor was littered with tablets and other medical supplies. A medical drip remained, fastened to a coat stand.

On the wall in the corridor outside was perhaps the most jarring sight in all Trostianets. Children's drawings brought from Russia were taped to the wall, gifts from schoolchildren in honour of Army Day, the day before Russia's invasion. The cards were decorated with pretty, colourful flowers and messages of support written in spidery youthful handwriting.

One was signed by Sasha P, first grade, and came with drawings in crayon and a printed message.

It read: 'Thank you, soldier, for making sure I live under a peaceful sky.'

9 APRIL

Lessons in survival against the odds, from the tortoise

TIM DOWLING

It's a nice morning – nicer than predicted – and when I step into the garden with a coffee, I find the tortoise sunning himself on the bricks.

'What's up?' I say, sitting on the bench. The tortoise fixes me with a reproachful look. It's really his only look. 'It could be worse,' I add. 'It's supposed to be raining.'

At this time of year I don't bring the tortoise in at night unless an unseasonable drop in temperature is forecast, and he doesn't emerge from his burrow under the ivy until it gets above about 12°C, so we don't see each other that often. Even so, I sometimes feel like he resents my fussing. It's a lot more stewardship than he's used to.

My wife was given the tortoise as a present when she was eight years old. Originally he was one of a pair, male and female.

'Were they, like, a couple?' I ask my wife later that day.

'Yes!' she says. 'They had an egg!'

In the end the egg proved unviable. One tortoise died. My wife's parents split up. Eventually the remaining tortoise was taken to my father-in-law's house in Cornwall, from which he promptly escaped. That should have been the end of the story.

'How long was he missing for?' I ask my wife.

'I don't know. Two years?' she says.

'That doesn't seem possible,' I say. She shrugs.

Two years later – allegedly – a Cornish farmer hit what he thought was a rock while out combine harvesting. The rock turned out to be the tortoise, heading south, a mile from his last known address. He was somehow completely unharmed.

'Have you seen the blades on a combine harvester?' I ask my wife.

'Bits of this may be apocryphal,' she says. 'I can't remember.'

After my father-in-law was alerted to the discovery, it was agreed that the tortoise would be adopted by the farmer. From then on the tortoise lived in a kennel with sheepdogs. According to legend he was very happy there, although this assessment is at odds with a narrative that includes regular escape attempts. The farmer painted a big white stripe on the tortoise's back every spring, so he could be spotted at a distance before he damaged any more agricultural equipment.

That really should have been the end of the story. But many years later the farm was sold, and the tortoise was returned to my wife's father, who was not thrilled about the reunion. Just a few weeks after getting him back, my father-in-law presented my wife with a large, heavy cardboard box.

'It was the day of my mother's funeral,' my wife says.

'I was there,' I say. At that point we'd been married five years, and I'd never heard anything about a tortoise.

'I thought he was giving me some kind of memento,' my wife says.

'He was,' I say.

When the tortoise emerged from hibernation, it seemed wise to let him do what he wanted. What he wanted was to thunk down the back step into the garden and destroy everything. That was 25 years ago.

After a couple of winters with us, the tortoise stopped hibernating, preferring a prolonged stretch of reduced activity in winter. We sometimes used him to prop open the kitchen door. But on sunny days he would stomp around, hoovering up grapes and biting the children's toes.

At some point we took him to a vet to make sure we were doing all we could for him, and that he wasn't as disconsolate as he always looked. The vet examined the tortoise thoroughly and returned a diagnosis: he was a girl.

'I've never understood this part,' I say to my wife. 'What made you think it was the female that died?'

'I don't know,' she says. 'I don't think it's that easy to sex a tortoise.'

When they were little the children called the tortoise Old Man. After the diagnosis we tried Old Woman for a while, but it didn't stick. He's just the tortoise.

'She,' my wife says.

'Yeah,' I say.

Out in the garden the low morning sun slips behind a cloud. The tortoise is still eyeing me with reproach. I go back inside and return with some radicchio leaves, dropping them in his path. The tortoise likes radicchio; at least he likes it more than I do. But he continues to stare at me with something like boundless regret.

'Anyway,' I say, lifting my cup. 'Here's to another 25 years.' I close my eyes against the returning sun and think: you'll be lucky.

25 April

Everything I thought before the birth of my son now feels naive and misinformed

RHIANNON LUCY COSSLETT

Five weeks ago my waters broke in spectacular fashion – the way they do in films, the way the National Childbirth Trust woman said you really didn't want them to break. 'It's too early,' I kept saying, again like some cinema cliché. During the rush to the hospital, our Uber got stuck behind a hearse travelling at a suitably funereal pace. The catastrophist in me assumed an omen. The writer in me rolled her eyes and thought: nice touch.

And so the boy, the bairn, is here (bairn is not a word I ever used before, but for some reason I cannot stop, as though my northern ancestors have risen up in me, conjured by all the drama). I am still adjusting to the fact that he is no longer inside me, that I thought I had five more weeks of kicks and punches, how I never got to see the reverse imprint of his hand on my skin. He is here and hardly anything is ready, and, despite needing some help from some magnificent doctors, he is all right and my life is transformed.

My colleague Eva Wiseman was right about the love feeling two centimetres from grief. I have been skinned alive. I weep at the merest trifle, as if I'm the baby. On the night we came home from the hospital, I cried and cried. I want a bumper between my new family and the world. I could have done without Billy Bragg's 'Tank Park Salute' coming on the radio in the kitchen: another microwave meal salted with tears. The love feels like terror too: of all the ways in which he could be taken from me ('It's the women who are blasé that we worry about,' said the discharging midwife).

But most of all, it feels like gratitude. For him: my dream come true. For his father. For the medical care, the costs of which in another place would have run, possibly, into millions. For our safety. The day after I had him, the Russians bombed a Ukrainian maternity hospital. Before my son's arrival, I had been reading of the women giving birth underground. 'Don't look at the news,' a friend texted, as I lay in a bay without my baby, who had been rushed to neonatal intensive care, listening to the sounds of labouring women, and she was right. I could not bear it.

How to articulate the transfiguration from not-mother to mother? I am the same person, and yet everything I wrote before feels naive and misinformed. It is as though I have been made party to some great secret. As though, when I stepped into the old, looming Victorian building, with its ghost sign saying 'women's receiving ward', just as my own mother and thousands of other women had before me, I was initiated. Though that could, of course, be the drugs.

I didn't have a birth plan. I was due to have a scan, to meet the obstetrician to discuss the best way forward. The hypnobirthing book I bought second-hand in an attempt to calm my fears regarding childbirth was clear in its views of the sort of delivery I should have. I am not so impressionable, and, when I skipped forward to read about the aftermath, the page proclaiming 'You've birthed a baby and you're a goddamn goddess' in a register I have come to dislike was decorated with – I kid you not – a smear of what looked like blood. Disgusting, but you could say it was the most honest thing in the entire book. There was, indeed, blood.

During my week in the hospital, I kept seeing glimpses through windows of the most beautiful spring skies, promising a world outside for the both of us, if he would only breathe and feed on his own. After a few days, I realised that I was not a prisoner; I could go out for a walk. In the lift I joked with a man about a discarded hat and how gross it would be if one of us put it on, and I was grateful that I could still hold a conversation that was not about my baby.

At the same time, he is everything, just as I am to him. My boy who could not wait, but whose eyes are scarcely open. Love, in the words of Sylvia Plath, set him going like a 'fat gold watch', but it has taken far more treatment than a 'slap on the soles' from a midwife to give him a healthy start in life.

In the small hours, in the bluish darkness of the ward, I sat next to his incubator and tried to remember lullabies, but amid the fear and the love and the painkiller fog the words had all vanished. Instead, as the machines beeped reassuringly and I stroked his skin through the small porthole, no longer able to be the ship that carried him, he got 'Here Comes the Sun'.

25 APRIL

Macron's appeal to unity succeeds but far right makes strong showing

ANGELIQUE CHRISAFIS

On the campaign trail in Denain, one of the poorest towns in France, Emmanuel Macron walked into a crowd of voters to 'take the pulse of the nation' and a woman pushed forward to sum up the mood. 'We're living in misery,' she said. Others shouted: 'This country doesn't work' and 'We've had enough'. When one father described not managing to make ends meet, Macron said: 'That's what I'm fighting for.' The man shot back: 'That's not the impression I have.'

Macron, a young, former banker, who had loosened labour laws and promised the biggest overhaul of the French welfare state since the war, was lauded internationally for making France a 'star economic performer' of the pandemic era – growth had bounced back faster than expected from the Covid crisis, unemployment was at its lowest level for more than a decade, and government caps on gas and electricity prices kept French prices from rising as fast as those in European neighbours.

But, as Macron got up close to voters in town squares across France in the past two weeks – keen to compensate for a persistent image as haughty and cut off from everyday concerns – he realised that the cost of living crisis and people's very real fears of making ends meet would play a greater role than he had anticipated in the campaign. His economic statistics on paper did not match everyone's felt experience on the ground. Six months earlier, the far right's Marine Le Pen had foreseen that workers on low and middle incomes felt they weren't being heard or understood. She styled herself as 'the candidate of a France that is suffering' and went under the radar across the countryside to listen to them.

In the final two weeks of the campaign, Macron tried to catch up by shaking hands and explaining his economic record, arguing that this was the first election in decades in which France's mass unemployment was not the central theme, because he had boosted job creation. But he found, by his own admission, 'people who don't feel they're being taken into consideration, who feel resentment ... who feel humiliated or looked down upon'. He said: 'I try to listen in an objective way.' He accepted that if he were to win re-election, things must be done 'more simply, more directly'. He said: 'We have to reconcile the working class with politicians.'

During the campaign, Macron conceded that if the French far right had risen to its highest ever levels in the presidential first round – with Le Pen and the newcomer TV pundit Éric Zemmour taking more than 30 per cent – it was because he himself 'had not managed to calm a certain anger'.

That anger will certainly be one of the main challenges in the next five-year presidential term. The *gilets jaunes* anti-government protests in 2018 and 2019 had shown that people's sense of injustice could spontaneously erupt into a large-scale and long-running protest movement that was not contained by traditional trade unions or defined by political voting patterns, but which pushed people to demonstrate every Saturday for months on end.

Some in Macron's government had initially felt this year's election would play out along the lines of moderation, 'reason' and science versus the 'hatred and division' of populists.

But it became clear in the final weeks of the presidential campaign that 'rationality' was not enough: there needed to be an emotional connection to people's everyday lives. Le Pen attacked Macron as 'power without empathy'. His brilliance at number-crunching and his professorial explanations of the efficiency of his policies were seen by some as technocratic abstraction. Macron accepted in the final days of the campaign that only getting level to French people's lived experience and emotional feeling would work. 'I'm very conscious of the precariousness, of the fragility, that you can lose everything,' he said of people who were struggling.

Macron said he had picked up on the signs of 'trauma' in a society where more than 140,000 lives were lost to Covid, and where voters' main worries were making ends meet, followed by the war in Ukraine and concerns about the climate crisis. 'It's the first time that even children have stopped me in crowds to ask me about the war in Ukraine,' he said, shocked, in the final days before the vote.

A 72-year-old former elected official in a village in the Oise, where a majority had voted Le Pen, said: 'People's mood can be summed up in one word: uncertainty. Uncertainty over health, over part-time job contracts, over how much you'll be overdrawn by the end of the month. Uncertainty over the prospect of nuclear war, and the planet burning.'

Against this backdrop of doubt towards the political class, Macron accepted that the country was fractured and divided. The immediate challenge is how a sense of unity can begin to be knitted back together and what form the parliament will take in June.

Analysts now carve French politics into three blocs. Macron is holding together a broad centrist bloc, which five years ago spread from voters on the social-democratic left to the centre right, and this time moved more to the right to take voters from Nicolas Sarkozy's old party of government. Then there is a far-right bloc – including not just Le Pen but the newcomer Zemmour, whose inflammatory anti-immigration rhetoric and warnings of society at war have left a lasting trace on the political debate. Finally, there is a bloc on the more radical left, led by Jean-Luc Mélen-chon, which is increasingly tapping into concerns over ecology and the environment.

But signs of disillusionment with politics persist, including the millions of voters who did not turn out at the ballot box. Analysis by the academics William Genieys and Saïd Darviche found that more than 61 per cent of French voters chose candi-dates in the first round whose message was 'anti-elite' – including Le Pen and Mélenchon, and many smaller figures, who had all argued that traditional political elites were stopping equality and hampering real democracy.

Macron argued that he could unite France 'in the important moments', such as the Covid crisis. He promised a new method of politics to take broader points of view into account. On the last day of the campaign, he promised 'to find a path and the reasons to make us live as a nation united'. His political opponents said they would hold him to the challenge.

29 APRIL

Keir Starmer the grownup needs to rediscover the radical youth he once was

ANDY BECKETT

Keir Starmer is a grownup. He is serious, capable, responsible, authoritative and realistic – or so he and Labour would like us to believe. Ever since he became leader, two years ago this month, one of his main goals has been to present himself as a much-needed political adult: repairing the damage done to the party by the supposed perpetual adolescent Jeremy Corbyn; poised to rescue the country from the naughty schoolboy Boris Johnson.

From his strict suits and haircut to his no-frills speaking style and carefully researched Commons questions, Starmer has sought to come across as a sober prime minister-in-waiting, a reassuring figure in troubled times. He is 59, and if Labour wins the next election, he is likely to be the oldest successful candidate for prime minister since Harold Macmillan in 1959. It's almost possible to imagine Starmer as a politician back in those more stable times.

This old-fashioned, rather severe persona has sometimes been pretty effective. We are in one of those periods now, with Starmer easily dismissing Johnson's shoddy homework in the Commons, and Labour ahead in the polls and expected to do well at next week's local elections. With the Tories seemingly running out of talent and policy options, a Starmer government is starting to become imaginable.

Yet at other times during his leadership, his 'grownup' act has fallen flat – and it could easily happen again. Next to Johnson's antics and the drama of the pandemic and Ukraine, any opposition leader would sometimes struggle to get attention. And Starmer, with his methodical, rather than intuitive, approach to strategy, his slightly yelping voice and stiff body language, is not a political natural. He is a workmanlike leader, partly because that's his character, as the modest but growing number of Starmer biographies make clear.

More importantly, his leadership style also reveals a lot about his party and our wider politics. Ever since Labour's crushing defeats and loss of confidence in the 1980s, to be a grownup Labour leader, in the eyes of most journalists, Labour MPs and strategists, has meant moving to the right. Neil Kinnock, Tony Blair, Gordon Brown and Ed Miliband led in very different circumstances, from the highly favourable to the near-impossible. But all reacted by shedding leftwing policies and acquiring more rightwing ones, by courting conservative interests and cutting adrift Labour's radicals.

Electorally, this approach only worked for Blair: a rare talent whose tenure also coincided with a particularly weak and divided Tory party. Otherwise, many voters, after initially being intrigued, have tended to conclude that Labour leaders who offer ideologically 'moderate' maturity are a bit boring, inauthentic, or not to be trusted. The same newspapers that help persuade Labour leaders to shift rightwards often then tell their readers that the party has not shifted enough. Kinnock, for example, got a good press for bashing the left in his early years as leader; but when he looked as if he might actually win an election, in 1992, the tabloids destroyed him.

Yet Labour's urge to seem grown up persists. Partly it's sustained by the conviction that a less respectable, more leftwing party would do even worse at elections – which is why it's so important both to New Labour veterans and Starmerites that the huge vote for Corbyn in 2017 is forgotten.

Behind this conviction is another layer of pessimism: a belief that Britain, by which the Labour grownups usually mean England, is fundamentally a conservative country. In this environment, the argument goes, Labour can only exist as a significant force if it looks safe and sensible. The importance of retired voters in general elections, and the collapse since 2010 in the proportion of them choosing Labour, from about a third to about a sixth, add to the pressure on Starmer to be conventional. In today's Britain, growing up, political maturity and the renunciation of leftwing politics seem to go together more than ever.

As leader, Starmer has reinforced this connection. In his youth, he was part of a radical collective that produced *Socialist Alternatives*, a short-lived 1980s magazine which argued presciently that the left should pay more attention to the environment and feminism. Yet on *Desert Island Discs* in 2020, he mocked his days at the magazine: 'We were out to change the world ... I said some things that were daft.' He had become less dogmatic, he continued, 'as I've grown up'.

But the idea that radicalism is always immature and naive is itself a form of dogma. During the 1990s and 2000s, when much of the West was relatively stable and prosperous under centrist governments, this cautious view of politics was fairly easy to justify. Yet today, with the climate emergency and capitalism lurching from crisis to crisis, it is the anti-radical position that often seems unrealistic. When the climate activist group Just Stop Oil began blockading fuel depots this month, Labour called for 'immediate nationwide injunctions' to halt the protests, because they 'cause misery for motorists'. This stance may please some voters at the local elections, but it's unlikely to seem wise in years to come. The same goes for Starmer's neglect of the young left that Corbyn mobilised, which could have been Labour's future.

In our era of flux, is there a chance that Starmer's leadership could change? In Oliver Eagleton's persuasive new biography, *The Starmer Project: A Journey to the Right*, his trajectory seems set: an idealistic lawyer protecting civil liberties gradually metamorphoses into a paternalistic party leader promising voters 'security'.

In theory, the latter offer still has radical potential, as one of the main causes of insecurity in Britain is our version of free-market capitalism. As leader, Starmer has repeatedly said that he wants an economy which is no longer 'rooted in insecurity and inequality'. Were he to become prime minister, however, the pressure to drop this goal would be considerable: many businesses have done very well out of Britain's harsh economic model. Taking advantage of the Tories' difficulties with some employers over Brexit, Starmer has already been trying to woo the private sector by calling Labour 'the party of business'.

To his admirers and lieutenants, such manoeuvres are simply grownup politics. If you want an end to Tory rule, they argue, this stern man in a suit is the person to deliver it. They may be right. But being a fully functional prime minister, like being a fully functional adult, isn't just about professionalism and authority. It's also about the ability to charm, communicate effectively, show empathy. We've yet to see those sides of him – if we ever will. Without them, a Starmer government, however welcome at first, will be hard work for him and for us.

7 MAY

'I yearned for a deeper, slower, more useful existence': dispatches from the Great Resignation

LAURA BARTON

Not long after I had left my job, and my marriage, and my home, in quick succession, I ran into an old acquaintance outside a local coffee shop. She had heard, of course, about the dismantling of my life, and now she looked at me, bewildered. 'You had it all,' she said, as she gripped her cup. 'And now you have ... nothing?'

For many years I had tried to live a life that made sense to others. I had swanned from a prestigious university straight into a job at a prestigious newspaper. I had got married young, to the man I began dating at 23, we had bought a beautiful home, got ourselves a cat, and begun to talk about starting a family. I had tried, very hard, all my life, not to put a foot wrong. And yet something inside me felt perpetually crushed.

With hindsight, the confusion my old acquaintance experienced outside the coffee shop seems understandable. To reject, so resoundingly, all the signifiers of happiness and success can be unsettling to observers. But still, my decision to walk away from the life I had built remains something of which I am proud. It was turbulent, and it was terrible, and I regret the hurt that was caused, but it was also the making of me.

The pandemic has encouraged many to perform an emotional audit of their lives; with a break from entrenched routine has come a recalibration of work and home, a recognition that life is perhaps too short to spend doing something you do not love. Last year Anthony Klotz, a professor at Mays Business School in Texas, coined the phrase 'the Great Resignation' when predicting the huge number of workers likely to quit their jobs. In the UK, that was one in 20 of us, but the phenomenon has been global – last November, the US Bureau of Labor Statistics announced that 'quits', as they are termed, had hit a record high, as 4.5 million American workers voluntarily left their jobs.

There are of course many reasons for this grand walkout. But it appears a striking number of people left their jobs with no plan to seek employment in the same sector, instead choosing wholly new lifestyles and careers. It makes sense that life-change memoirs should flourish in this context; those contemplating a radical new path perhaps seeking inspiration – or the steadying hand of a cautionary tale.

There is both to be found in Ben Short's April memoir, *Burn*. Short walked away from his role as a creative director for a London advertising company to work on the land – living, coppicing, hedge-laying and charcoal-burning in Dorset. 'I came to the woods over a decade ago,' he writes. 'I came to the woods because there was a fire in my head.'

'I was deeply unhappy,' he says today. 'Beset by anxiety and stifled and frustrated by a career which was supposed to be creative but often felt anything but.' Raised in Hampshire, he found that after 16 years in London the pace of the city had begun to pall. 'I yearned for a deeper, slower and more "useful" existence.'

Short's decision to rip it up and start again was not only rooted in frustration, it was also a way to address his crippling obsessive compulsive disorder. 'The illness was not a lot of fun,' he says. 'It basically took [away] a decade of my life. That said, it did give me a rocket-fuelled impetus to leave my career. I have been told many times that it was a brave move, but it had nothing to do with courage. It was a matter of survival.'

In one memorable scene, Short recalls the point where it became apparent that he must change his life. He is on a cruise ship in the Mediterranean, pitching for a new advertising account, when he suffers an acute anxiety attack. 'I felt like a boxer who had been knocked down a million times,' he writes, 'yet staggered back to his feet and was floored again in a bout lasting years. Inside I was pulp.'

In this form of memoir, immersion in nature is often presented as a salve – see also Caroline Van Hemert's account of a trek across Alaska in *The Sun Is a Compass*, Jon Krakauer's biography of Chris McCandless, *Into the Wild*, or Elizabeth Gilbert's *The Last American Man*, about Eustace Conway, who in 1977 moved from suburbia to the Appalachian mountains.

The idea of abandoning modern life in favour of something more traditional has long appealed to the disillusioned wage slave; there was the back-to-the-land movement of the 1960s and 70s, for instance. But the reality of manual labour after decades of deskbound life can be challenging, and rural life a rude awakening after the ready comforts of urban living. 'I'm very much a romantic by nature, so yes, there was an element of that,' Short concedes. 'Living in the woods did, initially, feel quite extreme. But I learned that when one's life is reduced to the basics – boiling water over a wood stove, hauling one's water from a well, washing in a tin bath – those tasks become rewarding in themselves.'

It was a similar experience for Siri Helle, author of *Handmade: Learning the Art of Chainsaw Mindfulness in a Norwegian Wood*, published in March. Some years ago, Helle inherited a plot of land and a log cabin, without water or electricity. When she set herself the task of building a privy, she found a new sense of purpose.

Since her late teens, Helle had led an unsettled life – she had moved 30 times in 20 years, made a few attempts at university, lived overseas, but found herself too restless to stick at anything. She was at agricultural college, studying to be an agronomist (a course she did in fact see through), when she first encountered the chainsaw. 'Someone just put it in my hands. And then when I came back to my cabin and I saw all the spruce trees my grandfather had planted, I realised it was the perfect tool for me.'

It was not easy. 'All the challenges in the construction, I had to handle them somehow,' she remembers. 'And sometimes I handled them by just throwing the tools aside and going for a long walk, and then I came back the next day and found a solution. But I think that can be a good mantra: it's just starting and trying.'

Like Short, Helle admits to harbouring some romanticism about the idea of working outside. 'But of course it's really difficult, and there are so many things to learn,' she says.

Still, the rewards can be vast. 'When I discovered that the manual labour and the creative challenges could be so fulfilling – that was life-changing. It gave me a feeling of accomplishment. I get it from writing as well, but it's different to getting it from something that's completely physical – and that's needed.' Today, Helle divides her time between work as a carpenter and as a writer, and says they make excellent bedfellows. 'I think it's very hard to demand we should choose just one path.'

'If you want to be a blacksmith or a carpenter, go try it!' says Bill Burnett, co-author (with Dave Evans) of *Designing Your New Work Life*. 'Maybe you will love it.' Burnett is executive director of the design programme at Stanford University in California and his approach to making a big life change is, accordingly, design-led. Most quitters leave a job because they hate it, rather than because they have the promise of something better – Burnett refers to this as 'running away from a bad thing', as opposed to 'running toward a good thing'. This rarely works out well, he says. 'What we tell people is: it's very dangerous to just throw everything up in the air, quit your job, and try to figure it out. Because there are bills to pay.'

A former Apple employee, Burnett encourages considering your career the same way one might design a new piece of tech. 'What do you do when you want to build a new product? You build a lot of prototypes,' he says. 'And you try a lot of experiments to see what's going to work.' If you follow the prototype approach, you'll road-test your new career before you quit your job in the bank. Perhaps you'll even acknowledge that sometimes it's OK to keep trapeze artistry as a hobby.

Lucy Leonelli was some way into a career in recruitment and in her late twenties when she had the nagging feeling that 'it was never really what I wanted to do', she says. 'I was having a good time, and doing well, and succeeding, but I wasn't living the truest version of myself.' She began to think about the person she'd been before corporate life. 'There was more colour in my life. I acted in pantomimes, I was a goth, I hung out with skaters and I rode horses. I was part of all these different worlds.'

Rather than walk out entirely on her career, she negotiated taking a gap year from her job, using the time to explore a range of other lifestyles and write a book about her experiences. *A Year in the Life: Adventures in British Subcultures*, which came out in January, is a nimble A-Z of different avenues – there are Essex girls, fetishists, LARPists (people who take part in live-action role-playing games) and vampires; there is a rollercoaster ride with a group of naturists. 'Writing a book meant having something to show for the year, and having a focus was really important,' she says.

Leonelli did return to her previous field, but she believes her year of exploration helped her enormously – she has fewer prejudices now, an openness to new situations and a ready confidence that meant that six years ago she had no qualms about moving to California. 'If I hate it,' she reasoned, 'I can always go back.'

Sometimes, though, the knowledge that you can't really go back is an important part of changing your life. I did not go back to my office job. I did not return to my marriage or my home. For a long time I lived in the state of nothing, trying to work out who I was, and how I wanted to live. I think, if we are lucky, all of us are given a moment to question the narrative of our lives. To wonder whether where we find ourselves is the result of our own choices, or of convention and others' expectations.

When this moment arrived for me, I'm glad that I took it. There have been many such moments since; new expansions in my career, time spent overseas, a period when I left London and later returned – decisions that might have seemed bewildering to others. But each time these moments come, I tell myself to take them. I tell myself to go into the woods. I tell myself to live more deliberately.

18 MAY

'I thought the UK was a good country': Sudan massacre refugee faces removal to Rwanda

DIANE TAYLOR

It took Mohammed over three years and a journey of more than 5,000 miles to reach the UK after fleeing a massacre in his village in Sudan.

Now, just over a week after arriving by kayak across the Channel, he is among the first tranche of asylum seekers facing forced removal to Rwanda, on the continent where his journey began.

A 'notice of intent', sent by the Home Office, warns that Mohammed (not his real name) has 14 days to register reasons why he cannot be relocated under the government's controversial new scheme. He is believed to be the first of about 50 asylum seekers in his position to speak out.

The 25-year-old told the *Guardian*: 'I wanted to reach the UK because I heard it was a place where I could be safe. We started hearing that the UK government was planning to send people who arrive in small boats to Rwanda but we didn't believe they would do this.'

He said the prospect of travelling to Rwanda, after fleeing Sudan via Libya, had triggered flashbacks.

'I thought the UK was a good country with a lot of humanity,' he said. 'I'm shocked that the Home Office is not treating me like a human being.

'I haven't been able to sleep since I arrived here. My trauma is getting worse and I've been having more flashbacks about what happened to me in Sudan and Libya since I arrived in the UK. It was so hard for me to escape from Africa and now the UK government wants to send me back there.'

Mohammed said he left Sudan in January 2019 following a brutal attack by the Janjaweed militia on his village. 'It was horrific,' he said. 'Many people were killed; girls and women were raped and others were kidnapped. Those like me who survived the massacre escaped as soon as we could.'

He travelled from Sudan to Libya and spent a year there, where he said he was exploited by traffickers. Libya is a popular transit country for refugees from places such as Sudan and Eritrea who are trying to reach Europe by crossing the Mediterranean to Italy.

'I was controlled by traffickers in Libya,' said Mohammed. 'They held us in some overcrowded, underground place and forced us to do farming work. After a year I managed to escape. Some people were shot when they tried to escape from the traffickers.

'Since that time in Libya I have developed a lot of breathing difficulties. I also have difficulty sleeping, suffer many flashbacks and suffer from a lot of trauma.'

In 2020 he crossed the Mediterranean, passing through Malta and other countries before reaching northern France. He said that for much of his journey through Europe, he had to sleep in the streets. After arriving in Calais, he said he and 10 other refugees from Sudan made repeated attempts to cross the Channel in a kayak designed for four people because they were too poor to pay smugglers for passage in a larger, sturdier dinghy.

'We tried many times to cross but sometimes our boat sank so we had to go back to France,' he said. 'Life was so hard in Calais, especially in the winter when it was very cold sleeping outside. Eleven of us finally managed to cross the Channel in a kayak. The journey was very difficult and we were lucky to survive because the waves were so high.'

They made it to Dover where Mohammed said they were processed by Home Office officials and tested for Covid. He and four other Sudanese men he travelled with were taken to a detention centre and given a notice of intent about being offshored to Rwanda.

'I was so shocked when I found out the government wants to send me and other refugees to Rwanda after all the years it has taken me to get here,' he said. 'I feel so sad after all that I've been through that I've been put in a place like a jail in the UK. It's not right in this world.'

The PCS union, which represents Home Office staff, is challenging the department's new offshoring policy along with NGOs Care4Calais, Detention Action and Freedom From Torture. Clare Moseley, chief executive of Care4Calais, said: 'The one thing that all refugees have in common is that something truly terrible has happened to them. Now they are facing the further trauma of deportation across the globe. Sending them to Rwanda will abuse their rights, cost taxpayers millions and break international law. We are fighting it and we need public support.'

A Home Office spokesperson said: 'The world-leading migration partnership with Rwanda means those making dangerous, unnecessary and illegal journeys to the UK may be relocated to Rwanda to have their claims for asylum considered and to rebuild their lives there. The first group of illegal migrants have received notices of intent. Depending on their circumstances, they will have up to 14 days to submit reasons on why they should not be relocated to Rwanda.'

22 MAY

Who is Anthony Albanese? How a working-class activist became Australia's PM

JOSH BUTLER

Anthony Albanese's election to Australia's top job will go down as one of the most remarkable in the nation's political history: both for the personal journey of the man who will move into the prime minister's residence and the circumstances in which he won the keys.

The student activist and political bomb-thrower from Labor's socialist left who famously spoke of enjoying 'fighting Tories', reborn as a centrist 'statesman' leader backing moderation on climate and tax. A boy who lived with his single mother on a disability pension in public housing, growing into a man who will occupy the highest office in the land.

'I want every parent to be able to tell their child no matter where you live or where you come from, in Australia the doors of opportunity are open to us all,' he said in his victory speech at Labor's election function in Sydney.

The 26-year veteran of the federal parliament has led the Labor party into government after nine years in opposition, breaking a streak of three straight election losses for the centre-left political organisation.

His story is well-known to anyone with a passing interest in Australian politics. He built an affable character, known simply as 'Albo' to many, garnering goodwill as a knockabout larrikin from a trendy industrial area of inner Sydney who liked rugby league, beer and rock music.

'I was raised with three great faiths: the Catholic church, the Labor party and South Sydney Football Club,' Albanese says. He often recounts his time as director of the Rabbitohs, helping the famous club get back into the national competition when they were ejected in 1999, and now spruiks his friendship with other Bunnies superfans Russell Crowe and Atlassian co-founder Mike Cannon-Brookes.

Leaning into the shabby-chic vibe of his electorate in the Grayndler constituency in Sydney, Albanese made himself a popular figure at pubs and concerts, spotted backstage or in the bar at festivals and music halls.

He has performed as 'DJ Albo', spinning selections of Nirvana, New Order and Taylor Swift at party fundraisers and charity events. Albanese was a regular on TV panels, sparring with Liberal opponents and even guest-hosting popular music video programme *Rage*.

But beneath the jovial exterior, Albanese has one of the more heart-rending personal stories in politics. Born in the Sydney suburb of Camperdown, he was told by his mother, Maryanne, that his father had died in a car crash. He lived with Maryanne – a disability pensioner with rheumatoid arthritis that he said 'crippled' her joints – in public housing.

'We didn't have much – but we had each other. And that was enough,' Albanese has often said.

It wasn't until Albanese was a teenager that his mother told him that his father was still alive and living in Italy. Albanese said he didn't want to find his father at that point. Maryanne died in 2001; in 2009, Albanese managed to track down his father, Carlo, and a half-brother and half-sister.

A senior figure in Labor for much of his political career, Albanese worked as New South Wales Labor's assistant general secretary for six years in the 1990s before being elected to federal parliament. He was a progressive voice for LGBTQ+ rights, marching in Sydney Mardi Gras parades and campaigning for equal rights for same-sex couples.

He rose up the ranks of the shadow ministry before becoming minister for transport and infrastructure after Labor's 2007 election win.

Albanese held the key position of Leader of the House following the 2010 hung parliament. He was also a key player in the 'spills' – challenges to party leaders – that saw Australia's prime ministership flip from Kevin Rudd to Julia Gillard and back to Rudd. In 2013, he tearfully called for his party to unite and stop tearing itself apart. 'I like fighting Tories. That's what I do,' he famously said at the time.

In Rudd's second government, Albanese became deputy leader and therefore deputy prime minister. It would be a brief tenure, with Rudd lasting just months before Labor lost the 2013 election. It was the last time Labor sat on the government benches.

Albanese loomed as a senior figure in the party as it lost elections in 2016 and 2019.

In 2013, Albanese won the popular support of ordinary members in a ballot but lost out in a vote of caucus colleagues. He put his hand up again in 2019, winning the leadership. After three straight election losses, Albanese set out to reform the party's strategy, setting an agenda to be a more conciliatory and cooperative opposition leader.

When the Covid pandemic hit, his push to avoid unnecessary antagonism attracted criticism from colleagues and the media, but the leader rarely wavered, confident in his belief that Australians had 'conflict fatigue'.

A strategic and disciplined campaign message was derided as 'small target' by many. But supporters called it 'smart target', not swinging at every issue thrown up by the Coalition government.

Despite wall-to-wall coverage of several 'gaffes' along the campaign, and a week in Covid isolation, Albanese looks set to win a majority government for Labor for just the third time in 30 years.

'We are still a party in which the child of a single mother in public housing can become a prime minister,' Labor's national president, Wayne Swan, said yesterday. 'And because of that, we are still a nation in which working people can see their dreams fulfilled. Just like Anthony has.'

24 MAY

Tech neck: what are smartphones doing to our bodies?

PASS NOTES

NAME: Tech neck.

AGE: Two years old.

APPEARANCE: The next stage of human evolution.

THIS SOUNDS EXCITING! ARE WE ALL GOING TO BE CYBORGS SOON? Not exactly.

THEN WHAT ON EARTH IS TECH NECK? It's the hunch you develop from staring at your phone too much.

THAT'S LESS EXCITING. And less deniable. It has been claimed by the Australian Chiropractors Association that our compulsive use of mobile devices is changing the shape of our bodies.

HOW? Let's say you hold your phone at an angle that makes you lower your head by 60 degrees. That adds approximately 27kg (60lbs) of weight through your spine. Now, imagine doing that for several hours every day. That's one messed up back.

HANG ON, YOU SAID THAT TECH NECK IS ONLY TWO YEARS OLD. Well, 'text neck' was identified as an ailment in 2011, but the pandemic made things so much worse.

IT DID? For month after month you were starved of normal human contact, and had to communicate with the rest of the world through your phone. And when you weren't doing that, you spent your time doom-scrolling in horror through a barrage of some of the worst news in modern history.

THAT SOUNDS JUST LIKE ME. Me too. And guess what? All that bad news was a pain in the neck.

WELL, ON THE PLUS SIDE PHONES HAVE ONLY HARMED US IN ONE WAY. Or two, if you count 'phone thumb', a condition where your thumb can become inflamed from prolonged texting.

OK, FINE, TWO WAYS. Or three, if you factor in the claim that blue light emitted by phones can interfere with melatonin production. Or four, if you count the eye strain you get from prolonged use. And a couple of years ago it was suggested that humans are growing bone spurs at the base of their skulls to counter all the terrible phone-related posture.

PLEASE, STOP! Want to know the good news?

YES! ANYTHING! The posture problem is easy to correct. You can do a simple stretch, where you interlock your fingers behind your head and hold your elbows against a wall.

THAT'S PROMISING. Or you could try holding your phone at eye level, to reduce the pressure on your spine. Or make an extra effort to stay active throughout the day.

THIS IS GOOD. I CAN DO THIS. Then again, there is a better way to combat tech neck.

THIS SOUNDS OMINOUS. You could always try not using your phone as much.

NEVER! THE HUMPS ARE WORTH IT! Suit yourself.

DO SAY: 'The best way to avoid tech neck is to put your phone down.'

DON'T SAY: 'You know, in a minute, after you've watched all those TikToks.'

13 JUNE

Sherwood review: the cleverest, most compelling show I've seen in years

LUCY MANGAN

The BBC's latest – and let me say up top, one of its greatest – drama series, *Sherwood*, opens with footage of the 1980s miners' strike. Arthur Scargill shouting, Margaret Thatcher speechifying (that pained and painful voice hurling you back into the past), police dragging people from the picket line, children screaming 'scab' at those crossing it. To anyone over the age of 45 or so, it feels like yesterday.

Which is very much the point. *Sherwood*'s six episodes (airing on Monday and Tuesday nights for three weeks) centre on two shocking murders that took place in real life in 2004, near where writer James Graham grew up, in the Nottinghamshire mining district of Ashfield. Out of these terrible events, Graham, as perhaps only a native – albeit one blessed with his talent – could, conjures a portrait as moving as it is convincing of a place steeped in historic grief and bitterness, full of personal enmities and festering wounds, but bound still by them all.

Alun Armstrong plays Gary Jackson, a National Union of Mineworkers (NUM) stalwart in a village dominated by the Union of Democratic Mineworkers (UDM), who, let's say, took a softer stance on striking and the privatisation of the coal industry. He is married to Julie (Lesley Manville), who is estranged from her sister Cathy (Claire Rushbrook), although they live next door to each other. When Gary is found dead in the street, killed by a crossbow bolt, the most immediate person of interest to the investigating officer – local boy made good ('Now I live on the outskirts of the village') Ian St Clair (David Morrissey) – is 'scab' Dean (Sean Gilder), with whom Gary had often and recently argued. But he also discovers that Gary's arrest records from 1984 are inexplicably redacted, even though the charges were dropped thanks to the intervention of Kevin Salisbury (Robert Glenister), one of the Metropolitan police officers sent from London to help local forces control the strikers. Salisbury's superiors send him up again from the capital to assist-without-assisting. There's also a connection to the local drug-dealing family, the Sparrows, whose son we have seen intimidating Gary. St Clair does not know that Cathy's stepson, who is about to go to prison, is into archery, because his dad (Kevin Doyle) didn't tell them and Cathy doesn't dare.

Over the way are the Fisher family, due to become more tightly bound to the main narrative next episode. Sarah (Joanne Froggatt) is standing as the local Tory councillor ('"red wall" fell, didn't you hear?') and is newly wed to Neel (Bally Gill). Her widowed father-in-law Andy (Adeel Akhtar, an absolutely heart-breaking mass of unspoken sorrow and need) is trying to get used to the new domestic order as Sarah remodels the garden and redecorates the house. 'What's an occasional chair?' he says, staring at the item she has proudly unveiled. 'It's a chair you sit on occasionally,' she snaps.

Everything you could hope for is here. It is the drama equivalent of bowling a strike: a writer knowing the setting and themes in his bones, a dream cast drawn to the richly allusive resulting script, each of those actors doing their best work in years (which, given the standards that Manville, Morrissey, Armstrong et al maintain, is quite something to watch) and their chemistry, with beautiful direction from Lewis Arnold and Ben A Williams, creating something even greater than the sum of its superb parts. It's even funny – because it's about people and because it has made those people real and because real people are, forever, even in their darkest moments, funny. When Salisbury tells St Clair that he has worked on 293 murders, to impress him with his credentials, Nottingham's finest replies: 'Well, London sounds fucking lovely.'

Without sacrificing story or suspense, and never paying less than meticulous attention to teasing out the knotty mass of relationships and the ramifications playing out around the village, *Sherwood* builds slowly – layer by subtle, evocative layer – into a magisterial state-of-the-nation piece. Forty years of emotion and history have been transmuted, lovingly and painstakingly, into art. It's the cleverest, most compelling and most moving thing I've seen in years. It should, and undoubtedly will, win awards for all concerned. But it should also last, enduring in our memories and set down in books about how to write, act and how best to conjure a specific world and make it universal, how to show us what we are and how we got here. It is, simply put, wonderful.

16 JUNE

There is a war on nature. Dom Phillips was killed trying to warn you about it

JONATHAN WATTS

Dom Phillips and Bruno Pereira have been killed in an undeclared global war against nature and the people who defend it. Their work mattered because our planet, the threats to it and the activities of those who threaten it matter. That work must be continued. The frontlines of this war are the Earth's remaining biodiverse regions – the forests, wetlands and oceans that are essential for the stability of our climate and planetary life-support system.

The integrity of these systems is under attack from organised crime and criminal governments who want to exploit timber, water and minerals for short-term, often illegal profits. In many regions, the only thing standing in their way is Indigenous communities and other traditional forest dwellers, supported by civil society organisations, conservation groups and academics.

My friend Dom knew how important this story was. It is why he took a year off to research a book, *How to Save the Amazon*, and it is why he took the risk of travelling to the bandit territory of the Javari valley with Bruno, who was one of Brazil's most effective, courageous and threatened forest defenders. It was to have been a book for everyone: accessible and useful, looking at solutions as well as problems. That was typical of Dom, whose journalism was always aimed at making the world a fairer, more accountable and enlightened place.

To my mind, this made him a 21st-century war correspondent as well as a witness to a crime that probably led to his death. Dom was no activist. He was a journalist's journalist, who wanted to find out what was happening and share it with everyone who might be affected. In this case, all of us.

If anything positive can come from the mind-numbingly horrendous news, it should be for more journalists to cover this frontline, especially in those regions controlled by leaders aligned with criminal interests.

Dom knew the threat posed by the president of Brazil, Jair Bolsonaro, who has encouraged illegal logging and mining, dismissed Indigenous land rights, attacked conservation groups and slashed the budgets and personnel of forest and Indigenous protection agencies.

Shortly after Bolsonaro won the first round of the 2018 presidential election, Dom shared his fears about the fate of the Amazon in a WhatsApp message: 'This is a very dark and worrying period and it's only going to get worse,' he wrote to me. 'My sense is that it is also going to become more dangerous for journalists.' But his real fear was for defenders living on the edge of the areas of the Amazon where criminals were trying to encroach on Indigenous territories and conservation zones. Dom was sure a second-round victory would give thugs a green light to step up their assault.

'If he wins, what will living here be like? It's like carte blanche to attack anyone his mob disagrees with,' he warned. Bolsonaro's election led Dom to focus more of his work on the rainforest and its defenders.

Separating the personal and the professional is impossible. Dom the individual was as important as Dom the journalist. He was much loved by his family and friends. I met him in 2012, soon after I first arrived in Brazil, and we immediately hit it off.

We connected through Bowie and Björk, and a love of nature and outdoor sports. Scrolling back through WhatsApp archives, many of the stories and pictures Dom shared are of spectacular views or wildlife he encountered: rays, whales, turtles and sharks seen during stand-up paddle outings around the coastline of Copacabana; capucins, marmosets and toucans encountered on hillside walks around Rio de Janeiro. With a group of like-minded friends, we made weekend hikes through the mountains between Teresópolis and Petrópolis, climbed the Pedra da Gávea to enjoy its stunning view of Rio and trekked up the slopes of Itatiaia for its stunning panoramas. More frequent were the bike rides. Early weekday mornings, we'd start the day with a cycle up to the

Corcovado, a lung-busting activity that became known as 'Christ on a bike'.

Despite a prodigious work rate, he found time for his friends. At a tough moment for me, Dom's prescription for the blues was a Spotify playlist of Walker Brothers songs, a recipe for anchovy paste spaghetti and a barrage of social invitations from him and his wife, Alessandra, to lure me out of a pit of misery. We shared happier times, too. The most memorable of innumerable get-to-gethers were his wedding party in Santa Teresa, where Dom and Alessandra radiated love and inspired joyous dancing, and my own wedding celebration, where every guest was asked to bring a word written on a stone instead of a present. For their gift, Dom and Alessandra chose 'Truth'.

That was his byword. Dom was a consummate journalist, meticulously researching and fact-checking any subject thrown his way. Covering topics from economics to art, he was a versatile writer, but it was his coverage of the Mariana environmental disaster that turned his attention to environmental issues, notably the devastating fires set by farmers and land-grabbers in the Amazon rainforest in 2019.

Undaunted and ever more alarmed by what was happening to the rainforest and its defenders, Dom upped his coverage of the environment and Indigenous rights. Last year, he took this commitment a step further, by taking a year off to write a book.

As usual, he left no stone unturned, which meant his grant from the Alicia Patterson Foundation was quickly used up on reporting trips, so he had to borrow money from his family in England to complete the project. The reporting trip to the Javari valley was to be one of the last. He had been to the remote reserve once before, in 2018, when he had met Bruno. Bruno persuaded Dom that attention needed to be focused on the forest communities on the frontline. 'It's not about us,' the burly, bespectacled man told Dom. 'The Indigenous are the heroes.'

The two men reunited earlier this month for a fateful trip to Javari. They appear to have been ambushed and killed on their return, most likely by an illegal fishing and contraband smuggling mafia that had previously threatened Bruno because he had helped Indigenous people to expose its crimes. The Brazilian authorities were slow to act: the police refused to put a helicopter in the air after the two men were reported missing, and the military said it had the capacity to search but wasted more than a day while waiting for orders.

This response by the army highlights how weak and misdirected states have become. National defence is stuck in the past – far too focused on borders and not enough on ecosystems. Meanwhile criminal gangs invade Indigenous and conservation areas with impunity. The failure of the state to defend forest defenders even as it gives a green light to illegal resource extraction suggests the government in Brazil has been captured by criminal interests.

In an election year in Brazil, everything is political. Bolsonaro has said, 'The indications are that something wicked was done to them,' but he has also accused Dom and Bruno of taking an 'adventure' that was 'ill-advised'. This is a common tactic in the war for nature. Those pushing the extractive agenda frequently trivialise, denigrate or criminalise land-defenders. They try to claim protests and exposés are isolated and unreasonable rather than an attempt to understand and confront structural problems on a global scale. When that does not work, intimidation and violence can often follow.

The killings will chill journalists and editors covering the environmental frontline, but I hope it will inspire rather than deter. What happened to Dom and Bruno is not a one-off: it is part of a global trend. Over the past two decades, thousands of environment- and land-defenders have been killed worldwide. Brazil has been the most murderous country during that time. Some of the deaths cause a global storm, such as those of Chico Mendes, Dorothy Stang and now Bruno Pereira and Dom Phillips, but most go under-reported and uninvestigated. If anything useful can come from the latest horror, let it be a recognition that these are not isolated cases. Let journalists examine the patterns that link these crimes, let us tell stories off the beaten track, and let us try to find solutions to the planet's problems, as Dom was trying to do.

24 JUNE

The *Guardian* view on the byelections: PM's end draws nigh

GUARDIAN EDITORIAL

To lose one Conservative seat may be regarded as a misfortune, to lose two looks like carelessness. Byelections on Thursday at either end of England saw Labour recapture a northern 'red wall' constituency and the Liberal Democrats storm a true-blue bastion in Devon. Unhappy with a blundering and lying prime minister in a cost of living crisis, the people spoke. The question is whether the Conservative party is listening. Mr Johnson's biggest asset was his ability to attract voters. He now repels them.

Electoral losses on this scale are unsustainable in the long run. The 12.7 per cent swing from Conservative to Labour in Wakefield would, if reproduced at a general election, deliver a Labour government. The Tory party would end up with 30-odd parliamentarians if it suffered the 29.9 per cent swing from Tory to

Lib Dems seen in Tiverton and Honiton. Yet Mr Johnson appears complacent, leaving Westminster for a week of summits abroad, with a promise that he will 'keep going'. Given that Conservative voters won't turn out for a Johnson-led party, this sounds more like a threat than a prediction.

The Conservative party chair, Oliver Dowden, had plainly had enough. He resigned, saying 'somebody must take responsibility'. He knew his boss would not. The cabinet could do worse than take their cue from former Tory leader Michael Howard, and tell the prime minister he should step down rather than risk being deposed. Perhaps Mr Johnson can convince colleagues that Thursday's results were just protest votes, to be reversed at the next general election. This is a risky bet.

Few voters know exactly what Sir Keir Starmer's Labour party or Sir Ed Davey's Lib Dems stand for. But both opposition parties think many more Tory seats will be theirs for the taking if Mr Johnson stays in office. Two in five Tory MPs apparently agree, voting to remove Mr Johnson earlier this month. Britain is seeing a new era of non-aggression between Labour and the Liberal Democrats. This is a good thing, as splitting the progressive vote has led to years of Tory hegemony.

Opposition voters at this moment appear willing to back whichever candidate is best placed to defeat the Conservatives. If local parties are ready to accept a level of self-sacrifice in a general election – Labour lost its deposit in Tiverton and Honiton as did the Liberal Democrats in Wakefield – then the Tories might find it impossible to win. There is a long way to go. The Wakefield result, as the pollster Sir John Curtice wrote, 'provides less than decisive evidence of a new enthusiasm for Labour'.

If something feels like a crisis, it is effectively a crisis. Voters face the fastest drop in living standards since the 1950s. Rail strikes over pay have brought the country to a halt. Shutdowns loom in classrooms, courts and post offices. Families see a government that is not ready to help in a timely fashion with rising fuel and food bills. Britons could muddle through, but the collective resilience required for them to do so is vitiated by the prime minister's divide-and-rule politics.

Mr Johnson should go. The only job he seems ready to work to save is his own. When he wrote of his hero Churchill that he was a 'spoilt, bullying double-crosser ... fascinated by only himself', the description applied to the author as much as to his subject. Conservative MPs fret about the lack of suitable candidates to succeed Mr Johnson. Hostile Tories clearly want a leadership challenge before next June. Almost anything would be better than continuing with the status quo. No amount of cabinet reshuffles or overblown speeches from Mr Johnson will change that. It is incumbent on Tory MPs – for the benefit of their party and their country – to find, swiftly, a better leader.

26 JUNE

A classicist at Glastonbury: 'Headbanging in raincoats? It's as English as *Gardeners' Question Time*'

CHARLOTTE HIGGINS

It's a cliché you overhear people saying to their first-timer friends as they enter the site: Glastonbury festival is a city, in which 200,000 people live for just less than a week and which has no purpose other than pleasure. It is, indeed, the sort of impossible city that you can imagine Jorge Luis Borges writing a story about.

But until you have climbed the hill to what they call the Crow's Nest, by the embers of the giant bonfire lit to mark the festival's opening, it is difficult to absorb the grandeur and absurdity of the fact that, almost as far as the eye can see, this broad valley is covered in tents and pavilions and stages and waves and eddies of innumerable people. There is a bit in Homer's *Iliad* where we are told that the campfires burning in the Greeks' camp at Troy are as bright and numerous as the stars on a clear night. This came to mind when I gazed down at the Glastonbury festival.

I have never been to Glastonbury before. These are the summer festivals I like: the Proms. Edinburgh – especially the book festival. Glyndebourne. It's not that I don't regard Glastonbury as culturally important; it's more that I dislike crowded places and have an old-fashioned respect for properly built sewers. Still, invited to taste the world's biggest music festival – a glaring gap in my experience – who am I to refuse?

Nevertheless, anxiety soon sets in. I throw myself on the mercy of my colleague Laura, who engineers for me, with touching patience, a list of recommendations from the bewildering line-up and a playlist. Packing is a whole other nightmare. 'Bring something fun,' says my friend Alicia, which leads to at least an hour's fruitless coat-hanger-flicking in charity shops. The only 'fun' item I possess is a jumpsuit, which I rule out: a hem coming into contact with the floor of a festival loo strikes me as undesirable. I post my packing list to Instagram in hope of tips. My inclusion of tweeds – a practical pair of trousers I sometimes use for gardening – is roundly derided.

On the road trip to the festival from London, I am initiated by my friend David into an undignified pre-Glastonbury ritual:

decanting 750ml of whisky into a plastic bottle in the car park of Frome Asda. (No glass is allowed at the festival.) But let's move on.

On my first day, I go to the Healing Field, which strikes me as being as good a place as any to start my exploration. Here, I join in with some Osho meditation, which involves breathing exercises alternated with bouts of cathartic screaming. I also sign up for the supposedly stress-relieving Alexander technique, find that gong baths are booked out and pass on the holistic palmist, who is sitting in his tiny enclosure with his shirt off, munching on a packet of Walkers crisps.

While inquiring about a cacao ritual (no idea), I meet a woman called Laura Bam Bam who recommends her laughter yoga class. This is not the yoga I know; it feels more like drama-class warm-up. One minute, we are doing a 'Dr Evil' cackle; the next, roaring like lions, then hooting derisively at an imagined post-Glastonbury credit card bill, which seems a sensible exercise given that tickets are £280. At the end, we lie down in a circle. Whatever comes is OK, we are told – and what comes is little tides of giggles, rising to big breakers of belly laughs. All these workshops are offered for free, or for donations. It is altogether delightful.

Later, David walks me to what is officially, if uninspiringly, called the South-East Corner, but which my friends call 'the naughty corner'. I have no idea where we are going – and my disorientation will continue, despite a map, not least because many of the festival stewards seem as confused as I am. This is unsurprising, I suppose, since this settlement didn't exist a week ago and will disappear again in a few days. (Plus, the distances are prodigious – on Thursday, I walk nearly 14 miles.)

The lights of a funfair – or, rather, of the Unfairground – twinkle through the trees. David conveys me to a bar called Maceo's, then ushers me, thanks to a wristband, round the back of the urinals to a backstage area. Beautiful drag queens glide past like exotic butterflies. David lifts a curtain that acts like a portal into another world – we are at the back of a club, NYC Downlow, the exterior of which I was just marvelling at. It's an entire building made to resemble a New York meatpacking warehouse from the 1980s, here in a field in Somerset. Two nights later, I will be in there, dancing in a dark, crazy crush of sweaty bodies. In my gardening tweeds.

Three nights later, I have a surreal montage of a night during which I stand in a field with a crowd while a giant spider hurls bursts of flame in my rough direction while a tiny Calvin Harris does his thing inside its body. (I cannot fathom it either.) Then we are back in NYC Downlow. When we leave, the gulls are circling in a blushing dawn.

What of the music? I find myself too old for Billie Eilish's wide-eyed injunctions to be grateful and not to judge each other. I absolutely love St Vincent, with her furious songs and her take-no-shit scowl. I bathe gratefully in Arooj Aftab's subtle harmonies, but find Phoebe Bridgers a touch too soulful for my mood.

From the back of the Pyramid stage crowd, I watch Wolf Alice as the drizzle sets in. Under these conditions, a British person at a festival, with their face-glitter, sequined jacket and bucket hat, is but a rain shower away from a British person on a walking holiday, with their sturdy boots and cagoule. A couple of people do some headbanging in matching yellow rain cloaks. It is as English as *Gardeners' Question Time*.

On Thursday, the day before the bands get going, I find myself at a stage called the Lonely Hearts Club, where I am supposedly meeting friends, but then not. Doing a set is a DJ called Sherelle. (Wikipedia tells me that her 'sets and mixes have been described as breakbeat, acid house and footwork'.) After a bit, I am into it, dancing on my own. Sherelle, dressed entirely in white, attacks her work with the seriousness of a librarian doing a spot of reshelving in the rare books section.

After Sherelle, I head to the cinema tent, the Pilton Palais, for a screening of *Orlando*. Here, I meet up with friends. We spend a long night grazing, pausing for mojitos, then burritos, then bhajis, then rum-and-apple, then doughnuts, before deciding on a whim to head to a drumming circle by the stone circle ('only built in the 1990s, but still very sacred', according to my friend Hannah). We take in a bit of trapeze and light candles in the peace dome, then head to the Glade, a stage beneath oak trees, for what is supposed to be a set by the DJs CamelPhat, but isn't. We weave our way into the crowd and dance for a bit anyway.

Later, wandering back to the campsite, one of my friends asks: 'What would Kenneth Clark have made of it? Would he have thought this was civilisation?' It's a good question. Glastonbury is either a highly advanced form of civilisation, or the opposite – a form of anticivilisation. The food, the toilet stench, the rubbish that piles up underfoot, the bodies, the sweat, the desire, the intoxication: everything that is raw and human is visible, on the surface, not buried or tidied away, as in normal life.

My bedtime reading here is Euripides' *The Bacchae*, a play about people who, impelled by Dionysus, leave the city behind and camp in the wilderness, worshipping, mostly peacefully, the god who presides over the state of being out of your head. Well: here we all are.

Summer

I read the 1973 *Roe* v *Wade* ruling to see what we lost. Everyone should

FRANCINE PROSE

As one more reminder of what we've lost, the text of the 1973 *Roe* v *Wade* ruling is unlikely to console us. Even so, I recommend downloading the pdf. In the wake of its overturning, this beautifully written document – which reads like a long-form essay – is not only interesting in itself, but now seems like another sign of how much has changed over the last half-century, in this case for the worse.

Drafted by Justice Harry Blackmun, the ruling includes a clear and persuasive summary of the history of abortion law. 'At the time of the adoption of our Constitution, and throughout the major portion of the 19th century, a woman enjoyed a substantially broader right to terminate a pregnancy than she does in most States today.' It tracks the centuries-old debate over when life begins, and dismisses the argument that a foetus is a person guaranteed the protections afforded US citizens. Throughout, it strikes us as the careful explication and clarification of a law, of legal precedent, unlike Justice Alito's ruling in *Dobbs* v *Jackson Women's Health*, which seems more like an expression of religious conviction masquerading as an unbiased interpretation of the constitution.

What's most striking about *Roe* v *Wade* – and its difference from the ruling that overturned it – is its eloquence. Blackmun's lucid, frequently graceful language reflects a commitment to decency and compassion. The judges are clear about the dangers of carrying an unwanted child or a high-risk pregnancy to term. They strive to see the issue from the perspective of those confronting a serious life crisis, and to imagine the devastating outcomes that pregnant women and their families may face.

'Specific and direct harm medically diagnosable even in early pregnancy may be involved. Maternity, or additional offspring, may force upon the woman a distressful life and future. Psychological harm may be imminent. Mental and physical health may be taxed by childcare. There is also the distress, for all concerned, associated with the unwanted child, and there is the problem of bringing a child into a family already unable, psychologically and otherwise, to care for it.'

The passage I admire most is the one in which Blackmun, at once profound and lyrical, describes the atmosphere surrounding the issue of abortion, the way our opinions are formed, and the pressures that the law must acknowledge and keep in balance.

We forthwith acknowledge our awareness of the sensitive and emotional nature of the abortion controversy, of the vigorous opposing views, even among physicians, and of the deep and seemingly absolute convictions that the subject inspires. One's philosophy, one's experiences, one's exposure to the raw edges of human existence, one's religious training, one's attitudes toward life and family and their values, and the moral standards one establishes and seeks to observe, are all likely to influence and to color one's thinking and conclusions about abortion. In addition, population growth, poverty, and racial overtones tend to complicate and not to simplify the problem.

And there it is: a superbly rendered catalogue of the factors that come to mind when we consider the factors that will now determine whom *Dobbs* will hurt most: poverty, race and life on the raw edges of human existence – an edge, one might say, on which *every* decision about abortion is made.

I understand that *Roe* has its flaws, though I disagree with the current court on what they are. Mid-century paternalism taints the idea that the decision to terminate a pregnancy be made by a woman *and her physician*; in most cases (excepting medical diagnoses and risk assessments) this difficult call doesn't always require a doctor's input. And the judges seem suspiciously quick to dismiss the notion that 'these laws were the product of a Victorian social concern to discourage illicit sexual conduct' – and by extension the suggestion that a man's views on abortion might reflect a desire to control female sexuality. But all of that seems minor and forgivable beside the icy piety of Justice Alito's ruling, or compared to Justice Thomas's concurring opinion: his barely veiled threats about the future of same-sex marriage and legal contraception.

In fact the distrust of – and ill will towards – women is nothing new. It permeates Justice Byron White's dissenting opinion on *Roe* v *Wade*, in which he offers *his* idea about why someone might end a pregnancy: 'Convenience, family planning, economics, dislike of children, the embarrassment of illegitimacy, etc.' *Convenience? Dislike of children?* White is only getting started. 'The court apparently values the convenience of the mother more than the continued existence and development of the life or potential life that she carries.' *Potential life?* And so we come to White's gloves-off moment, his disagreement with the court's contravening the states' attempts to 'protect human life' and instead 'investing mothers and doctors with a constitutionally protected right to exterminate it'.

Exterminate is a strong word. Alito's opinion is more tempered, but wholly lacking in Blackmun's empathy or the grace of his language. Alito's word-choice is revealing. The words 'human being' are invariably preceded by the word 'unborn' – as if the only humans relevant to the case are those who have yet to come into the world. After reading *Dobbs* we might conclude that the lives of the women forced to bear unwanted children had no influence on these deliberations. There are odd digressions – one about how definition of foetal viability changes when a community has a top-notch NCU – but the message comes through: a woman needs to be stopped by law from killing the person inside her.

In the 50 years between *Roe* and *Dobbs*, the US Supreme Court has forgotten that abortion involves human beings making tough decisions at difficult points in their lives. It has recast them as criminals conspiring to commit mass murder, killers who need to be stopped.

That was always the opinion of the protesters rallying outside abortion clinics, shouting insults at frightened, unhappy women and brandishing posters of mangled foetuses. How troubling now to learn that this opinion is shared by six of the justices presiding over the highest court in the land.

3 JULY

Women's rights have suffered a grim setback. But history is still on our side

REBECCA SOLNIT

As it happened, I was in Edinburgh the day *Roe* v *Wade* was over-turned, and the next day I caught a train back to London and took the short walk to the old St Pancras churchyard to visit the tomb-stone of the great feminist ancestor Mary Wollstonecraft, author of that first great feminist manifesto, *A Vindication of the Rights of Woman*. To be there that day was to remember that feminism did not start recently – Wollstonecraft died in 1797 – and it did not stop on 24 June.

Women in the US gained this right less than half a century ago – a short time when the view is from Wollstonecraft's memorial. I have regularly heard the opinions in recent decades that feminism failed or achieved nothing or is over, which seems ignorant of how utterly different the world (or most of it) is now for women to how it was that half-century ago and more. I say world, because it's important to remember that feminism is a global movement and *Roe* v *Wade* and its reversal were only national decisions.

Ireland in 2018, Argentina in 2020, Mexico in 2021 and Colombia in 2022 have all legalised abortion. So many things have changed in the last half-century for women in so many countries that it would be hard to itemise them all. Feminism is a human rights movement that endeavours to change things that are not just centuries, but in many cases millennia old. Resistance is neither shocking nor reason to stop.

Half a century ago it was legal in the US to fire women because they were pregnant. Marriage in most parts of the world, including North America and Europe, was, until very recently, a relationship in which the husband gained control by law and custom over his wife's body and nearly everything she did, said and owned. Marital rape was hardly a concept until feminism made it one in the 1970s, and the UK and US only made it illegal in the early 1990s. The 17th-century English jurist Matthew Hale argued 'the husband of a woman cannot himself be guilty of an actual rape upon his wife, on account of the matrimonial consent which she has given, and which she cannot retract'. Incidentally, the current US Supreme Court decision revoking reproductive rights repeatedly cites Hale, who is also well-known for sentencing two elderly widows to death for witchcraft in 1662.

The last decade has been a rollercoaster of gains and losses, and there is no neat way to add them up. The gains have been profound, but many of them have been subtle. Since about 2012, a new era of feminism opened up conversations – on social media, in traditional media, in politics and private – about violence against women and the many forms of inequality and oppression, legal and cultural, obvious and subtle. Recognition of the impact of violence against women expanded profoundly and brought real results. Last week's sentencing of R Kelly to 30 years in prison and Ghislaine Maxwell to 20 are the consequence of a shift in who would be listened to and believed, which is to say who would be valued and whose rights would be defended. Of people being included in the conversations in the courts of law who had not before been heard there.

The conversations are about violence and inequality, about the intersectionalities of race and gender, about the rethinking of gender beyond the simplest binaries, about what freedom could look like, what desire could be, what equality would mean. Just to have those conversations is liberating. These conversations change us in ways the law cannot.

You can take away a right through legal means, but you cannot take away the belief in that right so easily. Women in many US states have lost their access to abortion, but not their belief in their right to it. The uproar in response to the court's decision is a reminder of how unpopular it is.

It does not exactly return us to the world before *Roe* v *Wade*, because in both imaginative and practical terms US society is profoundly different. Women have far more equality under the law, in access to education, employment, institutions of power and political representation. We have far more belief in those rights and a stronger vision of what equality looks like. That the status of women is so radically changed from where it was 50 or 60 years ago, let alone in 1797, is evidence that feminism is working. And the Supreme Court's hideous decision confirms that there is still a lot of work to do.

6 JULY

I almost downloaded a pebble-identifying app – but some stones should be left unturned

ADRIAN CHILES

In the great outdoors, I find peace. Up hills, down dales, on beaches and cliffs and in fields and woods, I am a study in contentment. Just me and God's green Earth. And my phone. 'Put the bloody thing away,' implores a voice next to me, or in my head. But I can't comply.

It was the plane-tracking app that came for me first. Before I knew it, I couldn't simply enjoy any blue sky if it had an aircraft in it. Now, I had to know exactly where that plane was flying from and to. The app tells me when it left, when it will arrive and, for added interest, where else it has been that day, and yesterday, and the day before.

And that ship out there on the ocean blue, halfway to the horizon? Soon I didn't have to wonder where it was off to, either. I could know that, too. Instantly. The ship app goes one further – unbidden, it tells me where ships I once identified are now to be found. Why, only the other night, just nodding off, I was pinged interesting tidings about the SSI *Excellent*, a bulk carrier registered in the Marshall Islands (deadweight: 81,119 tonnes) that I saw in the Bristol Channel last summer. It had just left a city I had never heard of on the Yangtze for a port I had never heard of in Australia.

Things got better and worse with the advent of nature apps. No more wondering what that beautiful flower or tree is: take a pic and everything you want to know about it will be yours. Bird-song, too. Point, record, identify. Sweet.

But a straw has broken the camel's back. On my Twitter feed today, an advert popped up for – I kid you not – a stone-identifying app. Show it a pebble and it will tell you what kind of stone it is. Can't say I had ever wondered, but now you mention it ... I clicked to download, but stalled just in time. This madness has to stop.

An image of myself walking on an idyllic coastal path came to mind. Every other minute, I would glance at the sky or the sea – and then at my phone. Or I would stop to point the camera at a plant, or at a songbird, or – dear God – at a bloody pebble. Much more of this and I will grind to a halt completely. I will just stand there, checking, identifying, reading, paralysed by my own curiosity. As night falls, I will remain there, absorbed by my star-identification app.

It used to feel marvellous to live in an age of such easy access to facts, but now I am not so sure. For one thing, five minutes after I have looked up the name of a flower, or whatever, I have usually forgotten it. The next time I see it, I will have to look it up again. Curiosity needs to ripen awhile. If the thirst for a bit of knowledge is slaked in an instant, the fact tends not to stick.

Knowledge is wonderful, but wonderment is better. How I miss wonderment. How I miss those pre-app days; the joy of idle, unanswerable, vaguely asked questions such as: 'Which bird is singing that beautiful song?' An eminent theologian once said to me that if God were proved to exist, religion would die, because its power resides in the mystery. So, with planes, ships, flowers, trees, birds and who knows what else, the apps will have to go. I want my sense of wonder back.

7 JULY

The *Guardian* view on Boris Johnson's resignation: good riddance

GUARDIAN EDITORIAL

The good news is that the worst prime minister in modern British history is going. The bad news is that he has not yet gone. Boris Johnson fought to the end to remain in Downing Street as his reputation and his government collapsed around him. On Thursday, as more ministers resigned, including one who had been in office less than 48 hours, he bowed to the inevitable, resigning as Conservative leader while remaining prime minister until a successor is chosen.

Mr Johnson went grudgingly and without grace. He left with a speech outside No 10 that was at once breezy and bitter. It contained no note of contrition for his own misconduct as prime minister, or any syllable of awareness of why a party that had rushed to embrace him three years ago has rushed to rid itself of him now. His capacity to do damage to his party and the country has not yet ended.

Mr Johnson presided over three turbulent years in Downing Street. Some of the turbulence was wholly predictable from his past behaviour in journalism and politics, and was his own fault. Some was caused by seismic global events that few, including him, saw coming. He traded on his charisma, which helped lead to his election victory in 2019, but his approach to governance was never serious or strategic, as Brexit exemplified. His conduct as prime minister was incompetent, corrupt and shameful. He should have gone months ago.

He claimed to understand the British people but, as the past torrid weeks have shown, he never shared or understood their moral decency. He behaved like a president, not a parliamentary leader. He governed by campaigning, not through collective deliberation and delivery. He abused his office by rewarding cronies and doing deals with donors. To the last, he was incapable of giving a straight answer to a straight question. He has now destroyed three Conservative governments in six years and done much to damage Britain's international reputation. The party, and the British people, are well rid of him.

On Thursday, Mr Johnson departed in a defiant and petty address that lacked humility or any concern for anything other than himself. He brushed aside his ministers' 11th-hour pleas for him to resign over the Pincher affair as 'eccentric'. He condescendingly dismissed the concerns of MPs as 'herd instinct'. And he offered the barely concealed threat to his successor that he would 'give you as much support as I can'. If Tory MPs have not learned by now that Mr Johnson has no interest in or loyalty to them, they will never learn anything.

Instead, Mr Johnson cast himself as a leader betrayed, even referring to the Tories as 'that party', as though he was somehow not part of it. There was no note of apology, no word of thanks to any minister and no admission of even the slightest failure. This is all of a piece with Mr Johnson's repeated attempts to pretend that the vote for the Conservatives in 2019 was a purely personal mandate and not one for the party. This false claim lay behind his attempts this week to threaten an early election if he was ousted. It is a dangerous, almost Trump-like narrative, and we are unlikely to have heard the last of it, or of him.

The shock of this week to the Tory party will be very great. How it evolves, and under what leader, will begin to become clearer soon. But the process will not and does not deserve to be easy. Mr Johnson created an idiosyncratic Conservatism based on Brexit nationalism, active government, high borrowing and his personality. Few Tory MPs and few of the potential candidates share that approach. The new leader will also be chosen by Tory members who are whiter, richer, older and more southern than the country as a whole. It is a crossroads moment for the party.

Mr Johnson leaves, as usual, indifferent to much except himself. Except that, in one important sense, Mr Johnson has not left. He is still prime minister today. Extraordinarily, he rebuilt his cabinet on Thursday morning at precisely the same time as he finally prepared his own resignation. He intends to stay for some weeks – potentially up to the Tory conference in October. Under previous prime ministers, such transitions were relatively uncontroversial. That is not the case with Mr Johnson, and for a simple reason. They could be trusted. He cannot. Labour is right to threaten a confidence vote if he tries to stay. The Conservative party must act quickly and ruthlessly to kick Mr Johnson out conclusively.

8 JULY

The week Boris Johnson lost his grip on power

DAN SABBAGH

Last Thursday Boris Johnson headed home from the NATO summit in Madrid having spent several days in the company of world leaders. At the preceding G7 in Bavaria, speaking loudly enough for the camera to pick up, he had joked: 'Can we take our clothes off?' in a supposed riposte to an old shot of Vladimir Putin topless.

At NATO he had at least tried to think long-term, making a public promise to lift defence spending to 2.5 per cent of GDP by 2030. Yet his premiership ended one week later – by which time the only military comment he would make was to privately compare himself to a Japanese soldier who had refused to surrender for 29 years after the Second World War. The joke was remarkably apt.

The remarkable disintegration of his premiership began the moment he left the NATO photocalls behind. Chris Pincher resigned as a deputy chief whip the evening Johnson returned, after allegations that Pincher had groped two men at the Carlton Club in Westminster. The story was bad enough, but what followed was a disastrous series of evasions, half-truths – and even the sense that Johnson thought it all a joke.

On Friday last week, Downing Street said firstly that the prime minister had not been aware of any allegations against Pincher when he promoted him in February, and then hours later that he had not been aware of any 'specific' allegations.

Yet even that turned out not to be accurate as more complaints about Pincher emerged. Johnson's former adviser Dominic Cummings, long waiting for the opportunity to land the final blow, suggested Johnson had known all along and had referred to his colleague as 'Pincher by name, pincher by nature'.

More damning evidence was to follow. On Tuesday morning a former senior Foreign Office civil servant, Simon McDonald, said there had been a similar previous incident involving Pincher when he was a junior Foreign Office minister in 2019, and that Johnson had been 'briefed in person about the initiation and outcome of the investigation'.

Jason Groves, the political editor of the pro-Tory *Daily Mail*, began that day's briefing for lobby journalists by asking the prime minister's spokesperson: 'Will you be telling the truth?' – prompting a somewhat embarrassed civil servant to reply that they provided 'the information available to me at the time of each meeting'.

Johnson toured the tea rooms to try to salvage the situation. But as the Conservative MP Gary Sambrook revealed on Wednesday at prime minister's questions, Johnson sought to blame everybody bar the perpetrator.

According to Sambrook, Johnson said: 'There were seven MPs in the Carlton Club last week, and one of them should have tried to intervene to stop Chris drinking so much.'

Sambrook was applauded as he called on him to resign, but by then it was already clear Johnson's premiership was in the end game – even if Johnson was the last to see it.

The night before, Sajid Javid and then Rishi Sunak had resigned, releasing similar statements nine minutes apart that focused squarely on the issue of Johnson's character.

'The British people rightly expect integrity from their government,' Javid wrote in a statement published at 6.02pm.

Sunak wrote: 'The public expect government to be conducted properly, competently and seriously.' The statements looked coordinated even if both camps denied it.

Resignations of mostly junior ministers carried on at an extraordinary rate on Wednesday, the first coming while the new chancellor, Nadhim Zahawi, was doing a broadcast media round in the morning, and continuing through to the Welsh secretary Simon Hart at 10.33pm. By midnight the final departure count was more than 40.

It had been an easy day for Keir Starmer. At prime minister's questions the Labour leader read out an account from a victim of Pincher – 'he slowly moved his hand down in front of my groin' – in the deliberate style of a prosecutor. Then he pressed Johnson on why the former whip had been promoted in the first place.

From teatime ministers began converging on Downing Street, mostly to demand Johnson's head, and a handful to encourage him to stay. The prime minister saw them individually. Even Priti Patel, the normally loyal home secretary, said she thought he could not carry on.

It was expected that Johnson, having taken the temperature of his most senior colleagues, would conclude the game was up, as had Margaret Thatcher a generation before. There was even a scheduled early evening phone call with the Queen. But, remarkably, Johnson concluded for a moment that he could fight on.

In a final show of frustration and flexing of his waning power, he sacked Michael Gove from the cabinet while Gove's children and ex-wife Sarah Vine were watching *Love Island*. According to Vine, a columnist for the *Daily Mail*, Gove told her: 'The prime minister rang me a few minutes ago and told me it was time for me to step back. I said respectfully: "Prime minister, if anyone should be stepping back it is you."'

Downing Street said Gove had had to go because 'you can't have a snake who is not with you on any of the big arguments'. That night the *Sun* was told that Tory rebels would have to 'dip their hands in blood' if they were going to force out a prime minister who had won an election in December 2019.

A night's sleep and the fightback was over, although some could not wait. Michelle Donelan resigned as education secretary shortly before 9am on Thursday, after about 36 hours in post. She told Johnson it was the only way to 'force your hand'. Had she waited the length of a maths lesson, she might have changed her mind.

With more and more resignation letters landing on the doormat on Downing Street, officials stopped taking calls from journalists on Thursday morning, prompting the immediate suspicion that it was finally all over.

Johnson apparently got up at 6am to write a resignation speech, in which he would blame the 'herd instinct' for his departure rather than any particular misjudgment – over Pincher or parties or propriety.

It fell to the BBC's new political editor, Chris Mason, to tell the nation, taking a phone call from Downing Street while live on Radio 4 shortly after 9am.

On his return to the microphone, with a guest gently moved aside, a cool Mason said simply: 'The prime minister has agreed to stand down.'

18 July

The terrifying truth:
Britain's a hothouse, but one
day 40°C will seem cool

BILL McGUIRE

There's no getting around it, the UK's once equitable climate is falling apart. We are now firmly on course for hothouse Britain and the signs are all around us. Just three years ago, the mercury hit a record high of 38.7°C (101.7°F) in Cambridge. A year later, the Met Office mocked up a weather forecast for 2050, showing 40°C-plus temperatures across much of the UK. But the speed of climate breakdown is such that this future is already upon us. Today, the Met Office's first ever red extreme-heat warning comes into force for much of England, as ferocious 40°C-plus temperatures threaten to overwhelm ambulance services and A&E departments, and potentially bring about thousands of deaths.

And this is just the beginning. When our children are our age, they will yearn for a summer as 'cool' as 2022, because long before the century's end, 40°C-plus heat will be nothing to write home about in the climate-mangled world they inherit.

The brutal truth is that dodging dangerous, all-pervasive climate breakdown is now practically impossible. Even if all the promises and pledges made at Cop26 were kept, we would still be lucky to stay below a 2°C rise, and if tipping points are crossed and feedbacks kick in, the figure could be much higher. So, hothouse Britain is a reality, and the sooner we face this fact, the better. And be very clear, this isn't alarmist. It isn't what deniers are fond of calling 'climate porn'. This is simply how things are.

In the decades ahead, summers are set to get ever hotter and last longer, overwhelming the other seasons, and reducing winter to a couple of dreary months punctuated by damaging storms and destructive floods. Blistering heat will be the default weather for July and August, when a combination of high temperatures and humidity will make sunbathing and working in the open extremely unpleasant and potentially deadly. Our poorly insulated homes will provide little respite as they are turned into unlivable heat traps. Camping out in gardens and parks will become commonplace as baking nights make sleeping indoors impossible. Inevitably, increasing numbers of people will flee the cities to escape the heat-island effect that will transform them into unbearable saunas. A general migration northwards and uphill can be expected, as cooler conditions become a big property selling point.

But hothouse Britain is about far more than insufferable summer heat. Progressive climate breakdown will affect everyone and insinuate itself into every aspect of our lives. Transport and energy infrastructure will succumb repeatedly to the onslaught of extreme weather, making otherwise straightforward journeys increasingly problematic, and power outages a normal part of daily life.

Health and wellbeing services will buckle, as tens of thousands of the most vulnerable people struggle in the growing heat and humidity, cases of poisoning due to heat-related food and water contamination burgeon, and new diseases suited to the hotter conditions – including malaria and dengue fever – gain a foothold. An explosion in mental health problems is also foreseen, as living conditions become ever more desperate for many, and the strain on individuals and families takes its toll.

A confluence of desiccating drought, torrential rains and battering hail, flooding and new pests that thrive in the heat will take a massive toll on crops at a time when frequent harvest failures and climate wars will mean an erratic and unreliable supply from overseas. We have already seen price hikes and gaps on supermarket shelves as a consequence of the Ukraine conflict. Climate breakdown will bring far worse. One study predicts that by 2050 the world will need half as much food again, while crop yields could be down by as much as 30 per cent. This is nothing less than a recipe for widespread hunger, social unrest and civil strife, and the UK is unlikely to be immune.

Heat and drought will be the signature conditions of hothouse Britain, but there will still be rain. In the summer, downpours fed by convective storms will be so heavy that little rain will penetrate the ground, most of it flowing over the surface to feed lethal and destructive flash floods. Autumn and winter will see frequent incursions of powerful, damaging, storms and so-called atmospheric 'rivers', bringing rains that last for days on end, overwhelming catchments and driving river flooding on a biblical scale.

Coastal communities will fight a losing battle as bigger and more frequent storm surges, increasingly powerful waves and a remorseless hike in sea level supercharge cliff erosion and permanently swamp low-lying terrain. Sea level is now rising by a centimetre every two years, which is more than double the rate for the period 1993–2002. Within 80 years it will certainly be more than a metre higher, and could have climbed by two metres or even more. This would bring the North Sea far inland, threatening especially low-lying communities such as the Lincolnshire towns of Boston and Spalding.

Alongside rapid emissions cuts, the inevitability of climate breakdown makes adaptation desperately urgent. Now should be the time for massive government investment in resilient infra-structure and the preservation of health and wellbeing – but there is little sign of this. Our housing stock remains totally unprepared for the new summer temperatures and flood plains are still being concreted over for new estates; meanwhile, transport and energy networks continue to be dangerously exposed to the vagaries of floods, wind and excessive heat. No plans exist, either, for a national water grid that could ease future drought conditions. The bottom line is that every decision – from local government upwards – needs to be made in light of building resilience to climate breakdown as well as slashing emissions. But this just isn't happening.

If you are terrified by what you have read, then I have done what I set out to do. Too many of us still think that global heating will just mean that the world will get a bit warmer and that somehow we will muddle through. This is plain wrong. So be scared, but don't let this feed inertia. Instead channel the emotion and use it to launch your contribution to tackling the climate emergency. Things are going to be dreadful, but – working together – we still have the time to stop a dangerous future becoming a cataclysmic one.

18 July

The Tory leadership race

STEVE BELL

26 July

'Like seeing Stonehenge for the first time': the visionary genius of Vaughan Williams

ANDREW MANZE

Ask people about Ralph Vaughan Williams, whose 150th anniversary we celebrate this year, and you might be told either that he is hands down Britain's favourite composer or a parochial embarrassment whose music sounds like 'a cow looking over a gate' (to quote one critic). Both judgments are usually based on just two pieces: *Fantasia on a Theme by Thomas Tallis* and *The Lark Ascending*, which have appeared at or near the top of the Classic FM Hall of Fame poll for 20 years. In 1958, in the last year of his life, he was unquestionably the grand old man of English music, yet his last major work, the Ninth Symphony – to my mind a masterpiece – was written off by many critics as old hat.

Vaughan Williams has always been in and out of fashion. Many listeners have an 'a-ha' moment, whether it be one of enlightenment or rejection. Mine, the former, took place listening to his Fifth Symphony. Written during the dark days of 1942, it left its audience speechless, tearful and grateful for its message of peace and hope. But I knew none of this when, a blank-slate teenager, I put needle to LP and within seconds – a low drone in the strings, two visionary horns, some dreamy violins – I was hooked. And, if the symphony's first minute is not your thing, listen to the very last, a wordless hallelujah the like of which is heard at the gates of heaven. If you are still not charmed, keep reading. There are many sides to Vaughan Williams, as I quickly found.

The course of my love did not run smooth. I grew impatient with the *Pastoral Symphony* (No 3), staring into the vacant eyes of that cow, and the Fourth Symphony assaulted my tender ears. I hear both differently now. The *Pastoral* is a requiem for the men lost in the First World War, some of them friends and students of the composer. It was conceived on long, quiet evenings in northern France as the sun set over the battlefields where Vaughan Williams served as an ambulance driver. He witnessed things, as so many did, that he was never to speak of, except perhaps in music. The Fourth Symphony I now hear as a postwar expression of rage, dissonant from first to last, a hellish gate that might appeal to my previously unimpressed reader.

Vaughan Williams was slow to find his own musical voice. But from his late thirties he evolved into a one-man musical institution. He edited the Anglican hymn book *The English Hymnal*, cycled around country pubs collecting folk songs, was active in the English Folk Dance Society, though himself something of a galumpher, and conducted amateur choirs and professional orchestras with passion and the occasional burst of temper. As the Second World War neared its end, he was the one authorities turned to for 'A Song of Thanksgiving', to be ready for VE Day. And he was a beloved teacher who supported young composers financially and in other practical ways. He once had to bring to heel an orchestra which was openly laughing at a young, then unknown Benjamin Britten.

English through and through, Vaughan Williams was steeped in his country's literature and art, old and new. He set words of Housman and Kipling, Shakespeare and Herbert, and there is an opera on Bunyan's *The Pilgrim's Progress*. The closing scene of HG Wells's *Tono-Bungay* inspired the atmospheric end of *A London Symphony* and that 'old hat' Ninth Symphony was sparked by Hardy's *Tess of the d'Urbervilles*.

The scenario and music of *Job: A Masque for Dancing* (not a ballet – he disliked 'overdeveloped calves') were based on William Blake's *Illustrations of the Book of Job*, and the hall-of-famous *Tallis Fantasia* is gothic architecture in music. Vaughan Williams confessed that he himself sometimes did not know whether he had composed a piece or merely remembered it. He likened the process to seeing Stonehenge or Niagara Falls for the first time: it was as if he already knew them. The *Tallis Fantasia* sounds as if the musicians are reading not sheet music but runes carved on rock.

For some, however, Vaughan Williams's very Englishness can be a barrier. I have been lucky enough to perform his music outside the UK and see how it speaks to audiences who know nothing of its cultural roots. The most common reaction to hearing one of the symphonies is a sort of bemused appetite for more: how many of these are there? Why didn't we know them already?

Cultural roots lie deep and old. Dig deep enough, as Vaughan Williams did, and you find the roots of music entangled, shared even, with other cultures, on a bedrock of pentatonics, ancient modes, hymns, chorales and folk dance. And it is for that reason that I believe his music has lasted in our estimation and will for a long time, though fashions come and go.

30 JULY

'People are turning off': Muscovites put the war aside and enjoy summer

ANDREW ROTH

As Russia's war in Ukraine grinds into its fifth month, Moscow is a city doing everything it can to turn a blind eye to the conflict. It is a champagne-soaked summer like any other in the Russian capital, despite the thousands of dead and many more wounded in a war increasingly marked by acts of savage brutality.

In Gorky Park, outdoor festivals, cinemas and bars were all jammed on a recent evening, with young couples twirling to ballroom-dance music as others stopped for selfies along the Moskva river nearby. 'Yes, we are having a party,' said Anna Mitrokhina at an outdoor dance platform on the river. 'We are outside of politics. We want to dance and have fun. I can't worry any more and this helps me forget.'

Walk through the city and you might not even know the country is at war, a word that the Russian censors have banned from local media and that, even among many friends, has become taboo.

An Instagram influencer with more than 100,000 followers who was opposed to the war said she had decided to stop speaking about the topic because of the official restrictions but also the backlash she had received from subscribers.

'Nobody wants to hear about the war, the special military operation, any more. They tell me to stop talking about this and get back to normal topics like beauty and fitness,' she said, asking that her name not be used. 'Every time I mentioned it I would get so much hate in my messages. It hurts me, it hurts my business. I stopped mentioning it. It just doesn't exist for many people.

'What hurts the most is there is just no desire to talk about this,' she said. 'People are turning off.'

In a forthcoming paper shared with the *Guardian* titled 'How Public Opinion Is Hiding from the Truth', the Russian-based political analyst Andrei Kolesnikov and the Levada Centre pollster Denis Volkov write that the war has become 'routine' for many Russians.

'The inability to influence what is happening makes people think less about global political issues and focus more on everyday subjects, on life here and now,' the authors write.

If Russians were shocked by the outbreak of war in March, they said, then by June far fewer listed it as the most significant issue for the country right now.

And many had found it easier to join the 'mainstream' of support or indifference to the war, they added, calling it the 'most comfortable' position, and one that didn't force people to 'observe or, most importantly, think'.

After a wave of repression there are fewer voices speaking out against the war. But some remain.

At a table by the window in the Pushkin cafe, Alexei Venediktov is loudly decrying the conflict as 'catastrophic' as the staff look on with an air of concern. The former head of Echo of Moscow, the radio station that was shut down after its public opposition to the war, has now been declared a foreign agent. 'I was an enemy, now I am a traitor,' he says of his relationship with Vladimir Putin.

Venediktov had played a careful game for years, protecting his station's independence while maintaining good relations with Kremlin officials. That all ended after the invasion in late February.

'I told my staff that the closure of Echo was the price of our freedom,' he said. 'And your unemployment is also the price ... you wanted freedom; I provided it. Now we pay the price.'

He was also friends with people such as Margarita Simonyan, the head of the RT television network and one of the top media cheerleaders for the war. 'I showed her photos of the dead children in Mariupol,' he said. 'I could see her eyes get glassy. And then I heard what I hear from the television: "They did it to themselves. It's staged. It's Nazis." So we don't speak any more. I just don't understand how as a mother she can allow for this. And it's like that in every family.'

Those tensions are playing out in families across the country, particularly in big cities where younger generations are often liberal. At a small church attached to a monastery in north-west Moscow, Father Alexei says that for months he has had parents breaking down in front of him over family tensions due to the conflict, many asking for advice on how to quell family disputes or change relatives' opinions about the war.

'I can't tell you how many people have come to talk to me ... dozens, maybe hundreds,' he said. 'People are under immense stress. Families are being ripped apart.'

As those tensions often play out in private, Moscow is busy keeping up appearances, desperate to show that it is resisting sanctions and isolation as Western brands have fled the capital.

The country's first McDonald's on Tverskaya Street has been renamed as Tasty and That's It, a facsimile of the US fast food brand that also serves to keep Russians at work. 'Some things change, but stable employment remains,' a banner screams out. It reads like a rallying cry for a country keen to decry sanctions while ignoring the conflict that provoked them.

'I think our guys are top-notch,' said Dmitry, who had bought a double cheeseburger and large fries with several sauce packets still bearing the McDonald's logo. 'We can make all the same things, the same food, the same design, without the Western owners. I hope that they're all thrown out.'

But many people, especially those in business circles, recognise the hit the economy has taken and that the worst may be yet to come. 'My parents grew up in a country where there was no foreign competition and we know how that was,' said Alexander Perepelkin, the editor of *The Blueprint*, a fashion and culture publication, and a marketing director who regularly worked with foreign brands. 'It wasn't good.'

But for others, it is exactly the time to let loose. 'I've stopped talking about politics and the special operation after March,' said Marina Belova, who was eating at a paella restaurant along the Moskva on Wednesday evening. 'I fought with my parents and realised I could lose them and never change their minds anyway; it was extremely bitter and mean. I keep my friends close, I try to relax, not to think about the future. I hope that I can travel again soon. But I don't know what others will think of me, or what I will do if I meet someone from Ukraine abroad.'

Others seemed more motivated by rejecting what they claim is Western propaganda – in particular, accusations of atrocities – saying that how the war is run is out of their hands.

'We have nothing to feel bad for,' said Vadim Presnyakov, who was inline skating in the park. 'We are being told to feel guilty, but there is nothing that any of us could have done about what's taking place. And the more that you tell people to feel guilty, the more they will just reject you.'

The alternative is stark: events have panned out poorly for those who have offered even slight criticism of the war. Alexei Gorinov, a Moscow city councillor who spoke out against the war, was sentenced to seven years in prison this month for 'discrediting the Russian army'.

'The saddest thing is that I won't see my dog,' he told the Russian human rights defender Eva Merkacheva when she visited him in prison this week.

'She won't be alive by the time I am freed.'

2 AUGUST

I cried when England won. It's been a long journey for women's football – and for me

SUZANNE WRACK

When the final whistle went at the end of extra time, I pressed send on my on-the-whistle match report, put my face in my hands and sobbed. Big, loud, heart-rending, back-arching sobs.

It was not the first time I had cried around the Lionesses' stunning, swaggering run to a first major tournament trophy and I have not really stopped since.

It is hard to articulate just how much this victory means to me. When I started writing about women's football there was no full-time work available at any national newspaper for those wanting to cover the game.

I was asked to write a weekly column for the *Guardian* in 2017, on the eve of the Euros, at which Sarina Wiegman would guide the Netherlands to a home win. The headline on my first column? 'England's Euros adventure can deliver glory abroad and lasting impact at home'. My first interview? With Laura Bassett, the scorer of England's devastating late own goal in the World Cup semi-final in 2015 in Canada, who was heading to the Euros without a club after the collapse of Notts County.

Fast forward and, 1,093 articles later, I have just watched the game I have given everything to build – and that I care about very deeply – have a moment that will transform it as well as the resources and paid work available for covering it. Incredibly, it does not feel as if we are at the summit but at base camp, ready to roll, with all the equipment needed to reach the top.

There are people who have been pioneering this game far longer than I have – on and off the pitch. I came in as minds were starting to shift in the industry. I could sight potential openings; not that it was ever about that. Trying to fathom the feelings of Tony Leighton, Jen O'Neill and Cath Etoe, who are among those who have covered the women's game for decades, when Leah Williamson lifted the trophy on Sunday is impossible.

They very much had a hand on the trophy, too, as did so many others – I, perhaps, can claim a fingernail.

Every journalist covering a football team – men's or women's – gets to know the players and staff. We sit down with them and delve into their stories, sometimes asking deeply personal questions about their state of mind, feelings, tragedies, health and failures. You connect with many, with their stories, their passion, their unerring desire to push themselves to be the best. In women's football the players tell their stories freely, knowing that fans who connect with them may engage with the game and its journey to the front and back pages.

I have spoken to Chloe Kelly about the ACL injury that ruled her out of the Olympics, to Keira Walsh about how she wanted to quit football after the 2019 World Cup, to a tear-stained Ellen White after Team GB crashed out of the Olympics in extra time, at the quarter-final stage, her hat-trick not enough to earn victory over Australia. The list goes on.

Had the men's team won last summer, or should they go one step further at the World Cup in Qatar, I imagine many journalists who have covered the team for decades will have their emotions turned upside down in similar and different ways. We work late nights, long days and have many more unglamorous hours than Instagram-worthy ones. It is, of course, all worth it.

Women's football is decades, if not a century, behind the development of the men's game. At the moment it is still very, very reliant on and invested in an engaged media to help it grow. Of course the men's game needs the press, too, to maintain its deep stamp on society, but the fledgling nature of the women's game prompts far greater openness from players and managers who recognise the importance of a reciprocal relationship – we grow it and then it grows us.

So while tears and cheering in the press box may be unfamiliar, slightly frowned upon or seen as a little unprofessional, forgive those of us who were broken by events on Sunday. We know what this means for our jobs, our industry, the players, the game and for society more generally. Football is powerful and the broader impact of it 'coming home' thanks to a group of young women cannot be underestimated.

There are lots of people raising warnings, saying the opportunity to develop this wonderful sport off the back of this historic win and moment cannot be missed. They are right. Of course they are. But if there is one thing I know, it is that the people saying these things, the players on the pitch, the staff at clubs, the former players still championing the game, will not let the moment pass without a fight.

The FA banned women's football for 50 years, tried to smash the game out of existence, but those in charge back in 1921 failed. Instead they made sure that the gutsiest group of fighters would emerge to champion the game and grow it generation by generation.

That was a group of educated, intelligent, resilient and brilliant women, who would give anything, and have given everything, to see this sport succeed. A group who have given everything to see all girls have the right to play a game that has formed so much of who they are on and off the pitch; it's developed them as people and as important members of society in ways they could never imagine.

9 AUGUST

Truss and Sunak: completely unreliable narrators of their own campaigns

JOHN CRACE

Nice work if you can get it. Boris Johnson has just returned from holiday. Not that it would much matter if he had stayed in

Slovenia. It's not as if he's doing much at home. Thank God we're not in a cost of living crisis with fuel bills set to top £4,200.

Most prime ministers might have done things rather differently; seen out their last few weeks in office at No 10 with dignity and gone on holiday in September. But the Convict sees things through the prism of his own narcissism. So he takes his pleasures where and when he feels like it. He wants it. He takes it. He won't pay the price.

So we're left with a half-asleep government. Drifting pointlessly around in decreasing circles. And in place of responsible adults, the UK has been blessed with the tedium of the Tory leadership psychodrama.

It's almost as if the country is being gaslit by the Tories. That we are being presented with two possible leaders, both of whom are completely unreliable narrators of their own campaigns. In the blue corner we have Liz Truss. One day she says something, the next day she denies saying it. First we had Radon Liz insisting that people who lived in the north should be paid less. Then she said that she had been misinterpreted. Even though she had been quoted from her own press release.

Then, in the other blue corner, we have Rishi Sunak. Rish! is also completely hopeless. As the long shot in a two-horse race, he'll also say any old nonsense on the off chance it goes down well with the Tory members.

It's as if he and Radon Liz are two half-wits in search of a whole wit. But one of them – probably Truss – will be prime minister. Terrifying. Perhaps it's been a party political broadcast on behalf of the Labour party. What it definitely has also been is a shoo-in for this year's Darwin Awards. The Tory party's bid for self-extinction.

Sadly for us, we're not there yet and there are more hustings at which the same old – and some new – lies will be told.

Darlington was the only red wall location on this farewell tour. Host for last night, TalkTV's Tom Newton Dunn, tried to break the ice with a gag. The Tories seem to have a leadership contest every three years: so maybe everyone would be all back at another hustings in 2025. This was a little too close to home and almost no one laughed.

Then came Sunak. This was Rish! at his slickest. Much like the sales manager giving the keynote speech at the annual conference when he knows the entire audience is just waiting for the free bar.

There was a bit of establishing his northern credentials – tough for a boy from Southampton via Winchester – and then it was just the same pitch everyone had heard before. A bit on woke culture. A bit on hard work and patriotism as if they were a Conservative preserve and then a stretch on the perils of inflation. There was no limit to the savings he could make, so all state aid would come without any borrowing. It was a wonder he had been so inefficient in government.

Truss was altogether more wooden. Even though she too basically gave the same opening spiel as at all the other hustings, she managed to sound as if she was reading from a script for the first time. Though she did commit to making the UK free of the European convention on human rights. She didn't explain how she was going to square this with the Good Friday agreement.

Her attitude was more defensive than Rish!'s. She seemed to think Newton Dunn was some kind of leftwing plant. She wasn't going to get locked into a discussion of commie economics on handouts. Tax cuts would grow the economy and that was that.

Finally Newton Dunn wound things up. Two hours of our lives we will never get back. Until tomorrow when the exercise in futility continues. It's democracy, Jim. But not as we know it.

9 August

FBI raid on Trump's residence takes US into uncharted territory

ED PILKINGTON

The news that sent tremors across America broke at 6.36pm on Monday when the publisher of an obscure Florida politics website tweeted that the FBI had raided Donald Trump's Mar-a-Lago home, adding with a pinch of self-deprecation: 'TBH I'm not a strong enough reporter to hunt this down, but it's real.'

Eighteen minutes later another Florida resident responded to the news with more bombast. 'These are dark times for our nation, as my beautiful home ... is currently under siege, raided, and occupied by a large group of FBI agents,' the former US president said in a rage-filled statement.

More than 30 FBI agents, armed with a search warrant issued by a federal magistrate from West Palm Beach, are reported to have entered Trump's private residence and offices at his Mar-a-Lago club. According to NBC News, they stayed on site most of the day.

Despite Trump's cries of 'siege' and 'occupation' there was no bashing down of doors or loud flash-bangs for which the FBI is legendary. The search team had alerted the Secret Service agents guarding the compound in advance, ensuring an orderly execution of the warrant.

Once the operation began the FBI called Eric Trump, son of the former president, who, according to the account he gave to Sean Hannity on Fox News on Monday night, was the one who broke the news to his father. At the time, the pair were in Trump Tower, Manhattan, where the former president was preparing to be deposed in a civil lawsuit relating to his firm's financial bookkeeping brought by New York state. Eric Trump portrayed the search to Hannity in terms as lurid as those deployed by his father. 'They started ransacking an office, ransacking a closet,' he said. 'They broke into a safe! He didn't have anything in the safe.'

More details will have to emerge before Eric Trump's description can be assessed for accuracy. It will also take time for a full picture to be gleaned of the FBI's reasoning behind its actions, and whether or not that meets the exceptionally high bar needed to justify the first such raid on the residence of a former president in US history.

Within hours of the news erupting, Trump, his family and inner circle, and a slew of top Republicans across the country, had begun assailing the Biden administration and what they called the 'weaponised Department of Justice' for trying to thwart another presidential bid by Trump in 2024. Several prominent conservatives likened the search to the actions of a tinpot dictator.

Barely 18 months after the violent insurrection at the US Capitol following Trump's claims of a stolen 2020 election, rampant claims by leading Republicans that the justice department is using its formidable powers to interfere in the 2024 presidential election could also be incendiary. On Monday a crowd of angry Trump supporters gathered outside the Palm Beach club in a taste of what might come.

The search warrant granted to the FBI relates to official records, and to the investigation into whether Trump violated the Presidential Records Act. The provision requires the White House to preserve all paperwork and digital output arising from official business and to send it for safe storage to the National Archives.

The fact that the FBI sought a search warrant rather than a subpoena implies that it did not trust Trump to hand over or preserve official documents in his possession.

It has been known for some time that Trump has a vexed relationship with official documents. In June 2018 Politico was reporting that White House staff were being forced to sift 'large piles of shredded paper' and painstakingly tape them back together.

In a strange coincidence of timing, just hours before the raid began Axios released photographs obtained by the *New York Times* reporter Maggie Haberman which appeared to show a White House toilet clogged with wads of handwritten paper. Trump was fingered as the flusher.

The FBI's document operation itself stems back to January, when it was revealed that following protests Trump had returned 15 boxes of documents, gifts and letters to the National Archives. The following month the head of the archive at the time, David Ferriero, told Congress that the boxes included some 'classified national security information', so his staff had 'been in communication with the Department of Justice'.

Asha Rangappa, a former FBI special agent, pointed out that in such a well-trafficked location – and one popular with well-connected international visitors – as Mar-a-Lago, the presence of unsecured classified documents would present a 'national security threat'. That might help explain the DoJ's willingness to take such a dramatic and unprecedented step.

The *Miami Herald* said that the FBI's search warrant indicated that 'dozens of boxes' of alleged classified materials, in addition to the 15 already returned, were thought to still be stored at Trump's Palm Beach residence. According to CNN, the extra boxes had been identified in June when DoJ investigators travelled to Mar-a-Lago to meet two of Trump's lawyers to discuss potentially classified material.

At the start of the meeting Trump paid a visit and chatted to the investigators but without answering questions. His lawyers then took the DoJ officials down to a basement where boxes of documents were being stored; one source told CNN that some of the documents had been stamped 'top secret'. At the heart of the detective work that will now be done on the boxes carted away from Mar-a-Lago is the question that will need to be answered before the DoJ launches any formal prosecution – was Trump intentionally in breach of official records laws?

In the course of the 2016 presidential election Trump accused Hillary Clinton to her face of 'acid washing' or 'bleaching' 33,000 emails. He threatened to have the justice department appoint a special prosecutor to look into the matter, and his rallies were regularly filled with the chant of his supporters referring to her – 'Lock her up! Lock her up!'

In the end, the DoJ decided not to prosecute Clinton as it found no evidence of intent on her part.

A similar calculation is likely to be critical as investigators move forward. Under federal law anyone who removes classified information to an unauthorised location faces fines or imprisonment for up to five years, but only if they can be shown to have done so 'knowingly' and with 'intent'.

13 AUGUST

'She asked me, will they kill you if they discover you?': Afghan girls defy education ban at secret schools

EMMA GRAHAM-HARRISON

When inspectors arrive at the school gate, the older girls know the drill. They slip out of their classes, race to a musty room and huddle together for minutes that sometimes stretch into hours, hoping they won't be found by men who want them shut up at home.

The Taliban have banned secondary education for girls, the only gender-based bar on studying in the world. One year on from the withdrawal of US troops and the militant group's takeover of the country, learning algebra is now an illegal act of resistance.

'I have noticed plenty of changes in our students,' said Arezoo*, the headteacher of one Kabul school that decided to keep its doors open to high school girls in defiance of the ban. 'Psychologically they are under stress all the time, I can see in their eyes and behaviour. They used to come with lots of energy and excitement. Now they are never sure if this will be their last day in class.'

Some inspections last hours and the fear spills over. 'Even the younger girls [who are allowed in school] are affected. When we say the Taliban are coming and the older girls have to hide, the girls in third and fourth grade start crying.'

Taliban officials claim the ban is temporary, variously citing the need to change security, uniforms, teachers, buildings or the curriculum. But many Afghans remember the last time the group were in control, a 'temporary' closure of girls' schools endured for their entire six-year rule.

So as girls slid into depression, robbed of their dreams of becoming doctors, pilots, engineers, teachers or artists, women and men around Afghanistan began fighting back.

'I told my mother I had this idea, to reopen classes for high school girls,' said Jawad*, who manages a private school. 'She asked me: "Will they kill you if they discover you?" I told her no, they will probably just hit me. So she said: "Do it, you'll forget a slap in an hour or two."'

'Secret schools' have sprung up all over the country, as varied as the educators running them. Some are online classes, though they can reach only the minority of Afghans with smartphones and data access.

Some are private schools, operating much as they did before. Others are much more improvised efforts, designed to keep up morale and girls studying something in the hopes schools will reopen, rather than as a substitute for formal education.

'In the beginning everyone was crushed and disappointed, and they would even question the point of studying,' said Mahdia*, who set up a school teaching seventh grade classes in a mosque close to her semi-rural home near a provincial capital.

An engineer who recently graduated near the top of her class at one of Afghanistan's best universities, the 23-year-old worked on infrastructure projects until last summer, and misses her job terribly. But she sees little chance of being allowed back.

'For engineering a lot of our work is in the field and the Taliban are strongly against it for women. All my [female] classmates are unemployed, there is nothing for them to do.' So while she studies English and looks for scholarships to do a further engineering degree in another country, she has decided to teach local girls.

She negotiated with a mosque to hold the classes there – she comes from a Shia community that has avidly supported girls' education over the past two decades – and got practical support from an NGO, Shahmama, which provides textbooks and stationery, and is raising funds to pay the teachers a small stipend. 'I do this as a volunteer, to support the girls and create hope in their future, and the girls also give me hope,' she said.

The group includes one girl who was within weeks of finishing 11th grade when the previous government collapsed, three who were in ninth grade, 11 who were in eighth grade and six who were in seventh grade. 'Of course, sometimes we feel bad to be back in seventh grade, but it's better than sitting at home doing nothing,' said Zarifa*, who has gone back two years. 'We get to meet classmates and revise.'

Schools such as Mahdia's are beacons of hope in a bleak time, and many of their students are filled with extraordinary defiance against the armed men who cut short their studies. 'I have my argument ready if a Talib stops me. I will say: "You didn't study so you are like this, I have to study so I won't be the same,"' said Hasinat*, a seventh grade student.

But the compromises so many girls and teachers have made to be there – repeating grades, hiding from inspectors, swallowing the loss of their own careers – underline how much has been stolen from the women of Afghanistan by their new rulers. And many of the adults running these schools fear their work will not be able to continue indefinitely, because of financial and official pressure.

Illegal classes kept girls' dreams alive last time the Taliban were in power. Those who defied them include the journalist Zahra Joya, named as one of *Time* magazine's women of the year for 2022, and the educator and *Washington Post* columnist Shabana Basij-Rasikh.

They mostly went to primary school during Taliban rule, dressed as boys. Older female students are much harder to conceal, and Jawad is bracing for the day when the girls are discovered in class or their hiding place uncovered.

'Perhaps I can continue this risky job for a year or two but then I may get arrested, and when I do, what will happen to them?' he said.

Even if authorities decide to turn a blind eye to some schools – and they have given at least one prestigious private chain tacit permission to keep some of its branches open outside the capital – a financial crunch looms.

Secret schools all need private funding, and while some comes from NGOs, most rely on fees. Afghanistan's economy is collapsing, expected to shrink by about a third, and many families are struggling to find money for school even when it is a priority.

'The financial situation of the school is very bad since the Taliban. Students were paying 1,500 to 4,000 afghanis a month [£14 to £36], but most of those families left. We have new students now but they can't afford more than 500 to 2,000 a month mostly,' said the manager of one Kabul school.

Jawad decided to restart classes after mothers and fathers begged him to help. 'Education is everything,' said one father whose 10-year-old daughter, something of a prodigy, is newly enrolled in seventh grade there. 'Of course I have concerns for her and me, but I want my daughters to achieve their dreams, I don't want them to just become "aunties", sitting at home all day just asking their husbands for money.'

All names and some identifying details have been changed to protect the girls and their schools.

15 AUGUST

If we don't defend free speech, we live in tyranny: Salman Rushdie shows us that

MARGARET ATWOOD

A long time ago – 7 December 1992, to be exact – I was backstage at a Toronto theatre, taking off a Stetson. With two other writers, Timothy Findley and Paul Quarrington, I'd been performing a medley of 1950s country and western classics, rephrased for writers – 'Ghost Writers in the Sky', 'If I Had the Wings of an Agent', and other fatuous parodies of that nature. It was a PEN Canada benefit of that era: writers dressed up and made idiots of themselves in aid of writers persecuted by governments for things they'd written.

Just as the three of us were bemoaning how awful we'd been, there was a knock on the door. Backstage was locked down, we were told. Secret agents were talking into their sleeves. Salman Rushdie had been spirited into the country. He was about to appear on stage with Bob Rae, the premier of Ontario, the first head of government in the world to support him in public. 'And you, Margaret, as past president of PEN Canada, are going to introduce him,' I was told.

Gulp. 'Oh, OK,' I said. And so I did. It was a money-where-your-mouth-is moment.

And, with the recent attack on him, so is this.

Rushdie exploded on to the literary scene in 1981 with his second novel, *Midnight's Children*, which won the Booker prize that year. No wonder: its inventiveness, range, historical scope and verbal dexterity were breath-taking, and it opened the door to subsequent generations of writers who might previously have felt that their identities or subject matter excluded them from the movable feast that is English-language literature. He has ticked every box except the Nobel prize: he has been knighted; he is on everyone's list of significant British writers; he has collected an impressive bouquet of prizes and honours, but, most importantly, he has touched and inspired a great many people around the globe. A huge number of writers and readers have long owed him a major debt.

Suddenly, they owe him another one. He has long defended freedom of artistic expression against all comers; now, even should he recover from his injuries, he is a martyr to it.

In any future monument to murdered, tortured, imprisoned and persecuted writers, Rushdie will feature large. On 12 August he was stabbed on stage by an assailant at a literary event at Chautauqua, a venerable American institution in upstate New York. Yet again 'that sort of thing never happens here' has been proven false: in our present world, anything can happen anywhere. American democracy is under threat as never before: the attempted assassination of a writer is just one more symptom.

Without doubt, this attack was directed at him because his fourth novel, *The Satanic Verses*, a satiric fantasy that he himself believed was dealing with the disorientation felt by immigrants from (for instance) India to Britain, got used as a tool in a political power struggle in a distant country.

When your regime is under pressure, a little book-burning creates a popular distraction. Writers don't have an army. They don't have billions of dollars. They don't have a captive voting bloc. They thus make cheap scapegoats. They're so easy to blame: their medium is words, which are by nature ambiguous and subject to misinterpretation, and they themselves are often mouthy, if not downright curmudgeonly. Worse, they frequently speak truth to power. Even apart from that, their books will annoy some people. As writers themselves have frequently said, if what you've written is universally liked, you must be doing something wrong. But when you offend a ruler, things can get lethal, as many writers have discovered.

In Rushdie's case, the power that used him as a pawn was the Ayatollah Khomeini of Iran. In 1989, he issued a fatwa – a rough equivalent to the bulls of excommunication used by medieval and renaissance Catholic popes as weapons against both secular rulers and theological challengers such as Martin Luther. Khomeini also offered a large reward to anyone who would murder Rushdie. There were numerous killings and attempted assassinations, including the stabbing of the Japanese translator Hitoshi Igarashi in 1991. Rushdie himself spent many years in enforced hiding, but gradually he came out of his cocoon – the Toronto PEN event being the most significant first step – and, in the past two decades, he'd been leading a relatively normal life.

However, he never missed an opportunity to speak out on behalf of the principles he'd been embodying all his writing life. Freedom of expression was foremost among these. Once a yawn-making liberal platitude, this concept has now become a hot-button issue, since the extreme right has attempted to kidnap it in the service of libel, lies and hatred, and the extreme left has tried to toss it out the window in the service of its version of earthly perfection. It doesn't take a crystal ball to foresee many panel discussions on the subject, should we reach a moment in which rational debate is possible. But whatever it is, the right to freedom of expression does not include the right to defame, to lie maliciously and damagingly about provable facts, to issue death threats, or to advocate murder. These should be punished by law.

As for those who are still saying, 'yes, but ...' about Rushdie – some version of 'he should have known better', as in 'yes, too bad about the rape, but why was she wearing that revealing skirt' – I can only remark that there are no perfect victims. In fact, there are no perfect artists, nor is there any perfect art. Anti-censorship folks often find themselves having to defend work they would otherwise review scathingly, but such defending is necessary, unless we are all to have our vocal cords removed.

Long ago, a Canadian member of parliament described a ballet as 'a bunch of fruits jumping around in long underwear'. Let them jump, say I! Living in a pluralistic democracy means being surrounded by a multiplicity of voices, some of which will be saying things you don't like. Unless you're prepared to uphold their right to speak, as Salman Rushdie has done so often, you'll end up living in a tyranny.

Rushdie didn't plan to become a free-speech hero, but he is one now. Writers everywhere – those who are not state hacks or brainwashed robots – owe him a huge vote of thanks.

19 AUGUST

Country diary: The murderous wails of polecats in high summer

NICOLA CHESTER

Nothing seems to be sleeping in the heat. Our neighbour's bedroom TV plays a loop of old films, so clipped, forthright phrases drift into the night. Sparrows flutter uncomfortably in the eaves between us. Even the lullaby drone of the field-away combine harvester isn't soothing. Flints lie on our fields like broken crockery, and there have already been combine-sparked flint fires. We are all a bit jittery.

A sudden hysterical yikkering outside makes me sit up. The polecats are back! I go first to the window and then outside, grabbing the big lamp on my way, keeping it switched off. In high summer, jill polecats and their kits can be vocal for several nights, play-hunt-fighting in the arable.

The barley shifts and crackles up to the garden gate like a dry, restless sea. I stand and watch. There are more close, loud, murderous wails, yips and squabbling. These whirling dervishes must be just feet away. Subconsciously, I curl my toes in and tuck my nightdress between my knees.

The sound becomes a crescendo. In a moment of doubt, I switch on the lamp – perhaps it is cats after all, or fox cubs – and there is a face. The briefest snapshot: bright eyes in a Lone Ranger bandit mask, fierce, ferrety features, a teddy bear's ears and nose. It vanishes after the ripple of barley ahead, flowing its luxuriant, snatched-back stole of black-and-cream sable behind it. I hear myself gasp.

The former gamekeeper sometimes called them by their old names: 'fitch' or 'foulmart'. They have returned to southern England from a wild population in Wales, on their own terms, coming back to reclaim territory and their own right to roam. They are on the edge of my hearing when the combine reaches a gap in the hedge, raises its wide header on the turn with a roar and a flash of headlights, illuminating a plume of chalk dust like smoke.

I think of the glimpse of sable fur, a smouldering coat of fury, ash and white-hot embers. A thrilling fire starter of an animal. From behind me, canned laughter peals from next door's upstairs window.

One Welsh town offers a window on to the catastrophe facing Britain. But where are the politicians?

ADITYA CHAKRABORTTY

The little van trundles on to the estate, and out of the small terrace houses pour mums clutching a purse in one hand and a child in the other. They're not hurrying for 99 Flakes but for the essentials of life, such as bread and soap. Things that they can't easily afford anywhere else.

If you want a closeup of the cost of living crisis, don't ask an economist – speak to someone living it. The people in this queue in the town of Shotton, north Wales, have their monthly budgets memorised down to the last decimal place. 'Went down the shops this morning. Guess how much they're charging for a cucumber?' asks Deana. '£1.10.' There are gasps. One woman frets about feeding her ginger rescue cat, Thomas. A couple of years ago £2 bought 10 cans of his brand of cat food; today, she says, it's £4.95 for eight.

The mobile shop, from the local firm Well Fed, undercuts even the town's Iceland. Deana gets her cucumber here for 50p and walks home with a big bag of fruit and veg. She and her five-year-old boy won't go without for now, but within weeks she thinks they may have to. 'When winter comes – bang.'

By Deana's reckoning, the only thing standing between her and disaster is this summer's surreal warmth. Once that fades away then it's 'lights on at 3pm, heating on' – and fuel bills up by the kind of sum that will capsize her family. 'Am I going to get through this winter?' she asks unprompted. 'I don't really know.' I have rarely heard someone discuss the prospect of their own ruin in such an even tone.

Newspapers cover the cost of living as a crisis of economics, society or politics, but it is now larger than all those pigeonholes. Britain is sliding towards a humanitarian catastrophe.

That term is usually reserved for faraway countries devastated by hurricanes or drought, rather than rich societies whose citizens wear Apple watches and enjoy a cheeky Deliveroo. But if we use the UN definition of a humanitarian crisis as 'a singular event or a series of events that are threatening in terms of [the] health, safety or wellbeing of a ... large group of people', then that's exactly where we are heading.

By this time next week, the energy watchdog will have announced that fuel bills are set to rise by 80 per cent. As that increase comes into effect on 1 October, plus another in the new year, about 45 million Britons – two-thirds of our entire population – are projected to sink into fuel poverty. Westminster has gone AWOL. As inflation this week hit a 40-year high, the prime minister was sunning himself on a Greek island. Keir Starmer has spent months scraping together half a policy on gas and electricity bills, which is effectively a backstop for the big six energy firms. Meanwhile, daily life for millions of people is rapidly becoming unaffordable. Rents are shooting up, petrol remains expensive and, as Deana and her neighbours know, food prices are rocketing.

Over at the offices of the local Welsh Senedd member, Jack Sargeant, they've noticed a big change in the volume and type of requests for help they're getting. The usual targeted emails from familiar constituents are being replaced by Facebook messages sent by those who've never before got in touch. 'They're vague, because they don't know what to ask for – just that their mum needs help or their neighbour's in a bad way,' says staffer Ed Stubbs. 'And next week we'll get more, as parents start thinking about school uniforms.'

When a country in Africa is hit by a humanitarian emergency, the impeccably coiffed TV correspondents point out how long it has been teetering on the brink of disaster. What will they say here in their potted histories? In Shotton you might start the story in March 1980, when the giant steelworks shut and 6,500 locals were slung out of work in one day – at that time the largest industrial redundancy in western Europe. A much smaller plant today finishes steel that comes out of Port Talbot, while a couple of miles away is the real indicator of Shotton's present-day fortunes: an Amazon warehouse. Together with shops and food factories, it makes up a big chunk of the local labour market. For everyone else, there is Universal Credit and the kind of low-income ducking and diving that statisticians classify as self-employment. And I mean low income: in parts of this town, almost half of the kids are growing up in poverty.

Food banks began in the UK as a stopgap, yet donated tins and leftover bread have become a part of our welfare state. As Robbie Davison, who runs Well Fed, says: 'It's not food that people would choose for themselves. It's a model that says, "We know you're poor, and this'll do." That's right wing.' I have previously written about Davison and his alternative model of getting good food to everyone, regardless of their income. His business squeezes its profit margins to do meals on wheels and generous ready meals at £2 a pop, and he lobbies for councils and others to get on board.

At the local housing association, Clwyd Alyn, they now provide Well Fed's lunches for free to all staff. The scheme began this spring after the chief executive, Clare Budden, noticed that some employees weren't eating at work, while others were taking a lot of overtime to get by. Already paying in line with the market, Budden's team concluded that another salary rise would get part-taxed away. Free lunches on the other hand can save full-time employees about £100 a month. When I met Budden at Davison's kitchens, she had brought along Robin Rolfe, one of her guys in IT who noted that meal breaks were now more social than a sad sandwich eaten at a desk.

It was a rare moment of cheer before their thoughts turned back to the months ahead. Rolfe talked of starving his family's pre-pay meter of money. Budden has plans to give out hot-water bottles and blankets to her housing association tenants. 'I worry about some of our tenants not getting through the winter because they're not going to put the heating on.'

'This is wartime, in a modern age,' says Davison. 'All the lights will be on in the city centres; we'll still have all the trappings ...' Budden laughs: 'We'll still have the John Lewis ad and it [will make] us all cry and want to spend money we don't have.'

And on an estate on the other side of Shotton the signs will still warn against ballgames being played on the grass, and for pet owners to pick up after their dogs. But God alone knows what will happen to the families inside those small homes.

'You don't think strikes are the answer? What is?' RMT's Mick Lynch on work, dignity and union power

ZOE WILLIAMS

It is rare, these days, for the general secretary of a trade union, let alone a small one, to become a national figure. Yet Mick Lynch has done exactly that. The leader of the National Union of Rail, Maritime and Transport Workers (RMT), which represents 80,000 members, doesn't like flattery. Nonetheless, as the rail strikes in Britain enter their third month, he will concede that 'a lot of people are telling me I'm doing good'.

I meet him in the RMT's boardroom, round the corner from Euston station in central London, where the RMT recently had 1,000 people turn up at very short notice, to support a picket line in the dispute between railway workers and Network Rail. Lynch looks, in his own words, like 'the personification of what an RMT general secretary is': white, male, bald, 60. He is making the point that he hopes the RMT will be more diverse in the future. He also looks like a man in charge of the moment: relaxed, with an easy sense of humour. I can't think of a time in my life when that has been the stereotype of a trade unionist.

He has shot to prominence by going on TV and radio and running rings around everyone. Piers Morgan tried the most ridiculous attack line – why did he have a picture of a Thunderbirds baddie as his Facebook profile? Was it because he is a villain?

Lynch's detached, almost amused scorn spoke for many of us, not just about Piers Morgan, but also about how long we have been putting up with a media culture that means you can find 17 stories about the orphan/pensioner/dog who had their day ruined by a rail strike, but if you want a sober explanation of what the strike is about you will have more luck on TikTok. (It is about whether railway workers will accept what the RMT says is a real-terms pay cut over the next two years, plus the loss of one third of frontline maintenance roles and half of scheduled maintenance work. In short, they will not.)

'The state of journalism,' he says, shaking his head. 'The questions they ask are so ...' He chooses his word carefully. 'Dopey. They obviously don't know what trade unions are. They think that we are all these clichés that they perpetuate. I'm a baron. My members are pawns. I can just move them about according to who I want to annoy that morning. Which is completely the wrong way around: unions are very democratic. It sounds a bit pompous, but the members are sovereign in this union. They tell us what to do.'

The traditional attacks on striking transport workers – that they are out to stop hard-working people getting to work, that they are better-paid than you anyway – are failing to land. A poll during the strikes in June showed that 70 per cent of the public supported the railway workers getting a pay rise that took into account the cost of living. The classic, convoluted centre-left position, held by Labour – that the demands are fair but strikes are bad – has come unstuck; the same poll found that only 18 per cent of people were opposed to railway workers' right to strike. 'The bishop of Durham was on a panel with me last week, saying: "I identify with the issues, but I don't think strike action is the answer,"' Lynch says. 'But what is the answer? Do we pray, or play tiddlywinks, or have a sponsored silence? What is there for working people to do if they're not organised?'

Something has changed. Conservative MPs' insistence that railway workers' conditions are pretty good, actually, is no longer provoking kneejerk resentment; it is generating solidarity. At the launch rally last week for the cost of living campaign Enough Is Enough, Lynch brought the house down. 'Our message must be this ... the working class is back,' he said. 'We refuse to be meek, we refuse to be humble, we refuse to wait for politicians and policy-writers – and we refuse to be poor any more.'

Today, he says: 'They [the Tories] are saying: "Because you've got the final-salary pension, because you've got sick pay and decent holiday pay, because you've got the ability to negotiate and not just be consulted on your working time and working practices, that's all out of date. You're out of fashion." Everybody else in the country, at fulfilment centres or mega-warehouses, where they chase you around night and day, there's no dignity in the work, is saying: "Well, why am I treated like this? Why can't I have a union?"'

Lynch had no great ambition to lead the RMT, he says. 'I didn't want Bob [Crow, a lefty firebrand who died at 52 in 2014 of a heart attack] to pass on, and I didn't want Mick Cash to have to retire last year, but he did. So we're here. I didn't become an officer in this union till I was 54. I didn't have a trade union career. I was out doing my shifts. I was on the tools for 37 years, as an electrician.'

Lynch has never been on a trade union course. He says there is nothing special about him, or the way he argues. 'There's lots of people who could be in my position, doing what I'm doing. And that's what they find so shocking, middle-class journalists, present company excepted: that they meet somebody who might have read something in their own time, or is able to go toe to toe with senior people in industry while being on the tools.'

He was born in Paddington, west London, to Irish parents. It was a big family (he is one of five) with no money (his father, a shop steward, went on strike for seven weeks in 1971 and the hit on their income was unimaginable). He says he didn't notice, because he was the youngest and his siblings shielded him from it. 'But you weren't indebted. That was the key difference in working-class communities. People now are carrying debt that my parents would have thought: "That is impossible."'

He left school at 16 and did an apprenticeship. He rattles through his brothers' and sister's work – a painter-decorator, a teacher, a plasterer, a midwife – to illustrate that the horizons were fairly broad, especially with free tertiary education. There were a lot of jobs, and the workplace was quite attractive, before Margaret Thatcher came to power.

His childhood was happy, he says: 'I've got no complaints. We were a coherent family. My mum and dad didn't split up. None of us went to prison. We weren't in trouble; we were a respectable family. But, from my memory, there were a lot of families like that. Everyone paints working-class communities as being in crisis the whole time, as if there's no sense of humour, there's no fun or joy.'

He worked in construction until he was blacklisted for union organising, at which point he moved to the railways. As happy as he is to talk about the casualisation of the building industry, he is careful to underline that declining conditions are a problem for everyone. 'In your industry [journalism], people who are stringers or casualised find it very difficult. In universities, there's no security whatsoever [for early-career lecturers and researchers and, increasingly, with 'fire and rehire', for mid-career academics]. People are beholden to whoever's doling out the work.'

The reasons for this have to do with more than the decline of unionisation, he says. 'People have lost the ability to organise generally, I think, even in communities. Where I grew up, there was a residents' association, which had some of the most fearsome women you'd ever deal with – working-class women, who could stand up and articulate in front of councillors exactly the services they wanted.'

Then there is the fact we are two generations on from Thatcher. A lot of working people aren't old enough to remember the assumptions of the mid-80s, when 'you'd expect a level of dignity. You respected people for being workers and you had to respect workers' organisations ... People have been told that they should be grateful for having a job, grateful for earning a living. They've been told that if you can't earn enough in one job, to go and get a second job.'

But you could argue Tony Blair was even more influential than Thatcher, in terms of outsourcing and subcontracting on a huge scale. Now, the NHS, TfL and many other employers get their cleaners from a third party, while local authorities subcontract their housing duties to housing associations and their social care duties to exploitative providers. The results have been catastrophic for working and living conditions.

In the care sector, for example, you will find workers paid the minimum wage in 15-minute segments and expected to provide the car and fuel to get them from one appointment to the next – yet they don't strike, 'because it affects people who need their care'. Plus, of course, poverty wages strip away the option of forgoing pay.

On this point, he has a gripe about the EU: 'Everyone told us the European Union would solve all this.' This riles me a bit: however we got here, it wasn't via Brussels. The RMT was a pro-Brexit union. It is not affiliated to Labour and can't be held responsible for the party's fudge, but it still contributed, I think, to the split on the left over Brexit that left Boris Johnson looking like the one with the answers.

He deflects that: the RMT is a small union; it wasn't that influential; in any case, he still opposes the EU for its lack of democratic levers. 'But I'm not making the point about remain or leave. Frankly, I find all that tedious now. The point I'm making is that we can't wait for court judgments and policy decisions. What I'm trying to encourage, with Sharon Graham [the general secretary of Unite] and Dave Ward [the general secretary of the Communication Workers Union] and others, is we've got to put the industrial flag up.'

The RMT's next campaign will be for cleaners in the transport industry. Lynch wants to get other unions involved, for cleaners in the NHS and beyond. The long game is to 'punch a hole in subcontracting and make it really expensive. It's a means of exploitation and people are fed up. Labour have got to say: "We believe in in-house work."'

He rattles off a list of other things the opposition should say: end low pay; end the housing crisis with municipally run, municipally owned council homes; end food poverty. 'You've got to get people to identify with you, through values.' He shrugs off Keir Starmer's proposal to freeze the energy price cap as insufficiently radical: 'That's gonna cost £60 billion. So we're gonna take that money off ourselves and give it to those companies to subsidise the price they're charging the people they're getting the money off.'

He would rather the government sequestered North Sea gas and capped the wholesale price. I run this past a friend later, who remarks sarcastically: 'It worked for Hugo Chávez.' The Venezuelan president nationalised important industries in the 00s, but by the time of his death in 2013 the country was struggling with high inflation and endless shortages. But socialist chaos looks a lot less scary in the middle of a crisis of late-stage capitalism.

Lynch was attacked in various newspapers last week as a Putin apologist, after accusing the EU of empire-building and saying: 'There were a lot of corrupt politicians in Ukraine.' That was true before Volodymyr Zelenskiy, but has also been one of Putin's attack lines. It is hard not to see it as a response to his popularity, an attempt to discredit him, but he is sanguine about it.

'Anyone that knows me in this organisation knows that I condemned the Soviet Union; I thought it was a murderous death cult. I never played with any of the symbolism of red stars and hammers and sickles. All oppressive regimes, without exception, are oppressive of workers and peasants. And then people tell me I'm a Putin apologist? I'm not. Putin should stop the war, get out of Ukraine and respect the sovereignty of that nation.'

It is unrealistic at this point to think that we can avoid a Liz Truss government, however long it lasts. She has promised to go to war with unions, pledging legislation within 30 days to curb union powers; Grant Shapps, the transport secretary, has chimed in to threaten redundancies. 'So they're escalating the battle. We're going to have to respond in kind. But this will need a union-wide response. It needs the Labour party, because they are the movement. We're going to need the support of the community and the whole of Britain's public opinion. It's got to be bigger than my trade union, because we're not able to do this on our own.'

24 AUGUST

'I can't believe this is happening': Ukraine marks 31 years of independence

ISOBEL KOSHIW

As Ukraine marks 31 years of statehood, Kyiv's streets are a far cry from the way they looked six months ago when thousands were fleeing in panic and military checkpoints operated on most corners.

The very real feeling of imminent death – which jolted the population into mounting a large-scale, voluntary resistance – has subsided outside the frontline areas in the south and east. Most restaurants and businesses in the capital have gradually reopened. But like Kyiv's tree-lined streets and summer clothes, the physical aspects of life returning to normal have not outweighed the inner pain many Ukrainians are experiencing – brought home even more by the muted public holiday.

'As I'm speaking to you now, I have goosebumps. People I know, my godson even, is fighting at the front. There is no celebration today. I can't even believe that this is happening,' said Yana Pasychnyk, a choral singer in one of Ukraine's national choirs.

Wearing a traditional Ukrainian blouse, Pasychnyk was heading home after performing hymns for Ukraine at Kyiv's St Sophia Cathedral. 'I'm constantly worried and praying that our skies remain blue, and I understand that people are giving their lives for this,' said Pasychnyk.

Her feelings are common. This year's public holiday is not being met with the traditional parade in Kyiv and countrywide town-square celebrations. Ukraine has banned gatherings amid security concerns. The country and its Western allies say Russia plans to step up attacks on civilian infrastructure around independence day.

Ukraine's general staff has warned Ukrainians not to ignore the air raid sirens, the frequency of which caused them to lose potency within the first few weeks of the war.

Visits to a Kyiv metro during two of the four sirens on Wednesday found only about 20 people on their phones, waiting out the sirens, while dozens more waited for trains undeterred, as they did before the war.

The twists and turns of Ukraine's independence period, during which there have been six presidents and two revolutions, have forced Ukraine to adapt to a rollercoaster of economic and political changes.

The future of the Ukrainian state is almost entirely dependent on continued Western military supplies to fight Russia and financing to sustain its economy. Western support in turn derives from Ukrainians constantly agitating and demonstrating continued resistance.

Ukraine's president, Volodymyr Zelenskiy, wrote on Instagram that Ukraine was marking independence day during a war for independence and he hoped one day soon Ukrainians would be able to congratulate each other on victory day, too.

Ukrainian forces managed to push Russian forces out of the north of the country. The frontlines remain relatively stable in the east and south, of which Russia now occupies 20 per cent. The military losses on both sides have been phenomenal, considering the timeframe.

Ukraine says it has lost almost 9,000 men, though the figure is impossible to verify independently. Russia has not yet named a total. The US believes Russian losses amount to at least

15,000 men, while the Ukrainians put the figure at more than double that.

Ukraine's defence minister, Oleksii Reznikov, told CNN that Ukraine is past the worst of the war. Reznikov said: 'We are in a stage of stabilising all the battlefield or battle lines with the small moving of the units, and we made a lot of good deterrents there.'

Russia's defence minister, Sergei Shoigu, contradicted Reznikov's assertion that the lack of movement along the frontlines was a result of Ukrainian successes. Shoigu said Russian forces were deliberately slowing down their offensive to prevent civilian casualties, a statement he first made in May.

Though it is difficult to measure their accuracy, two recent polls indicate the mood of Ukrainians chimes with Zelenskiy and Reznikov's confidence. The polls put the number of Ukrainians who believe Ukraine will be victorious over Russia at between 90 per cent and 98 per cent. But for at least some Ukrainians it is difficult to muster faith in the idea of victory, despite the reams of positive messaging each day.

'I think this is all a geopolitical game and I don't think Ukraine has a chance of winning,' said Alla, a 40-year-old Buddhist teacher, sitting on a bench in central Kyiv. 'If you had a family and some massive guy came along, would you put them out to be slaughtered? It's all very sad.'

Thirty-one years ago, Ukraine's parliament voted for the country to leave the Soviet Union and break from Moscow's control. It was its first successful attempt after two previous failures. Ukrainians had long considered themselves a nation denied a state by various imperial powers, primarily Russia.

When independence was declared in 1991, there was no bloodshed. However, Ukraine's deputy KGB chief at the time, Yevhen Marchuk, later said in interviews that central command in Moscow had attempted to thwart the process, seeing it as an affront.

This strand of KGB thinking is what some believe has led to Russia's violent invasion this year, having been absorbed by Russia's president, Vladimir Putin, once a KGB operative, and members of his inner circle.

'If we stopped fighting that will be the end,' said Yaroslav Dmytrovych, 27, who was setting up a stand of rental bikes. 'Russia has no freedom of speech. I want to live in Ukraine where it's more interesting, happier and there are more opportunities.

'At the moment I feel OK. The sirens have ended. But everyone is waiting for something to happen and we don't know what it will be.'

29 AUGUST

The Edinburgh fringe is too long, too expensive and too gruelling. It must change or die

BRIAN LOGAN

With litter strewn across the streets, the heavens opening, and drawn faces on every comic who didn't make the awards shortlists, there's a post-apocalyptic feel to the end of this year's Edinburgh fringe. Is it just the bin strike and the undeniable fact that the festival is far too long? 'The only thing that should last a month,' as the comic Sarah Keyworth joked, 'is a month.' Or is there more to it, a sense – long brewing, ever harder to ignore – that the fringe festival model is broken? 'Ultimately,' as the comedy producer Owen Donovan tweeted, 'it comes down to a lot of people having a shit time, both those on and offstage.'

I've spent my whole professional life loving the Edinburgh fringe, a wonder of the cultural world. Where else do creativity, youthful resourcefulness and idealism, the urge to experiment and the need to hustle, ever come together so intensely – and in such glorious profusion? And with a gorgeous castle-on-a-freaking-volcano backdrop to boot? But in recent years, my enthusiasm has been increasingly smothered by caveats: that the fringe is too absurdly expensive for artists, to a degree that excludes many; that it's insufficiently diverse; that it can be overwhelming, gruelling and lonely for many of the people taking part.

This year, these conversations felt louder than ever. A new generation, and rising standards around access and inclusion, have understandably lowered tolerance for the fringe's peculiarities – the impossibly high turnover of shows, say, or the whiter audiences than you find in London (where many of the participants make their living), or all that sitting tightly packed in dank underground catacombs, having first scaled some impossibly steep cobbled slope to their front door. Add to this audience numbers being down 25 per cent on pre-pandemic years, the diminution of mainstream media coverage, and the disappearance of several features (the fringe app, the Half Price Hut, the Total theatre awards) that helped level the event's uneven playing field, and more artists are asking themselves: is it worth the candle?

For some, the answer is still yes. It's not just a myth that the festival is a seedbed for the entertainment stars of tomorrow. To cite only recent examples, Channel 4's *Taskmaster*, the BBC's *Starstruck*, and *Alma's Not Normal*, and *This Is Going to Hurt* – they all have their roots on the fringe. (See? I didn't even mention Phoebe Waller-Bridge ...) Would they have happened anyway? Maybe –

but I'd give some credit to that #edfringe atmos, the premium it places on experiment and novelty, the cross-fertilisation of creativities at play. Could that be easily recreated elsewhere? I'd like to see you try.

And make no mistake: there were a good few Waller-Bridges and (that other go-to example of Edinburgh star-making) Tom Stoppards in embryo this August. In theatre, Haley McGee proved a real tour de force with *Age Is a Feeling*, tracing our journey from young adulthood to death, while Karim Khan won the Popcorn prize with the 'vital and moving' *Brown Boys Swim*. In comedy, Leo Reich's satirical stand-up on Gen Z self-absorption announced the arrival of an extraordinary talent. And Jordan Gray – working-class, trans and supernova-ing from the stage – told audiences on Friday night: 'This has been the best month of my life.' The fringe can still have that effect on people, from all backgrounds.

But it's never just about the talent. It's about the get-together. It's about taking the temperature of where the culture is at, and where it's heading. The eclipse of the great white male? That's here in theatre (Brokentalkers' *Masterclass*) and comedy (Jayde Adams's *Men, I Can Save You*). Fracturing mental health as we stagger out of a pandemic and into a country teetering on the brink? Good luck finding the comedy shows that don't address that. Woke – and the war on it? The fringe is a crucible for that conversation, in maverick shows by rookie talents (Sam Nicoresti's *Cancel Anti Wokeflake Snow Culture*) and in the debate about the cancellation of veteran comic misanthrope Jerry Sadowitz.

That all happens elsewhere, too, you could argue. Yes, it does – but there's value in creating spaces where it can happen in concentrated form. Where, for just a few weeks a year, art and ideas are the conversation, not the afterthought. I was struck by the novelist Elif Shafak's response to the attack on Salman Rushdie a fortnight ago, which she construed as an attack on the literary festival itself: 'One of our last remaining democratic spaces ... where one can both speak one's mind freely [and also] hear someone else's story.'

At a time when cultural spaces are closing, the study of the humanities threatened, funding for the arts shrinking, nuance falling out of fashion and censoriousness on the rise, we need to defend events like the Edinburgh fringe, where art, imagination and play are amplified and celebrated, not undermined.

But to defend it, we need to reform it. It's not right that artists must ransom their futures to the cost of their Edinburgh accommodation, and that many (particularly those from backgrounds already marginalised in the arts) can't afford to come at all – or don't feel welcome when they do. These concerns are not being adequately addressed, in part because there's no central authority with sufficient jurisdiction to do so. The fringe is unregulated, wonderfully so, you might say, when it's working. But – spoiler alert – laissez-faire only takes you so far. The lack of anyone to take responsibility is a problem right now.

The Edinburgh festival started with a noble vision 75 years ago, to heal the wounds of war with the balm of culture. Is that a dream worth fighting for? Or should we accept – as Tim Crouch suggests in his fringe hit *Truth's a Dog Must to Kennel* – that live performance, and our liberal aspirations for it, are a busted flush? Is persisting with the fringe, in Crouch's formulation, 'like keeping your dead mum in the freezer to claim the pension'?

Let's thrash it out. A statement posted yesterday by the fringe's eight major producing venues protested about the 'soaring accommodation costs' that threaten the fringe's sustainability. We need a constitutional convention, these venues urged, at which everyone – Edinburgh city council, local residents, the Fringe society and the EIF, Creative Scotland, the Arts Council, performers and representatives from their industries – assembles to map a route forward. We're now approaching 'change or die' territory. And 'die' would be a terrible waste.

For all its problems, the fringe is a jewel in the crown of this country's – and the world's – cultural life. We would miss it if it were gone. Let's create a festival fit for the heroes who year after year bring their dreams, their creativity and their – still, in spite of everything, but for how long? – indomitable spirit to Edinburgh.

31 AUGUST

A peaceful yet radical social transformer: Mikhail Gorbachev leaves a blazing legacy

ARCHIE BROWN

Mikhail Gorbachev was the most significant political leader of the second half of the 20th century and one of the greatest reformers in Russian history. By the time he resigned as president of the USSR during its final throes, he had played the decisive role in making Russia a freer country than it had ever been. The new tolerance and liberties at home, together with the transformation of Soviet foreign policy, emboldened the peoples of eastern and central Europe to send their communist rulers packing and to reject Moscow's overlordship. As Gorbachev was also the most pacific of all Soviet leaders, not a shot was fired by a Soviet soldier while the Warsaw Pact countries achieved independence from 1989, when the Berlin Wall fell in November that year, or when Germany was reunited in 1990.

There is a popular fallacy in the West that the Soviet Union had reached crisis point by 1985, that the Communist party's politburo chose Gorbachev as general secretary because he was a reformer, and that therefore he had no option but to undertake radical changes. An authoritarian regime is in crisis when its laws and commands are no longer obeyed, when there is persistent mass protest and, in particular, when such social unrest is accompanied by open splits within the political elite.

But none of this was present in 1985 – in fact, such unrest did not occur until a few years into Gorbachev's *perestroika* reforms. Far from crisis leaving no option but reform, it was radical reform that provoked crisis. The new freedoms enabled the repressed grievances of 70 years, including ethno-national grievances, to rise to the surface of political life.

The idea that poor economic performance in the mid-1980s had forced reform through is belied not only by the country's quiescence under Gorbachev's predecessor, Konstantin Chernenko, but the fact that Gorbachev prioritised political over economic reform. This did nothing to improve conditions in the command economy – for in the new political climate, commands could be circumvented or ignored, and people became free not merely to grumble in private but to complain in public about queues and shortages.

It was as late as 1990 that Gorbachev embraced a market economy in principle, stressing that it should be of a social democratic type. However, by then he had lost much of his earlier political authority and did not take the risk of moving to market – and higher – prices for basic foodstuffs and utilities, so the Soviet economy ended in limbo, neither centrally controlled nor market-driven.

Yet Gorbachev's political reforms were extraordinarily bold. He had an unusually open mind for any political leader, never mind a Soviet Communist party general secretary. The *glasnost* (greater transparency) Gorbachev advocated from the outset of his leadership developed, with his blessing, into a freedom of speech and, increasingly, of publication. By 1989, literary works whose very possession in underground or foreign editions had been a criminal offence were published in Moscow in huge print-runs – among them George Orwell's *Nineteen Eighty-Four* and even Aleksandr Solzhenitsyn's *The Gulag Archipelago*. Dissidents were released from prison and exile and the rehabilitation of those unjustly repressed in the past (begun under Nikita Khrushchev and abandoned by Leonid Brezhnev) was resumed. Gorbachev encouraged a new freedom of communication across frontiers. That included an end to the blocking of foreign broadcasts and a developing freedom of travel.

During less than seven years in the Kremlin, Gorbachev achieved the kinds of reforms that no previous Soviet leader would have contemplated. The changes were also beyond the wildest dreams of Western leaders in 1985 (as Margaret Thatcher acknowledged) and of Soviet reformers at that time, as I know from my conversations with them.

That did not prevent some of those same reformers casti-gating Gorbachev by 1990 for his supposed 'half-measures' and transferring their allegiance to Boris Yeltsin. He began in 1985 as a communist reformer. By 1988 he had turned into a systemic transformer. As he put it in 1996: 'Until 1988 I had the same illusions as previous reformers. I believed that the system could be improved. In 1988 I realised we needed systemic reform. The system had to be replaced.' That was not merely a retrospective judgment. Addressing a closed meeting of regional party secre-taries in April 1988, Gorbachev asked: 'On what basis do 20 million [party members] rule 200 million?' He answered his own question: 'We conferred on ourselves the right to rule the people!'

Two months later he startled most delegates at the 19th party conference by announcing that contested elections for a new legislature with real powers would take place not later than the spring of the following year – and in March 1989 they were duly held. They marked an end to 'democratic centralism', for party members were allowed to compete against one another on fundamentally different policy platforms. This was merely a first step in trial-and-error democratisation, but after it, the Soviet Union could never be the same again.

That the Soviet communist system ceased to exist was not an unintended consequence of Gorbachev's actions, for he and his most like-minded associates consciously dismantled that system. What Gorbachev did not intend was the dissolution of the Soviet state. He strove to keep as many republics as possible within a 'renewed union' by negotiation and voluntary agreement and turn what had previously been a pseudo-federation into a genuinely federal state. He failed in that endeavour, but resisted calls from party and state officials, including the leadership of the KGB, to maintain the union by force.

Gorbachev was in failing health in recent years and saddened by the way his greatest achievements were being destroyed. As a boy in a peasant household in southern Russia, he had been especially close to his Ukrainian maternal grandparents. War between Russia and Ukraine in 2022 was for him the ultimate devastating blow. In one of his last interviews a few years ago, he was asked what he thought his epitaph should be. His answer was: 'We tried.'

6 September

At least Liz Truss's dull delivery skills will make oncoming crises seem less dramatic

MARINA HYDE

Well, there it is. The UK's third prime minister in just over three years is Liz Truss, the troubling result of a lab accident in which a community-centre asset-stripper was crossbred with a Live-Laugh-Love decal.

Her predecessor, Boris Johnson, left Downing Street this morning after an arrogant, lie-heavy speech, in which he displayed his character development after three years in office – precisely zero. None of his children were there (it's actually quite a small street). He remains a short king over the water for any number of Conservatives who somehow still yearn to be shackled to a wildly underachieving narcissist who openly despises them. There's being psychologically beaten, and then there's ... that.

A few hours later, Truss flew to Balmoral to meet the Queen, who she once wanted to abolish but now finds it more personally convenient to revere. Presumably Her Majesty asked Truss to form a government in the same way you might ask a telemarketer if you can call them back in five minutes. It's always good when people explain what the Queen's outfits mean; I assume that today's choice telegraphed amused relief that she could be the only person spared having to hear Truss butcher a reading from Ecclesiastes at her funeral.

Truss uses the word 'delivery' a lot for someone whose own delivery would lose the Bafta to an HGV announcing 'This vehicle is reversing'. The vocal that will be delivering all the bad news to you this winter is slightly less appealing than a dental drill, if any of you are lucky enough to still have a dentist. Can you Auto-Tune the spoken word? I'd make Simon Cowell my comms chief if I were her. Truss does at least seem capable of reversing, having made 'no handouts' a central feature of her campaign. The current best intel on her energy plan suggests that she might allow energy companies to avoid a windfall tax by freezing bills at the current level and setting the unit price centrally, meaning the taxpayer will be giving the handouts to the energy firms, who will be able to reward their shareholders with huge dividends and themselves with huge bonuses.

Anyway: let's take a snapshot of the UK that Florence Olivier is taking charge of. Nigel Farage has just launched a personal red-white-and-blue gin range – a reminder that 40 per cent proof spirits are the perfect accompaniment to the ongoing fallout of his political philosophy. He says his gin is 'a taste of Brexit'; certainly, the blue liquid is the precise shade of the contents of a chemical toilet. Elsewhere, *This Morning* has pivoted its 'Spin to Win' competition in the direction of 'full dystopia', with desperate viewers now offered the chance to have the peppy morning magazine show pay their apocalyptic energy bills. The Conservative party's forever war is still raging, with less than half its MPs supporting Truss, and the leadership contest having landed its winner a smaller percentage of members' votes than even Iain Duncan Smith, back when they tried that Dadaist experiment.

Nevertheless, former Tory leaders have been weighing in with good wishes for Truss. There may well be a day when my reaction to any vanilla interjection from David Cameron is not to shout to an empty room: 'You did this! You're the reason we all live in the upside-down! YOU OPENED THE GATE!' That day, however, was not yesterday. The current bookies' favourite to replace Liz Truss as Tory leader is ... Boris Johnson.

All in all, a nation in rude political health, and absolutely not a deeply necrotic political culture where a significant number of grownups spent two days wetting their pants over a comedian pretending to take Truss seriously. Incidentally, if any of this feels somewhat downbeat, do consider that polls indicate a full 50 per cent of the UK are disappointed that Truss is the new PM, against 22 per cent who say they are very or fairly pleased. Maybe look at this column as an attempt to 'deliver' to the majority.

Goodbyes-wise, it's farewell to Priti Patel, floating off in the hope of a better life on the backbenches. Sayonara, too, to Nadine Dorries, who seems to have identified the moment of maximum opportunity for a peerage outside of a dream sequence. And the seal on the 'brain drain' description remains unbroken with news that Lord Frost, the worst negotiator since France sold Louisiana, will also not 'serve' in a Truss cabinet after rejecting two roles. Just assume he'll be trying to unpick this decision in two months, like he did with his own Brexit deal.

Bright spots? Boris Johnson, a terminally immoral liar who turned out to be a terminally immoral liar, is no longer in office today. It is properly positive that none of the four offices of state in the country is likely to be held by a white man for the first time in history, no matter how some might prefer to dwell on whatever downsides they have decided to see in that. The shameful, thoughtless political limbo in which the increasingly panicky country has been left all summer is now over. Truss finally has no choice but to make contact with reality. Quite how many parsnips any of that will butter in a couple of months' time is unclear – but it'll need monumental political skill not to make a cheery 'we are where we are' sound like a 10-year stretch.

Liz Truss's faith in the power of markets will be tested to destruction by a winter of strife

RAFAEL BEHR

Liz Truss enters Downing Street unencumbered by much expectation of success. Even the party that picked her is full of people whose first choice was someone else. Many of them think it should be the man she is replacing – the one who was discarded as a venal liar and an electoral liability.

Boris Johnson has a stake in Truss's failure. The worse things get in his absence, the fonder he imagines the nation's hearts will grow for him. He says he will support the new government 'every step of the way' but he says all kinds of things. He once said there were no lockdown parties in Downing Street.

Truss's authority over her party now has to be negotiated with MPs who think Conservative members chose unwisely, while relying on the loyalty of a faction that thinks there should never have been a contest in the first place.

Polls of non-Tory opinion show little confidence in the new prime minister's ability to rise to the challenge. Her supporters say she can confound low expectations, citing as proof the fact that she has already outmanoeuvred the people who thought she was a loser. Whatever her deficiencies, she is demonstrably smarter at politics than a lot of her detractors.

The Trussites (Trussians?) say their candidate has the essential quality of effective prime ministers – pragmatism about the means to achieve goals that are set with unyielding conviction.

The creed is summarised by Mark Littlewood, director of the libertarian Institute for Economic Affairs, and a friend of the new prime minister, as an intuition 'that the state has a greater propensity to do harm than good'. Kwasi Kwarteng, the new chancellor, has written that 'Liz is committed to a lean state', while preparing to throw tens of billions of pounds at the problem of soaring energy bills.

That all tallies with my experience of having argued with Truss about politics on a handful of occasions. There is no problem to which she wouldn't prefer a free-market solution, but she sees voter demand for government protection as a sad fact of political life. She seems to view that appetite with indulgent frustration, as if the coddled public needs its hands gently but firmly prised from nanny's skirts.

In that respect, Truss represents an intellectual departure from both of the last two Tory prime ministers. Theresa May came to power promising a government that would busy itself dousing 'burning injustice'. She interpreted the Brexit referendum result as an expression of anger by people who felt 'left behind' by the march of globalisation.

Johnson agreed. His levelling-up agenda was conceived as a deployment of state power to repay all the leave voters clustered in former Labour heartlands who had lent the Tories their votes in 2019. Truss takes a different view of that ballot.

In a short victory speech on Monday, she explained how the result of the last election was down to natural alignment of British and traditional Conservative values: 'freedom, low taxes, personal responsibility'.

In other words, the nation has been crying out for the very things that Truss herself believes to be the foundations of sound government. Armed with that convenient belief, the new prime minister is going to test a proposition that is common among her own MPs but eccentric elsewhere – that the only thing wrong with Conservative governments over the past 12 years is that they haven't been *Conservative* enough.

It is a habit of mind that radical Tories share with revolutionary communists, who can always excuse the slide of Marxist regimes into bankrupt tyranny with the claim that the theory wasn't properly applied or its correct operation is thwarted by unbelievers and malign foreign states.

Truss is supported by Brexit Bolsheviks who are convinced that their revolution is at constant risk of sabotage by unrepentant remainers in Whitehall. The prime minister's own analysis of Britain's economic malaise relies on the idiosyncratic view that policy has been focused too narrowly through a 'lens of redistribution' and is not interested enough in growth. Apparently, the obstacle to an enterprise boom has been a picket-line of socialist chancellors who were only pretending to be Tories.

Paradoxically, the Trussonomic remedy to stagnation requires an attitude to public debt that has more in common with the Labour left than the fiscally conservative right (although the two sides propose different targets for their borrowed munificence).

The new government's political strategy appears to be pumping money into the system to induce a sugar rush of growth before too many households and businesses are ruined by inflation and rising interest rates. When Keir Starmer complains, Truss will accuse him of deficient patriotism – talking the country down instead of helping lift it up. She can pilfer bits of Labour policy that look popular.

The plan involves riding out a winter of industrial strife as public sector wages stay frozen, and weathering voter fury as basic services stop functioning. It also relies on financial markets not deciding that the whole thing is bananas and junking Britain's currency and its debt.

Could it work? Truss has been underestimated before. It's a long shot, but swing voters might be more inclined to give the benefit of doubt to an unfamiliar new prime minister than Westminster malcontents whose contempt has been hardened by familiarity. A dogged sense of purpose could feasibly earn an embattled leader grudging respect from people who can see there are no easy options. But the ideological aversion to government intervention will inhibit the prime minister whenever events demand drastic state action, as they will again and again.

The people who are certain that Truss is the right choice to steer Britain through the coming storm base that view on the one opinion she has that is least appropriate to the task at hand. Her special quality is supposed to be pragmatism in pursuit of conviction, but those two things now pull in opposite directions. It is a formula for government that lurches all over the place, then comes apart at the seams.

9 SEPTEMBER

The loss of the Queen will test a divided Britain

MARTIN KETTLE

The death of a monarch is an entirely foreseeable event, the solemn formalities hardwired into the rituals of dynastic succession. But it is also an event that is difficult, partly for the simple reason of good manners, to anticipate with any accuracy at any particular time.

With the death at Balmoral of Queen Elizabeth II, a prepared but nevertheless shocked nation finds itself at such a moment, and it is important that our troubled politics and our wounded civil society face up to it as calmly and sensibly as possible, because this event will resonate politically and constitutionally for years to come.

Elizabeth was on the throne for so many years that, through no fault of her own, she made this process difficult. She reigned longer than any other monarch in British history, and by a considerable margin. She is the only one to have reigned for more than 70 years, a span that is unlikely to be repeated in the foreseeable future. Until yesterday, she was the only monarch that the vast majority of us had ever known – you have to be at least 75 to have any memory of George VI's reign. This is a big, big event for Britain.

She presided over a system of doing monarchy that in some ways felt timeless, but which was in fact adaptive and distinctive. Her staying power and her skill at keeping her distance have bequeathed a model of monarchy that will not be easy for Charles III to replicate, especially if, as is distinctly possible, he fails to earn the breadth of respect that Elizabeth enjoyed.

The signs were suddenly ominous yesterday. It is unusual for Buckingham Palace, normally so tight-lipped and uncommunicative on such matters, to volunteer the kind of frank statement on the monarch's health problems that it put out. It is even more unusual for the scattered and sometimes warring members of the royal family to descend en masse to the monarch's bedside at Balmoral.

This is the moment, nevertheless, for which the new monarch has long prepared, and it will be marked by change at least as much as hallowed continuity. But it is a process of change in which the many institutions of British society, not just the palace, are entitled to have their say.

Even monarchy evolves, albeit slowly. It evolved under Elizabeth, as it evolved under George VI. It will certainly evolve further under Charles, who is determined to slim down the numbers of working royals and who is also certain to find himself ceasing to be head of state of many Commonwealth countries. Yet, outside the palace walls, a collective taboo seems to have evolved when it comes to discussing the future of British life without Elizabeth.

There was an egregious but revealing example of this habit as recently as January. During the Partygate furore, Keir Starmer stood up in the Commons and drew a contrast between the lax attention to Covid rules in Boris Johnson's Downing Street and the punctilious and poignant observance of those rules by the widowed Queen at the funeral of Prince Philip during the pandemic in 2021.

It was a contrast that millions had grasped for themselves, but it drew an immediate reprimand from the Commons Speaker, Lindsay Hoyle, who told Starmer: 'We normally would not, and quite rightly, mention the royal family. We do not get into discussions on the royal family.'

This is an infantile stance for a senior parliamentarian. Parliament may not be supposed to get into discussions on the royal family, but everyone else in the country does. So, of course, do the press, which knows that the royals – whether in the form of the exemplary Cambridges, the troubled Sussexes, the disgraced Andrew or the continuing allure of Diana – sell. It passes belief that parliament should have such a pointless self-denying ordinance on the system of constitutional monarchy on which its own supremacy rests.

The idea that Britain's way of doing a monarchy is the only possible model is nonsense. Ours is the only European monarchy that is also the head of an established church. Partly for that reason, ours is the only one that has an elaborate coronation to mark a new reign. If Liz Truss had been a Swedish political leader, she would have travelled to see the speaker of the Riksdag this week to be appointed as prime minister, not the monarch. Sweden's king has no role in summoning or dissolving parliament either, and he does not give royal assent to legislation.

These are among the many terms and conditions of constitutional monarchy that a grownup country might reasonably discuss, particularly at the end of a long reign such as Elizabeth's. The list would certainly include the many forms of royal prerogative powers that are exercised by Britain's prime minister, but which the Johnson era helped to make controversial.

Do not underestimate the upheaval in British life that this dynastic moment will trigger. Elizabeth II spent 70 years as a low-key but extremely effective unifying force in a nation that is visibly pulling itself apart. Her passing will remove that force, which her heirs cannot assume they will be able to replicate. In its way, this succession will be one of the biggest tests to face modern Britain. Politics needs to be involved.

9 SEPTEMBER

Thousands make pilgrimage to palace to mourn the Queen and greet the King

DANIEL BOFFEY

The stream of people, bouquets in hand, hugged the palace tight. Slowly, dutifully, they skirted the perimeter wall of Buckingham

Palace and its 39 acres of gardens in what seemed to be inexhaustible numbers, some among them perhaps feeling a little self-conscious and awkward, others proud of being part of the moment, happy to catch the eye of those around them.

From Birdcage Walk, at the south-east edge of the palace, clockwise the thousands went, flowing by the palace estate, around Hyde Park Corner and on to Constitution Hill, to emerge in an orderly fashion, guided by polite police officers in traditional helmets, so they might lay their floral tributes in front of the famous front gates or tie them to the black rails.

On completing their pilgrimage, the mourners joined a heaving crowd around the Victoria Memorial, refreshed by ever more people as the day went on, from every walk of life, of every age and ethnicity.

Among this cross-section of British society, a scattering of wide-eyed children. Hoisted high on to shoulders or pushed in buggies. Told that they were witnessing something they would remember for the rest of their lives, and that school could wait.

But what will they remember? It won't be tears and overwhelming grief. There wasn't much of that. This was not the death of Diana, Princess of Wales. Not a tragedy of that type. No hysteria or anger or anyone to blame. What then will pierce the consciousness of a young child about the end of the second Elizabethan era?

It might be the sweet smell that filled the air, the roses, tulips, peonies and sweet peas, bouquets big and small. Neatly, tidily, some still in freshly cut plastic wrapping, spread out in front of the palace. Often with notes of appreciation. Expressions of thanks, of respect. 'We are so grateful for your dedication and wonderful example,' read one. A soft and comforting aroma.

It might be the gentle murmur of the crowds, quite peculiar in a mass of people so large, or that, when the heavens briefly opened, no one left. That those in front of the palace – where a teenage Princess Elizabeth had slipped into the crowds with her sister, Margaret, on VE Day 77 years ago – merely buttoned up their coats and opened up their umbrellas as one. An immediate canopy that disappeared almost as quickly as it had appeared. An astronaut above would have witnessed it as a slow-motion wink from the centre of London.

Or might a young child at the palace on Friday remember in the years to come the peculiar sight of men and women lifting their phones into the air, like periscopes poking out from the ocean of people, trying to catch their very best image or video of the extraordinary scenes materialising? Or the red tunics of the soldiers guarding the empty palace? Many among the crowd said they were most moved, however irrationally, by the emptiness of the famous balcony.

The arrival of the new king at the palace in his royal Bentley might also make a mark on a young mind. Shortly before 2pm, King Charles III, fresh from Balmoral and the deathbed of his late mother, stepped out of the car with his wife, Camilla, the Queen Consort, to greet and shake hands for the first time as monarch. One woman gave the new king a peck on the cheek. Charles then took time to view the floral tributes, placing an arm around his wife, before walking on through the gates as a bugler sounded. The royal standard – raised only when the monarch is in residence – was flown for the first time to mark King Charles's presence. 'God save the King,' some shouted. But most kept quiet.

Respectful solemnity was the order of the day, as it was elsewhere in the UK as people reflected on the loss of a constant in their lives.

Gun salutes took place across the country, including in Hyde Park, at the Tower of London, Cardiff Castle, Edinburgh Castle, Hillsborough Castle, in York, Portsmouth and Gibraltar. A round was fired every 10 seconds, 96 to represent each year of the late monarch's life.

There was a spontaneous round of applause from those gathering in Edinburgh. Jan White, 56, was one of hundreds of people who stopped to watch the gunfire salute on the busy Princes Street. 'It was moving, it was touching,' she said.

Even at royal residences where no formal events were planned, the people came. In Windsor, Trevor Skerritt, 59, from Guildford, said he felt drawn to visit to pay his respects because of what he believed the Queen represented. 'For most of us, she's been the only monarch we have known,' Skerritt said. 'She has given us solidity, she's kept the royal family going through thick and thin.'

In Balmoral, two monks from the Theravada Buddhist centre in Aberdeen, dressed in orange-brown robes, took a bouquet of sunflowers to the gates. 'After the Second World War, the country was in a difficult time,' said one of them, Sujan, 45, originally from Nepal. 'She was a figurehead, someone you can trust. You can't trust politicians.'

In parliament, Liz Truss nevertheless sought to capture the moment, reflecting that for many, if not all, this was a time to take stock and to reflect. 'On the death of [the Queen's] father, King George VI, Winston Churchill said the news had stilled the clatter and traffic of 20th-century life in many lands,' the prime minister told the House of Commons. 'Now, 70 years later, in the tumult of the 21st century, life has paused again.'

13 SEPTEMBER

This is a Britain that has lost its Queen – and the luxury of denial about its past

AFUA HIRSCH

This will be remembered as a watershed moment in British history for two reasons. First, for the death of Queen Elizabeth II. Second, for what happened next: the voices of those colonised in the name of the British crown being heard, not as a fringe, exceptional view, but as a clamouring chorus of global trauma.

I had prepared for this moment as a time when I would not be free. I have no idea how I actually feel about the passing of Queen Elizabeth – the only British monarch I have known in my lifetime – because for all my life deference and admiration have been drilled into me as mandatory.

I had expected that those of us minoritised in Britain would understand this as a test of our loyalty, patriotism and Good Immigrant status. We would therefore fall into two categories: those who sought to pass the test, by enthusiastically toeing the line of national mourning, and those too conscious of the harm Britain's power has caused, who would stay silent.

But it turns out that tone policing is no longer tenable. Social media have been saturated by the harrowing memories of a legacy the British establishment has refused to acknowledge. The plunder of land and diamonds in South Africa, crimes that adorned the Queen's very crown. The physical suffering that continues from violence inflicted by her government in Kenya, even as her reign was celebrated for having begun there. The scars of genocide in Nigeria, events that took place a decade into her rule. In Britain, minoritised people are remembering this Elizabethan era through the lens of the racism that was allowed to thrive during it. Shooting the messenger – the radio host and former footballer Trevor Sinclair was quickly hung, drawn and quartered for voicing this perspective – has failed to quell the tide of global truth-telling.

The burdensome task of truth-telling – to a hostile Britain more used to hearing that its past is glorious – has always fallen unequally on the descendants of empire. Yet as I write, our stories are continuing to be erased. During her reign, the BBC tells us, colonies 'gained independence', but there's no mention of those who were imprisoned, shot and killed in the struggles – from the Gold Coast to Cyprus, India and Malaya – that were required to win it.

This trauma is not recalled with a single voice. One of the effects of the empire that Queen Elizabeth personified is that it is unevenly remembered within our communities. People who were enslaved were taught that their assimilation into the culturally superior empire was a form of advancement. Families such as mine in Ghana experienced the violence of colonialism, and were then educated to believe it was justified.

I will never forget visiting Independence Arch in Ghana. This was the nation proud to have been the first black African people to successfully break free from empire, and here was the physical focal point of that freedom – an archway bearing a symbolic black star. When I looked inside, I found a reality check: a plaque dedicated this freedom to none other than Queen Elizabeth II.

I understood it as a lesson that even in our freedom, we are not free. We are expected to be grateful for having been colonised. We are racialised, and then expected to prove that racism exists. Even as black British people continue to die at the hands of the state, such as the unarmed Chris Kaba, news of the black community's mourning is obscured by the more important story of royal mourning. To the extent that it's ever acknowledged that black lives matter, now is certainly not the time.

Yet I sympathise with those who feel the Queen's loss. Under her reign, many latched on to the stabilising sense of cultural continuity. To lose that is to feel disrupted and uncertain. For me, it's a familiar anxiety – Britain's empire by definition redrew boundaries, and swept aside generations of tradition. Our parents and grandparents were recruited to Britain for its benefit, the terms and conditions of which my generation are still trying to make sense. We know how it feels to lack cultural continuity. Others in Britain enjoyed it at our expense.

If continuity is an abstract subject, the other trappings of royal symbolism are more concrete. There were pompous reflections last week with the idea expressed in the *Economist*'s obituary that the Queen 'came from good Hanoverian blood'. If that sounds like a white supremacist idea, that's because it is.

When I am attacked for applying reason to what is obviously an emotional situation, one of the allegations will be that I dare speak of race, when the real oppressor is class. And yet here we come to the other mainstay of royal ideology – the Queen was the class system personified. Her role, and that of the King who succeeds her, is to sit at the apex of a class system, in a hierarchy anointed by God. In some cases, it's hard to distinguish this from the idea that she was indeed a god herself – the British tabloids began seeing her omnipresence in rainbows and old-lady-with-a-hat-shaped clouds hovering benignly over the land.

Change has come, but the systems of race and class that delineate our destinies remain. The genius of our monarchy is that it transforms people who have the most to gain from dismantling those systems into passionate subjects of the crown instead.

If it were possible to set all of this to one side, maybe I would like to mourn the Queen, the hard-working old lady who has been the symbol of my country for my, even my parents', entire lives. But I can't separate her from a reign that refused to acknowledge this reality, let alone attempt to change it.

Nor do I get to opt out of the emotional labour of processing the memories that other British people refuse to acknowledge. Until now. Last week, Britain lost the luxury of long-lasting denial, at the same time as it lost its Queen.

19 SEPTEMBER

It was a very modern pilgrimage – a people's quest that led to this historic day

IAN JACK

Great state occasions inspire an elevated kind of journalism, which does its best to match the mystical rituals of the ceremony and reflect or shape what it perceives as the national mood. 'Two rivers run silently through London tonight and one is made of people,' the *Daily Mail*'s Vincent Mulchrone wrote – memorably, as it turned out – in January 1965 of the queues to see Winston Churchill's lying in state. 'Never safer, better guarded, lay a sleeping king than this, with a golden candlelight to warm his resting place, and the muffled footsteps of his devoted subjects to keep him company,' the BBC's Richard Dimbleby told his radio audience in February 1952, when the coffin of George VI lay in the same ancient hall.

The *Guardian* has often taken a less Shakespearean approach. Its reports of George VI's lying in state, witnessed by nearly 300,000 people over three days, are lively with detail. Some aspects of queue behaviour still apply: there are ways of jumping it. In 1952, the jumpers honourably included 'nurses who had been on night duty' and, perhaps less forgivably, 'the boys and masters of Westminster School', who had been led in through a side door. Other things belong to history. Telephone boxes overflowed with pennies from husbands taking 'a minute to explain that they would be home late'. A party from a girls' college in Berkshire had arrived through the snow by taking an early morning 'workmen's train', evidence of their enterprise in an age when 'workmen' travelled early and the middle class came late.

Other newspapers carried similar details. What marked out the *Guardian* was its wryness, its refusal to get carried away. It was a Manchester paper, after all. On the night before the King's funeral, the London correspondent toured the streets twice to gauge the kind of people who were prepared to wait for hours in the cold to have the best view. At 10pm, he noticed the groups that had set up camp in the Mall were mostly elderly women – 'some were old women and some were very old women with memories of Queen Victoria's funeral'. At 2am, he saw the last of the queuers emerge from Westminster Hall to ponder 'whether to wait for the procession or go home to bed. Bed is winning.' In the meantime, Whitehall had filled with one-night-only pavement dwellers using old blankets, mackintoshes and in-memoriam editions of that morning's papers to protect themselves against a bitter wind.

'Everybody was stoutly clad but everybody was cold,' the London correspondent wrote, and the question naturally arose, as it has naturally arisen several times in the 70 years since, more pressingly since the whole affair can be watched at length without leaving home: *why?* Why freeze in the cold overnight for a fleeting sight of a gun carriage; why queue for 16 hours to walk past a catafalque in 60 seconds? The *Guardian*'s correspondent observed that when a reporter asked the question, he was 'disconcerted to find that the kind of people who sit up all night ... answer in clichés or in headlines that were considered the latest thing in Northcliffe's day. "It's cold but we shall see it through." "I've seen every royal procession since ..." or "Been waiting three hours – feels like three days."'

By 'Northcliffe's day', he meant the first 20-odd years of the newspaper Lord Northcliffe founded, the *Daily Mail*, and when I visited the queue last week I have to admit that a part of me wanted to discover that the relationship between the *Mail* and the royal crowd persisted. In fact, so far as I could tell, it didn't. People spoke articulately and sincerely and freshly, in the sense that their words seemed unborrowed. They nearly always mentioned the fellowship that had been created by the act of walking and stopping – walking and stopping again and again – on the four or five miles along the Thames to Westminster. 'It's like a kind of pilgrimage,' one woman said, and that was how it often looked: a pilgrimage with Essential Waitrose and Pret a Manger carrier bags, takeaway pizzas and coffees, and the occasional beer. A pilgrimage without self-flagellation or any major discomfort beyond sleeplessness, tired legs and sore backs. As the *Guardian* said in 1952, 'mourning' wouldn't be the right word for a crowd that was 'cheerful but decently subdued'.

At Southwark Park on a warm Saturday afternoon, the pre-queue queue set off at a cracking pace, tramping along a chicane of rubber mats and temporary fencing that folded back and forth across the grass, a kind of treadmill in which we were the only moving parts, the distance between us and the bandstand hardly wider after 15 minutes' brisk walking. The estimated time of the journey in prospect was 14 hours, but despite this a young woman kept shouting at us like a friendly sergeant major. 'Move along now! Keep it up! Well done!' I think she was south Asian, or of south Asian heritage. There have been estimates of the multicultural nature of the crowd (mine is: a lot less multicultural than the average London bus), but none so far as I know of the police, stewards and marshals who directed and channelled the crowd from A to B.

The police were almost entirely white; the stewards and marshals with very few exceptions black or brown. Most were from India, Pakistan, Bangladesh and Sri Lanka, and their languages included Hindi, Punjabi, Telugu, Tamil, Gujarati and Bengali, as well as English. Private security firms pay them the standard living wage of £9.18 or £9.50 an hour, depending on their age. Many held the recently created post-study work visa that enables them to stay in the UK for two years after their graduate or (more usually) postgraduate studies have ended. In 2020-21, UK universities attracted more than 84,000 students from India alone.

In Southwark Park, I asked a few of them what they made of the crowd they were guiding towards the dead queen. They estimated that most were over 50, that 10 per cent were African or African-Caribbean and another 10 per cent south Asian or Chinese. They were all very friendly. There had been no trouble.

'Why is England so crazy about the Queen?' a student from Hyderabad asked. Her companion, from Ahmedabad, had an answer. The Queen was clearly popular; leaders became popular when they did good for their people; ergo, the Queen must have done good for her people. 'She was a great woman; she deserves the respect.' It was tremendously logical, needed no poetry, and will do for the time being.

Picture credits

Plate 1
top: Peter Summers/Getty
bottom: Dan Kitwood/Getty

Plate 2
top: Anadolu Agency/Getty
bottom: Aris Messinis/AFP/Getty

Plate 3
top: Fadel Senna/AFP/Getty
bottom: Aris Messinis/AFP/Getty

Plate 4
top: Roberto Schmidt/AFP/Getty
bottom: Christopher Furlong/Getty

Plate 5
top: Dan Kitwood/Getty
bottom: Jane Barlow/PA Wire

Plate 6
top: Guy Levy/BBC/PA Wire
bottom: Dan Kitwood/Getty

Plate 7
top: Gareth Cattermole/BFC/Getty
bottom: Tom Jenkins/Guardian

Plate 8
top: Sean Smith/Guardian
bottom: NASA, ESA, CSA, and STScI

Index